# A GUIDE TO
# VOCATIONAL
# ASSESSMENT

# A GUIDE TO VOCATIONAL ASSESSMENT

by

## Paul W. Power, Sc.D.

Associate Professor
Director, Rehabilitation Program
University of Maryland, College Park

**University Park Press**
Baltimore

**UNIVERSITY PARK PRESS**
International Publishers in Medicine and Human Services
300 North Charles Street
Baltimore, Maryland 21201

Typeset by Brushwood Graphics
Manufactured in the United States of America by The Maple Press Company
Design by S. Stoneham, Studio 1812, Baltimore

**Library of Congress Cataloging in Publication Data**

Power, Paul W.
A guide to vocational assessment.

Includes bibliographies and index.
1. Vocational rehabilitation. 2. Disability evaluation. I. Title. [DNLM: 1. Rehabilitation, Vocational. 2. Counseling. 3. Disability evaluation. HD 7255 P887g]
HD7255.P68 1983      362.4'0484'0287      83-16696
ISBN 0-8391-1718-3

# Contents

*To Richard Baker, David Bachrach, and Charles Robinson, each of whom has maintained the highest professional standards for assessment and who are continual sources of influence; and to Barbara, Jonathan, and Lucinda for their patience during this book's development.*

# Preface

This book originated from the many years of teaching a graduate course in vocational assessment and also from the numerous national workshops on evaluation conducted for rehabilitation counselors and other allied health professionals. It developed from the conviction that many helping professionals could conduct either informal or formal beginning vocational assessments of their clients if only they had the necessary knowledge and skills. Whether seeking a job, exploring possible satisfying avocational pursuits, or attempting to achieve new career directions in mid-life, people need positive feedback on their productive capabilities. Disabled people, in particular, should learn about their remaining capabilities as soon after the traumatic, handicapping event as possible. A disabling experience usually brings feelings of frustration, disappointment, hopelessness, and even inferiority. A vocational evaluation can alleviate some of these feelings by providing timely feedback on what the person can do. To perform assessment at the initial contact with handicapped individuals can be a significant factor in determining ultimate rehabilitation success (Crystal et al., 1980). Rehabilitation assessment can also bring hope. But in order to give useful information, helping professionals must know about the many evaluation approaches that have been developed to assist disabled people gain a better understanding of their potential. Importantly, professionals must also have the skills to apply this knowledge to the many varied opportunities that disabled people offer in an assessment situation.

Recent historical developments in rehabilitation have facilitated the necessity for helping professionals to enlarge their own job-related skills. Since 1970, remarkably new directions have been established in vocational rehabilitation. The Rehabilitation Act of 1973 emphasized both client involvement in the rehabilitation process and improvement of services to the severely disabled. In 1978, the Comprehensive Rehabilitation Amendments expanded employment options for handicapped individuals and brought renewed attention to the counselor/client relationship in vocational rehabilitation planning.

To meet all of these renewed or revitalized demands in rehabilitation, helping professionals should not only perform their job in the best possible way, but also acknowledge new opportunities to help their clients toward a more productive life. Vocational assessment is one such opportunity. This book presents many approaches and guidelines that enable rehabilitation professionals to perform an adequate assessment and yet still meet the daily responsibilities of their particular jobs. The topics of the 14 chapters represent areas of assessment that are most relevant today in the 1980s. Each chapter is designed to assist professionals not only in acquiring knowledge about evaluation, but also in learning how to apply this understanding to their clients. Each chapter concludes with a case study of a disabled person. These case studies apply the particular assessment approach in the chapter to someone in need of rehabilitation planning.

This book is primarily for those who have little training in vocational or rehabilitation assessment, but who face opportunities to evaluate clients' productive- /employment-related capabilities: students who are pursuing undergraduate or graduate training in the human services or rehabilitation professionals, such as allied health practitioners, physical and occupational therapists, rehabilitation nurses, employment counselors, social workers, and counselers who have been hired by a rehabilitation agency but have had little academic training in rehabilitation. At the same time, much of this book's content is also intended for professional work evaluators or rehabilitation counselors who want to enhance their assessment skills or learn new approaches to understanding the work potential of the severely disabled. This book contains basic information about evaluation as well as detailed assessment approaches or particular diagnostic measures, which are important for exploring the work potential of difficult clients. Examples of this specific evaluation information are found in Chapters 7–9.

Helping professionals must have the interest and motivation to provide a client with information about productive capabilities as soon as possible after initial contact. As many disabled persons progress toward rehabilitation goals, they will have to be referred to an assessment resource center for a more thorough and sophisticated evaluation. Many clients will also receive the special services of a psychologist, who may perform a thorough evaluation of intellectual and personality functions. Although all of these services are necessary and extremely beneficial, they do not eliminate the necessity for the helping professional to do a beginning vocational assessment early in the treatment rehabilitation process. For those who also believe that an early exploration of a client's physical and intellectual capabilities can be of invaluable assistance to appropriate rehabilitation planning, this book is especially appopriate.

During the many workshops in vocational assessment that I conducted over the last 5 years, practitioners in rehabilitation or related allied health fields frequently provided insight into how assessment could be conducted without affecting other job responsibilities. Or, they elaborated on the feasibility of a particular evaluation approach. These insights and elaborations are incorporated into this book, and I am particularly grateful to the large number of dedicated persons who have taken time to understand how they can further grow as skilled helping professionals by assisting their disabled and handicapped clients in becoming more aware of their work- and performance-related strengths. I also want to thank my wife, Barbara, who not only typed the manuscript but who also greatly encouraged me to develop the chapters throughout this book.

## REFERENCES

Crystal, R.M., Growick, B.S., and Whitten, C.R. 1980. Concentrated assessment and diagnosis in rehabilitation entrance. J. Rehab. July, August, September, pp. 33–37.

# Introduction

This book explains how vocational assessment approaches can be utilized. Application of evaluation knowledge is based on understanding: 1) the meaning of vocational rehabilitation; 2) the role of assessment in the rehabilitation process; 3) a current conceptualization of vocational evaluation; 4) the target areas and components of vocational assessment; 5) the need for a personal philosophy of assessment that lays the base for everyday practice; and 6) the different roles that can be adopted by the rehabilitation professional during assessment. Each of these areas is discussed in this introduction.

## REHABILITATION: ITS MEANING AND SCOPE AND ROLE OF ASSESSMENT

Rehabilitation is viewed in the 1980s as a process of restoration—a way to help an individual toward practical goals where opportunities for self-dependence and personal satisfaction are possible. It is not only problem-centered but also is focused on adjustment. Moreover, rehabilitation aims at reducing disability conditions that restrict activities or cause handicaps, developing competencies necessary for adequate role performance in family, social, and occupational areas and helping a person to participate in the life of the general community. It can also be viewed as a process of remediating a skills deficit. Anthony (1980) believed that:

> The goal of rehabilitation is to assure that the disabled person possesses those physical, emotional, and intellectual skills needed to live, learn, and work in his or her own particular community (p. 7).

Rehabilitation, consequently, has more than one goal, although for decades many considered that rehabilitation efforts should only be directed to assist individuals who could be totally self-reliant in producing their income. The ideas of rehabilitation have grown "into the concept of enabling a person to return to or to attain as much function and independence as possible" (Crowe, 1976, p. 30). It is no longer tied to manpower needs and is based both on productive output and productive living. With this perspective, rehabilitation efforts are devoted to help handicapped clients become more productive until they are able to function adequately in varied settings. Vocational goals are still most important in rehabilitation, yet other functional outcomes are included. These can be activities in which a person is capable of engaging on a regular basis and which require the use of time, strength, and mental or physical faculties. Such activities might be, for example, sheltered employment (transitional or long-term, homebound employment), self-employment or employment by others, volunteer work, and programmed day tasks.

The scope of rehabilitation has widened to those clients who are severely disabled and for whom the traditional work structure of time and output might not be feasible. The increase of acceptable outcomes affects the extent of the delivery of rehabilitation services and necessitates that more relevant approaches for delivering these services be examined. This is particularly true of the role of assessment in the rehabilitation process.

The rehabilitation process is a form of social technology to assist someone in making the transition from patient to rehabilitant. The traditional role is usually characterized as dependent and passive, ("You do it for me") while rehabilitant behavior conveys participating and initiating, with a dominant focus on residual strength and capabilities. If disabled individuals are to achieve functional outcomes, they must become rehabilitants. The shift not only depends upon the person's ego strength, the attitude of family members toward rehabilitation, and the degree to which rehabilitation programs meet specific needs, but also on the quality and extent of the assessment early in the rehabilitation process. An evaluation that reaches out to involve the client in rehabilitation planning, emphasizing what the person *can do*, rather than the extent of his or her limitations, will considerably facilitate the client's development to worthwhile, rehabilitation goals. Assessment, then, is a dynamic of the rehabilitation process as well as an integral part of the client's rehabilitation.

Traditionally in the rehabilitation process, assessment is performed soon after the client makes a request for vocational services. If the disabled person is to be referred to an evaluation center, then he or she may wait for a considerable length of time because most centers have long waiting lists. Therefore, in order for clients to remain motivated enough to pursue rehabilitation goals, rehabilitation professionals should conduct a beginning assessment so that any hopes for rehabilitation achievement are not dispelled. An assessment performed soon after the initial client contact that provides the disabled person with a renewed awareness of productive-oriented strengths and capabilities becomes the first step toward the development of an effective rehabilitation plan.

## A CONCEPTUALIZATION AND TARGET
## AREAS OF VOCATIONAL ASSESSMENT

Vocational assessment is a comprehensive, intradisciplinary process of evaluating an individual's physical, mental, and emotional abilities, limitations, and tolerance in order to identify an optimal outcome for the disabled or handicapped person. Evaluation is a method of acquiring information—a process to assist individuals in identifying their functional competencies and disabilities. It evaluates such factors as the disabled individual's vocational strengths and weaknesses, which in turn could be found in the areas of personality, aptitude, interest, work habits, physical tolerance, and dexterity. Assessment is also prognostic because it attempts to answer such questions as whether a client will be able to work or what kind of productive activity the individual will be able to do. An added evaluation goal is to identify those services needed to overcome the functional disabilities that are barriers to successful performance.

In regard to understanding rehabilitation as an alleviation of a skills deficit, Anthony (1980) stated that the assessment process:

> ...yields information about the disabled client's level of skills and the skill demands of the community in which he or she wants or needs to function. This information enables the rehabilitation practitioner to work with the client to develop a treatment plan designed to increase the client's strengths and assets or to identify an environment more suitable to the client's functioning (p. 9).

The process of rehabilitation assessment, therefore, is mainly one of diagnosis and prediction, assisting both professionals and the client, in a relatively short time, to gain information concerning promising directions for client development. Evaluation can generate a course of action for a disabled individual that may range from competitive employment to effective productive activity within his or her own home. Although not all individuals are able to move toward competitive employment, different recommendations for all clients could be included within the goals of assessment.

In the process of vocational assessment, the word "comprehensive" is emphasized, for evaluation incorporates medical, psychologic, social, vocational, educational, cultural, and economic data. When exploring a person's capabilities, the helping professional seeks information on such broad client characteristics as: work interest, general intelligence, physical capacity, work tolerance, and special aptitudes. Obtaining this information often requires the involvement of professionals or experts in several areas, and data collected by these other professionals may be used in rehabilitation assessment.

Information in rehabilitation assessment can be obtained both formally and informally. Informal assessment includes observing a person's behavior in a variety of situations, conversing with the client, or getting information about the client from other sources. Formal assessment is comprised of such processes as the interview, mental testing (e.g., intelligence, aptitude, ability, personality, and interest tests), work samples, job analyses, and situational assessments. The choice of an approach depends, of course, on the objectives for the assessment. No one of these methods can do everything because each deals with a specific, limited facet of a many-faceted problem. When the rehabilitation professional understands each approach, it can then be used or adapted to provide optimal information for planning.

The interview is a person-to-person experience in which the professional obtains information relevant to rehabilitation goals. It can follow a structured or unstructured format and is a way for the client to learn about his or her own strengths and weaknesses as well as to recognize those abilities and aptitudes which may facilitate or militate against training demands. It is often the most useful way for many severely disabled clients to learn the information needed for rehabilitation planning.

Psychometric tests have been utilized in assessment for many decades and are usually easy and inexpensive to administer. Yet, their validity with disabled and handicapped persons can be questioned. Most tests were normed on populations other than the disabled, and in a rapidly changing labor force, future job applicants may have very different characteristics from those that typified the standardization sample. Also, there are crucial differences between the demands of the test situation and the demands of the work or production situation (Neff, 1966). For example:

> In the test situation, attention, concentration, and motivation are maximized and under continuous control, while in the work situation these variables truly vary and are under very meager control (p. 684). Even with these difficulties, tests are widely used and are able to provide some very useful information for rehabilitation assessment purposes.

Work samples are close simulations of actual industrial operations, no different in their essentials from what a potential worker would be required to perform on an ordinary job. Through performance on a work sample, tentative predictions about future performance can be made. This approach has a strong reality orientation and provides an opportunity to observe actual work behavior in a reasonably controlled situation. But, there are still unresolved problems of reliability and validity, and there is uncertainty as to their predictive efficiency.

The job analysis approach focuses on a description of the work to be performed and not on the characteristics of the worker. The work or task is observed very carefully, and detailed descriptions are written on what can be very complex activities. Although this method of assessment can be over-analytical, it is important to understand the detailed set of job requirements for a person whose potential for work is being evaluated.

The situational assessments, like work samples, are based on an effort to simulate actual working conditions. The main orientation of the situational assessment, however, is toward work behavior in general. It asks such questions as: Can a person work at all and get along with co-workers? How does he or she work most effectively? What are his or her strengths and weaknesses as a worker?

## A PHILOSOPHY OF EVALUATION

Approaches to effective assessment must be developed not only from acquired knowledge and continued experience but also from a personal philosophy that embodies strong convictions about helping disabled clients. These convictions provide a direction to evaluation and represent assumptions that, in turn, generate attitudes toward how assessment will be performed. Often, the attitudes of the professional toward the assessment situation and the client can become more important than the content of the assessment itself. The author has identified an assessment philosophy that has been formulated from working with clients of varied disability conditions. In order to stimulate the thinking in the direction of developing an individual philosophy of vocational assessment, the central issues of this philosophy are discussed as follows:

1. Assessment should be integrated into the counseling process and the continued interaction that takes place in rehabilitation between the professional and the client. Often, clients have the expectation that they must place themselves completely into the helping professional's hands to provide answers to finding a job or obtaining suitable training. This belief is expressed in such statements as: "I will put all the responsibility on you, and when you are through, you will be better able to tell me what I should do." If clients are to feel better about themselves, they have to feel some sense of autonomy and control of their future. When vocational evaluation is integrated into the counseling process, clients are helped to identify and understand the attitudes and feelings about themselves that mitigate against successful living and employment. In counseling and vocational evaluation, limitations are recognized. More important, strengths that can be utilized for productive living can be discovered.

2. During the vocational process, rehabilitation professionals must not only evaluate general employability factors, i.e., work habits, physical tolerance, intellectual and achievement levels of functioning, and the ability to learn, but also the client's social/emotional competence. A disabled individual's constellation of attitudes and behaviors may be more influential in determining future success than other work-related factors. People lose jobs primarily because of deficiencies in work behavior and not just because of skill deficits as such. For example, mental functioning should not be considered in isolation, but must be weighed with the person's motivational and personality structure. Assessment should take into account the social and cultural factors that impact on either achievement functioning or training. How an individual is likely to function on future tasks is often based on personal attributes that have known predictive ability. Such traits could be the disabled person's coping styles, mo-

tivation, relationship to others, an understanding of self, the manner of adjustment to disability, and the ability to profit from experience.

3. Disabled persons frequently magnify partial inadequacy to a totally nega-tive view of themselves. Consequently, the helping professional should conscientiously use esteem-enhancing efforts during assessment, par-ticularly in the initial interview. The assessment process is not only one of diagnosis but also an opportunity to give positive feedback to clients. Such information can help handicapped individuals to achieve a renewed under-standing of themselves and assist them in identifying personal capabilities that can generate productive outcomes.

4. Assessment should include a multifactoral approach, which promotes the examination of a wide variety of client characteristics. Intervention de-cisions in rehabilitation should not be based on a single attribute, such as educational or work achievement. Other factors, i.e., family network, adjustment style to disability, or social relationships, can be included to learn how an individual is going to adjust to a work or similar productive situation. A more comprehensive exploration, then, demands broadening the rehabilitation professional's knowledge of evaluation approaches.

5. Finally, what is good for the agency is not necessarily always beneficial for the client. The dimensions of vocational rehabilitation have been expanded in the 1980s to include goals that comprise transitional employment or more productive use of leisure time. Often, the agency has the view that unless a client can meet traditional employment demands, assessment is not going to be valuable. Broader expectations for what the client could possibly do can generate a more helpful attitude during assessment.

The preceding beliefs have given a decided focus to the author's as-sessment efforts. They also influence the different roles that a rehabilitation professional may assume when performing evaluation.

## ROLES OF THE COUNSELOR DURING ASSESSMENT

When rehabilitation professionals begin to evaluate either the client's eligibility for services or capabilities for work-oriented productivity, they assume certain roles that will impact on the client. Each role conveys definite responsibilities. One of the primary responsibilities is to be a communicator, namely, someone who can establish a helping, interpersonal relationship with a client. This relationship should transmit empathy, trust, and the conviction that the re-habilitation professional is very willing to listen to the viewpoint and needs of the client. If such a relationship is established, then generally the client will readily respond by providing much needed information that relates to the building of a rehabilitation plan.

The rehabilitation professional is also a provider of information. Feedback to clients should usually focus on what they can do, considering the limitations of the disability, and not what they cannot do. Each evaluation approach should be used to help clients understand their remaining strengths and how these strengths can be used either in the work sector or in avocational activities.

Another necessary role of the rehabilitation professional is that of a reinforcer. In attempting to cope with a disability, clients face many frustrations and setbacks. The reality of perceived failure could be an everyday occurrence. These perceptions and disappointments lower their self-concepts and contribute to their belief that there is probably not much opportunity to become a wage-earner. The helping professional should take every chance during assessment to provide some needed feedback on the client's capabilities. For example, when the disabled person reveals how a certain adjustmental problem was handled, the professional can give needed support to those efforts, or even when the adaptive attempt failed, can compliment the client on the courage to discuss a disappointing experience.

Of course, one of the primary responsibilities during assessment is to be an evaluator—to know how to diagnose and then make predictive statements about rehabilitation outcomes. This role necessitates a comprehensive knowledge of diagnostic approaches, but more concisely, presumes that the helping professional understands human nature. Acquiring this information is gained not only by standardized approaches to psychometric testing, but also by the professional's intuition, willingness to listen to what clients are saying, and understanding of what it means to experience a disability.

## CONCLUSION

The purpose of rehabilitation assessment is to plan a course of action. It involves exploring a person's strengths and weaknesses and discovering how the individual's potential for vocational adjustment can be enhanced (Wright, 1980). Approaches in assessment are never used to measure people themselves, but characteristics of people, such as verbal skills, self-confidence, and intellectual capacities.

Importantly in vocational rehabilitation, evaluation has a comprehensive perspective, for it considers the physical, intellectual, and emotional components of personality as well as the influence of the environment on an individual with a disability. A person cannot be fragmented, and the interrelationships of feeling, mental functioning, and body capabilities must always be considered. The most useful assessment approaches include understanding all three dimensions; and, underlying any assessment approach should be the client's participation in the evaluation process. To assist handicapped people in becoming productive implies that not only are various ways utilized to gain information about possible functioning but also that the disabled person has the opportunity both to understand the diagnostic information and to make decisions from this information. What are the varied assessment approaches that can tap the client's intellectual and emotional resources? How can the disabled person become integrally involved in the evaluation process? These are questions which are answered in this book.

## REFERENCES

Anthony, W.A. 1980. A rehabilitation model for rehabilitating the psychiatrically disabled. Rehab. Counsel. Bull. 24:6–14.
Crowe, S. 1976. The role of evaluation in the rehabilitative process. In: R. Hardy and J. Cull (eds.), Vocational Evaluation for Rehabilitative Services, pp. 29–39. Thomas Publishing Co., Springfield, IL.
Neff, W. 1966. Problems of work evaluation. Pers. and Guid J., 44:682–688.
Wright, G. 1980. Total Rehabilitation. Little, Brown and Co., Boston.

# A GUIDE TO VOCATIONAL ASSESSMENT

chapter 1

# PERSPECTIVES IN VOCATIONAL EVALUATION
## Evaluating for Productivity and Successful Job Placement

Vocational rehabilitation embraces many activities—assessment, counseling, job preparation, and job placement. Each has an integral part in what is called the rehabilitation process. As mentioned in the introduction to this book, the principal aim of this process is to assist clients in reaching productivity, especially in employment areas. Underlying both client development and the achievement of these goals is a comprehensive and current evaluation of the client's capabilities.

Client assessment is the first step and the vital link to all successful rehabilitation activities. Many of the mistakes made in job placement could be avoided if an appropriate and accurate evaluation was performed. Assessment can also become a stimulus to the reluctant rehabilitation professional who considers job placement an undesirable task. A knowledge of what the client can do often encourages the professional to look for job possibilities that are in harmony with this awareness.

The rehabilitation professional, however, usually sees the client some months after the occurrence of a chronic illness or disability. That encounter implies that clients have brought much of their past, particularly in the areas of vocational functioning, to the present moment. They then look ahead to possible directions for a satisfying future. Figure 1.1 conceptualizes this process. As suggested, individuals frequently proceed through stages in their childhood, adolescence, and early adulthood before following a particular career direction. Ginzberg (1972), Super (1957), and Tiedeman (1961) formulated theories which identified this vocational development. Other theorists emphasized more situational/economic issues as the facilitators for the development of career patterns. Whatever theory is followed, the client with a disability usually presents himself or herself as someone who has been functioning in some kind of vocational environment. Such pre-disability, work-related characteristics are not completely extinguished by the disability experience; rather, they serve both as guidelines for current functioning and also as foundation areas for renewed or further vocational development.

An exception to the sequence outlined in Figure 1.1 are persons who are disabled from birth. Although their vocational development may be slower, they still have the same potential and, perhaps, actual vocational behaviors as the newly disabled. But in contrast to the latter population, the life of the congenitally disabled has not been suddenly disrupted by a traumatic, disabling event. Adjustmental patterns have been formed, although few persons handicapped since birth never adapt to their own limitations.

Table 1.1 shows a more elaborate model of vocational functioning, which establishes a broad framework for vocational assessment. The model specifies the areas that needed to be identified in evaluation. It depicts an individual's possible vocational functioning at a fixed point in time, usually at the initial interview with a client. Any model, however, is developed from certain assumptions, and this model of vocational functioning is based on the following:

1. Work satisfaction depends upon the extent to which individuals find adequate outlets for their abilities, interests, personality traits, and values (Super, 1957)
2. Occupations are chosen to meet needs. The occupation that is chosen is that field or area that the person believes will best meet the needs that most concern him or her (Hoppock, 1976).
3. An occupational choice is determined by the individual's socioeconomic level, age, abilities, personality characteristics, education, and by the opportunities to which he or she is exposed.
4. Vocational preference, the situation in which people live and work, and

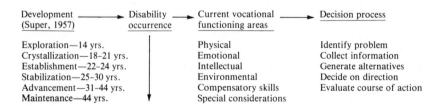

| Development (Super, 1957) | Disability occurrence | Current vocational functioning areas | Decision process |
|---|---|---|---|
| Exploration—14 yrs. | | Physical | Identify problem |
| Crystallization—18-21 yrs. | | Emotional | Collect information |
| Establishment—22-24 yrs. | | Intellectual | Generate alternatives |
| Stabilization—25-30 yrs. | | Environmental | Decide on direction |
| Advancement—31-44 yrs. | | Compensatory skills | Evaluate course of action |
| Maintenance—44 yrs. | | Special considerations | |

*Figure 1.1.    Pre-disability vocational functioning.*

Table 1.1.   Model of vocational functioning

| Vocational functioning | Vocational and independent living tasks/demands |
|---|---|
| *Client physical characteristics* | |
| General appearance | Work appropriateness<br>Employment interview |
| Stamina | Work tolerance<br>Work full-time<br>Work part-time<br>Light physical activity<br>Sedentary work |
| | Work pace |
| General health status | Working conditions<br>Current level of response to work location (hot, cold, humidity, noise, hazards, and other atmospheric conditions) |
| Motor coordination<br>Eye/hand/foot coordination<br>Finger dexterity<br>Mobility | Work demands<br>Transportation<br>Mobility in work space<br>Self-care |
| Personal hygiene | Work appropriateness |
| Physical limitations | Ability to meet work demands<br>Necessary job modifications |
| *Client intellectual characteristics* | |
| General level of knowledge | Knowledge of work demands<br>Awareness of entry requirements |
| Educational development | Level of possible training<br>Language development<br>Mathematics<br>Level of reasoning |
| Aptitudes<br>Verbal/speech<br>Numerical<br>Spatial perception<br>Form perception<br>Conceptual ability | Communication demand<br>Complete employment forms<br>Hold job interview<br>Ability to abstract and calculate<br>Measuring ability |

*(continued)*

Table 1.1.    *(Continued)*

| Vocational functioning | Vocational and independent living tasks/demands |
|---|---|
| Work experience<br>Homemaking<br>Leisure time<br>Avocational activities | Skills and competencies developed<br>Safety consciousness<br>Ability of person to return to former job<br>Transferable abilities and skills to a work situation |
| Decision-making ability | Initiative in work areas<br>Take opportunities for job and work development |
| Memory | Ability to retain instructions<br>Training capability |
| Attention span | Ability to follow work directions<br>Training capability |
| Work habits | Attendance<br>Promptness<br>Speed of production<br>Use of time |
| Interests | Preferred type of jobs<br>Preference for certain types of work activities |
| Values | Perception of work for life functioning<br>Work habits<br>Expectations for self in job situation |
| Disability-related knowledge | Understanding of assets and disability limitations in relation to work |
| *Client emotional characteristics*<br>Mood/Temperament<br>Indifferent<br>Apathetic<br>Cooperative<br>Eager<br>Self-assured<br>Interested | Relation to supervisors and other people<br>Frustration tolerance<br>Adjustment to strains and pressures of work environment |

*(continued)*

Table 1.1.   *(Continued)*

| Vocational functioning | Vocational and independent living tasks/demands |
|---|---|
| Needs[a] | Change orientation |
| Responsibility | Adaptability |
| Security | Ability to take risks with self |
| Social status | Openness to alternatives |
| Variety | |
| Supervision/Authority | |
| Recognition | |
| Creativity | |
| Independence | |
| Achievement | |
| Good working conditions | |
| Advancement | |
| Autonomy | |
| | |
| Attitudes | Sense of responsibility |
| Toward self | Successful job performance |
| Toward others | Relationship with others |
| | Self-confidence in work situations |
| | |
| Motivation | Seeks rehabilitation goals |
| | Energy on job |
| | Achievement level |
| | |
| Adjustment to disability | Confidence in self as worker |
| | Accepts limitations |
| | Dependent or independent role |
| | |
| *Environmental factors* | |
| Family situation | Family members supportive of rehabilitation goals |
| | Family accepting of occupational choices |
| | Family recognizes client capabilities |
| | |
| Available financial resources | Current finances are sufficient to meet client needs |
| Workmen's Compensation benefits | Will job/occupations meet client financial needs? |
| SSI | |
| SSDI | |
| Primary souce of support | |
| | |
| *Client special considerations* | |
| Medications | Attention, concentration, stamina, and safety on job |

[a]Lofquist and Dawes, 1969.

*(continued)*

Table 1.1.   *(Continued)*

| Vocational functioning | Vocational and independent living tasks/demands |
| --- | --- |
| Aids | Transportation<br>Can drive own car<br>Can take public transportation<br>Needs assistance for transportation |
| Certificates/Licenses/Union membership | Job opportunity |
| Precautions | Job and work flexibility<br>Job/work modification |
| Social skills | Work demands<br>Relationship to others |

self-concept change with time and experience, making occupational choice and adjustment a continuous process.

5.  The experience of disability represents a transitional period in the sense that many behaviors common to the pre-disability state are gradually replaced.

6.  The changes that the onset of disability usually precipitate frequently have traumatic implications for the family, organizational, or work system in which that individual is embedded.

7.  Work itself may not be central to the life-style or aspirations of some persons and, for many, it has connotations that repel rather than attract (Zytowski, 1965).

8.  Prevalent career choices, which are primarily based on research studies utilizing samples of boys and men, may be applicable for girls and women. Although research that is more longitudinal in scope is needed on girls and women, current vocational practices should recognize the distinctive needs of women as well as minimize sex role bias.

The main headings of the model in Table 1.1 are: *Client physical characteristics, Client intellectual characteristics, Client emotional characteristics, Environmental factors,* and *Client special considerations.* The content of the model is developed from various sources, including Hoppock (1976), Knefel-kamp and Slepitza (1976), Lofquist and Dawes (1969), and Super (1957), as well as the author's own extensive professional experience in vocational evaluation. The model includes all disabled people, namely, those who were born with a disability as well as those who became disabled because of an accident or crippling illness. The model also includes women. Most women are becoming a part of the labor force outside of the home, and many of them will become disabled and want to return as wage-earners.

## EVALUATING FOR SUCCESSFUL JOB PLACEMENT

One of the most important activities in vocational rehabilitation is job place-ment. The reality of assisting clients in obtaining gainful employment should influence each step in the rehabilitation process. It begins at the time of referral and the first interview and extends through every step taken together with the client, including the last follow-up contact. Assessment, training, and voca-tional or adjustmental counseling can each be carefully viewed in the per-spective of placement. Over the years, job placement has maintained the viability and growth of vocational rehabilitation. At the same time, this activity in rehabilitation has created the most concerns for the rehabilitation pro-fessional and potential employers.

Many rehabilitation professionals view their job responsibilities as being comprised mainly of counseling or case coordination. Performing job de-velopment tasks or generating employer awareness about hiring the disabled is considered by many to be an unwelcomed activity. In turn, many employers today claim that clients referred to them for possible jobs are, in reality, not ''job ready.'' Yet, one of the continuing facts in rehabilitation is that when a rehabilitation professional engages in job and employer development activities and refers clients who have the immediate capabilities to hold a particular job, such jobs are usually obtained, even in a tight labor market.

Job placement is in itself a process within the overall rehabilitation process. Usually, the process of job placement includes client assessment, job development, employer development, client development, and follow-up. Vandergoot et al. (1979) have conceptualized the rehabilitation process in a refreshing manner as ''productivity enrichment, productivity realization, and career enhancement'' (p. 17). Job placement is viewed as a central focus for each of these three components. Productivity enrichment, for example, in-cludes information development, strategy development, and strategy imple-mentation with such identified tasks as using occupational and labor market information, evaluating client skills and needs, establishing occupational goals, and utilizing community resources. Underlying each component is the assumption that an appropriate assessment of the client's capabilities has been made.

Assuming that client assessment is the indispensable, initial step and prime consideration for job placement, then this evaluation should be per-ceptively, efficiently, and comprehensively conducted. It is a responsibility, moreover, that can frequently be performed by the rehabilitation professional whose primary job task is not work evaluation. Issues related to the assessment responsibility are discussed in Chapter 2.

The diagnosis for job placement can be structured in such a way as to allow the rehabilitation professional the opportunity to gain necessary information in an easily understood manner. This structure develops around the general concept of *work readiness*. There is much confusion in the 1980s regarding the definition and application of work readiness (Vandergoot, 1982). Bitter (1968) believed that it is a general term relating to an individual's personal attributes to the world of work. But job readiness, he suggested, is more specific; namely, it is the extent to which an individual's qualifications fit the skill requirements of a particular job. Sinick (1969) distinguished "employability" from "placeability." Employability refers to someone who possesses the requisite skills and work personality; placeability refers to the perceived attractiveness of an applicant to an employer.

Although the concept of work readiness needs clarification, readiness can be understood by exploring the client's skills, behaviors, and psychologic traits as these attributes interact with the environment (Vandergoot, 1982). These guidelines for the evaluation of job placement should include the terms work readiness, employability, and placeability, which provide at least a perspective for assessing client characteristics relevant to labor market conditions.

## Work Readiness

There are different methods for determining work readiness. The general approaches, which are explained in greater detail later in this book, include:

1. Analysis of work history
2. Analysis of educational and social data
3. Interviews with client and family
4. Medical and psychiatric consultation
5. Psychologic testing
6. Work samples evaluation
7. Analysis of part-time or temporary work experience
8. Analysis of on-the-job training experience

Any one or a combination of these eight approaches can be utilized when determining either employability or placeability. There are more specific guidelines to follow when exploring job readiness.

## Determination of Employability

During the initial interview, an assessment has to be made as to whether the client is ready for work. Although the model of vocational functioning presented earlier in this chapter provides a broad structure for assessment activities, more specific questions must be asked in order to ascertain whether an individual has the ability to meet the varied requirements of jobs and occupations. Walls et al., (1979) developed the Vocational Behavior Checklist, which identifies seven areas of employment-related capabilities. Bolton (1982) precisely defined these areas as described below, and they are quite useful for understanding employability issues.

*Prevocational skills* The client's vocational interests and potential, knowledge about his or her need for work and what a job is

*Job-seeking skills* Behaviors needed for locating and applying for employment, i.e., understanding ads, and completing applications

*Interview skills* Behaviors needed to conduct an effective interview with a prospective employer; includes understanding the interview situation, responding, and asking appropriate questions

*Job-related skills* Skills which someone should have in order to adjust to a job situation, such as following rules and adjusting to the work environment

*Work performance skills* Behaviors of starting to work on time, following instructions, working safely, using and caring for tools, etc.

*On-the-job social skills* Getting along with others, for example, and constructively handling criticism

*Union and financial security skills* Company policies; obtaining pay, overtime, union functions, insurance, and benefits.

From these seven areas, questions develop for assessing the potential for employment.

### Physical Questions

Is the client at the maximum level of physical capacity?

Can the client travel to and from a job? Use public transportation?

Can the client work a full workday? A full work week?

Can the client meet the physical demands of the kind of work sought (Current level of performance in strength, climbing, stooping, reaching, talking, and seeing)?

Does the client understand the nature of his or her disability?

Is the client aware of activities and situations that would tend to aggravate the disability or impair general health, such as cold, heat, work location, humidity, noise, hazards, and atmospheric conditions?

Does the client know danger signs, like fatigue or coughing, as warnings that rest or treatment may be necessary?

Is the client aware of the need for periodic examinations or further treatment?

Is the client capable of living independently?

Would the client's personal appearance be acceptable to employers and coworkers? Poor personal grooming, dirty clothes, or inappropriate clothing are three major problem areas.

Does the client have a number of unfortunate personal mannerisms (tics, failure to maintain eye contact, etc.)?

### Psychologic Questions

Do the client and family accept the client's limitations?

Do the client and family recognize the client's capabilities?

Is the client sincerely motivated toward employment?
Can the client adjust to the strains and pressures of a work environment?
Does the client react appropriately to supervision?
Can the client get along with others, such as co-workers and supervisors?
Is the client a dependable worker, i.e., attendance, promptness and appropriate use of time?
Are the client's personality traits in keeping with the usual job tasks?
Are there personal or social problems that might affect the client's performance on the job?
Does the client regularly engage in any antisocial or seriously maladaptive behaviors?

### Occupational Questions

Are the client's aptitudes, skills, knowledge, and experience commensurate with usual job requirements, current and future?
Can the client do the job; namely, what is the client's capability for productivity, speed of learning, and ability to do accurate and efficient work?
Is the client aware of wages and hours?
Are the nonmonetary, psychologic rewards of working in keeping with the client's needs, values, and long-range goals?
Does the client have an occupational goal; namely, is he or she oriented toward employment?
How does the client feel about work?
What jobs has the client held, for how long were they held, when did the client leave and what were the reasons given by the client for leaving?
What aspects of the job were most satisfying to clients and why was this so?

### Socioenvironmental Questions

Do the important people in the client's life accept the client as a worker?
Would the client's family be supportive of the client as a worker?
Is the client presently receiving monetary benefits because of the disability?

With all of these employability-related concerns, the amount of exploration depends on the client's problems, needs, and the barriers that exist to achieving productivity. Yet, it is not only the physical, psychologic, occupational, and socioenvironmental areas that make the difference between readiness or lack of readiness for most types of employment; really, the attitudes and feelings of the client are far more important determinants of employability (Forrest, 1963). An evaluation of job readiness should include an assessment of the person's fundamental system of values and the clients' basic feelings and perceptions about themselves, especially as these feelings and perceptions relate to work. From this information, the professional can gain a beginning idea of the client's motivation. All in all, personality factors take on tremendous importance insofar as readiness for work is concerned. During the evaluation, attempts must be made to assess how these attitudes affect performance and what, if anything, can be done about them (Forrest, 1963).

## Determination of Placeability

Placeability is the ability of the individual to meet the hiring requirements of employers, particularly as defined by personnel officers. An individual can be employable without being placeable. For example, a client who possesses many job-related skills, but may not be able to obtain a job in a particular geographical area. Criteria for placement readiness include:

1. To what extent can the client participate in the job-finding process? Most chronically unemployed people fail to seek work with sufficient frequency. Interviewing the client should reveal the reasons for this failure, such as fear, lack of financial need to work, and lack of a job goal. Job frequency probably does depend on job opportunities to some extent.
2. Does the client know and utilize sources of job leads?
3. Can the client develop a resume or a personal information packet?
4. Can the client satisfactorily complete a job application?
5. Can the client present himself or herself adequately in a job interview?
   a. Can the client make his or her capabilities clear to employers? Can the client account for problems, such as periods of unemployment? Most clients are handicapped in an employment interview by an inability to explain some of their problems in such a manner that would induce a perspective employer to overlook or accept such problems. Typical problems are age, history of institutionalization, history of lengthy unemployment, physical handicap, and poor work history (Walker 1966).
      Also, an evaluation of whether the client can explain his or her skills to an employer is needed because employers basically hire job applicants for skills that they are known to have. During the job interview, clients need to explain their skills, usually in a very brief period of time.
   b. Is the client reasonably free of mannerisms that annoy the employer? This area can be easily evaluated by simply looking at the client and deciding whether his or her personal appearance would be acceptable to employers and co-workers.
6. Would the client continue a job search if met with some rejections?
7. Would the client conduct himself or herself appropriately if starting work tomorrow?

An explanation of placeability also includes such job market factors as: 1) unemployment rate in the client's skill area; 2) availability of jobs in the geographic area; 3) union requirements; and 4) wage requirements. During the evaluation process, the rehabilitation professional should keep these factors very much in mind.

## Standardized Measures To Assess Employability

During the past 15 years, varied assessment resources have been developed to explore the client's potential for employment. What follows is a list of measures which the author has identified as particularly useful.

*Functional Evaluation Form*    The form[1] includes background information; medical characteristics; physical characteristics of hand dominance, grasp, coordination, balance, reach, and ambulation; transfers; transportation; communication; work samples of writing; desk activities; keyboard control; telephone use; filing; tape recording; microfilming operation; use of a Xerox machine; and architectural barriers as well as work tolerance and fatigue level. Also covered is the person's level of self-care, for example, dressing, bathing, hygiene, eating, hand manipulation, household activities, and transfers. The amount of time the activities take should also be considered.

There are 50 items on the self-care scale. The client is given a score to help define in numerical terms the degree of severity of his or her disability. Zero points are given for an activity requiring maximum assistance; 1 point for moderate assistance; 2 points for minimal difficulty; and 3 points for complete independence in an activity. Assistive or adaptive devices are then given to the client.

*Employability Evaluation Form*    The Employability Evaluation Form[2] is a general guideline measuring a client's job readiness. It can be used for clients who have never worked or who have specific problems as a result of their disability (e.g., Family Problems, Transportation Problems, etc.) The form, a checklist, covers the following measures: Work Skills, Transportation, Child Care, Education, Health, Family, Appearance, Dependability, Attitude toward Work, Initiative, Work Habits, Relocation, Work Interests, Learning Ability, and Communication.

The rehabilitation counselor or placement specialist fills out the form based on client observations. The process takes approximately 30 minutes. The counselor/job specialist can provide additional comments as desired.

---

[1]The Functional Evaluation Form can be obtained free of charge from the Job Development Laboratory at George Washington University in Washington, D.C. The form can also be obtained from: Mallik, K., and Sablowky, R. 1975. Model for placement J. Rehab. Nov/Dec: 41 14–21.

[2]The Employability Evaluation Form can be obtained from Oklahoma Goodwill Industries, Inc., 410 S.W. Third St., Oklahoma City, OK 73109. Phone: 405-521-2778.

*Employability Information Sheet*    This sheet[3] provides the rehabilitation professional with important background information for placing clients in jobs. It requires the counselor to obtain basic information about the client's history (vocational objective, disability, minimum salary desired, etc.). The sheet is then sent to the placement specialist at the rehabilitation facility. It takes approximately 20 to 30 minutes for the rehabilitation counselor to fill it out.

*Placement Readiness Checklist*    This checklist[4] can be used by work evaluators and work supervisors to determine whether a client is ready to seek employment. The checklist consists of positive and negative statements in regard to a client's work behavior in such areas as Punctuality, Acceptance of Unpleasant Tasks, Interactions with Co-workers, and Tension Aroused by Close Supervision. A Summary section on the form requests that the evaluator check off those areas in which the client shows particular interest.

The checklist is usually filled out by the work evaluator and the client so that areas of weaknesses and strengths as well as employment goals can be discussed openly. The checklist is then reviewed with the placement supervisor. The form takes approximately 5 minutes to complete.

*Service Outcome Measurement Form*    This form[5] assesses a person's employability after rehabilitation services. It consists of a series of items assessing personal characteristics and 23 items rating functioning in four broad areas: Economic/Vocational Status, Physical Functioning, Adjustment to Disability, and Social Competency. A fifth area assesses the difficulty of rehabilitating a particular individual.

The form is completed by the counselor or case manager. Four criteria were used in its development and are pertinent for those who would use it. First, the form should require no changes in service delivery. Second, it should not need sophisticated electronic data-processing equipment. Third, the form should require little in-service training. Finally, the form should not require more than 10 minutes to complete.

*Employability Plan*    This plan[6] is used by work evaluators for persons who do not have any work history or have a disability that greatly interferes

---

[3]The Employability Information Sheet can be obtained from the Bureau of Vocational Rehabilitation, Rehabilitation Services Commission, 924 North Cable Rd., Lima, OH 45805. Phone: 419-228-1421.

[4]The Placement Readiness Checklist can be purchased from the Peninsula Lodge Co., 146 N. Marion Ave., Drawer PP, Bremerton, WA 98310. Phone: 206-377-0059.

[5]Information about the Service Outcome Management Form may be obtained from the Dept. of Institutions, Social, and Rehabilitative Services, Rehabilitative Services 24, P.O. Box 25352, Oklahoma City, OK 73125. Phone: 405-521-2778.

[6]The Employability Plan can be purchased from Peninsula Lodge Co., 146 N. Marion Ave., Drawer PP, Bremerton, WA 98310. Phone: 206-377-0059.

with chances for employment. The plan covers such areas as barriers to employment, skills, and training that a client presently possesses and a plan of action to overcome employability barriers. Required social services, the client's occupational goal, and the projected date of completion are also covered.

The work evaluator uses the plan to realistically assess the client's strengths and weaknesses, the services provided, and the occupational goal that has been decided upon by the counselor and client. The work evaluator fills out the form with the client. The process takes approximately 5 minutes.

*Job Readiness Scale*   This scale[7] assesses a client's job readiness. The system uses the following levels of job readiness: Placement, Pre-Placement, Work Adjustment, Work Activities and Activities of Daily Living (ADL) Skills.

Ratings on the scale correspond to levels of placement. The scale measures the client's attendance, punctuality, relationship with supervisors, relationship with co-workers, appearance, and independent functional abilities. Each staff member at the Madison Opportunity Center is assigned to a unit that works with clients within a specified level. At the end of a 3-month period and after reviewing the client's case at the unit meeting (state vocational rehabilitation clients are reviewed every 20 days), the counselor/case manager completes the scale for his or her clients. If the unit decides to move the client into a higher or lower level, the counselor responsible for that level would also be present at the meeting.

The client signs the review and the rehabilitation plan, which is part of the scale. This signature indicates that he or she has discussed it with the counselor. The scale is also signed by the client's counselor and the level coordinator and is then filled out by the counselor/case manager and reviewed with the client and level coordinator. It takes approximately 15 minutes to fill out the form. However, this may vary according to the needs and functioning level of a particular client.

*Job Readiness Test*   This test[8] determines whether the client is ready to seek employment and the areas in which the client needs to improve. The test asks the client to repond "yes" or "no" to job readiness statements concerned with such things as the employment application and the job interview. The test takes a client with a sixth-grade reading level approximately 10 to 15 minutes to complete.

---

[7]The Job Readiness Scale can be obtained from the Madison Opportunity Center, 2841 Index Rd., Madison, WI 53713. Phone: 608-274-8060.

[8]The Job Readiness Test can be obtained from the Bureau of Vocational Rehabilitation, Rehabilitation Services Commission, 924 N. Cable Rd., Lima, OH 45805. Phone: 419-228-1421.

***Readiness Planning Checklists I and II***     The checklist[9] provide the rehabilitation professional with a systematic case management tool for monitoring a client's job readiness.

Checklist I is divided into four sections or steps, each relating to specific stages in the client's rehabilitation program.

*Step 1*     General assessment is made at the time of intake and application of services.

*Step 2*     Readiness factors that can be assessed during the client's evaluations are cited. After the evaluations, "acceptable" "unacceptable," or "not applicable" is determined.

*Step 3*     The planning and implementation of the client's readiness plan is devised and implemented. Columns marked "Service Needed" and "Source" plan the client's services. Columns marked "Start" and "End" monitor the client's progress through these services.

*Step 4*     The client's readiness following completion of services is assessed. The job goal is entered at the top of the column, and then each criterion is reassessed as "acceptable," "unacceptable," or "not applicable."

Checklist II can be used in the later stages of the rehabilitation process toward actual placement in a specific job. In the first column, criteria relating to self-placement are listed under headings of "Self-Placement Skills" and "Environmental Factors." As in Checklist I, the client's readiness in each criteria is assessed by marking "acceptable," or "unacceptable." The second column is for planning and implementating all services that will move the client closer to readiness. As in Checklist I, the columns "Service Needed" and "Source" plan the individualized placement strategy for each client. Columns marked "Start" and "End" monitor the client's progress through these services. The last two columns are reserved for listing all individual client and rehabilitation professional responsibilities for tasks mutually agreed upon as needed for facilitating job placement.

Vocational assessments are made by the rehabilitation professional at different points in time. The length of time required for filling out Checklists I and II depends upon the extent and type of data the counselor has already gathered on the client.

The checklists are a mutually written agreement between the rehabilitation professional and the client. In this way, the client shares in the placement process with the rehabilitation professional's guidance.

## CONCLUSION

The principal focus of any assessment performed in vocational evaluation should be the goal of job readiness, which includes employability and place-

---

[9]The Readiness Planning Checklists I and II can be obtained from David Vandergoot, Human Resources Center, Albertson, NY 11507. Phone: 516-747-5400.

ability concerns. As explained in this chapter, the criteria for both of these concerns indicate what should be evaluated. The emphasis is on the client's behavior, and through an evaluation of this vital dimension of human functioning, the client can gain important insights into what is realistically needed to obtain and maintain employment.

## CASE STUDY

*José is age 26, born in Tijuana, Mexico, September 15, 1956. In 1968, he came to the United States, where his parents immigrated as "green card carriers." José is not a United States citizen, has not applied for citizenship, and is himself a "green card carrier" for work purposes. José is married, he lives with his wife and infant daughter, and they are expecting a second child. They live in an apartment, own their own car (which is debt-free), and reportedly subsist on $385 per month.*

*José reports he was educated in Tijuana, Mexico in Spanish to approximately the eighth grade. He feels his school progress was excellent until coming to the United States, where he was expected to comprehend ninth-grade course work in English. He reports having one course in "English as a Second Language" during his first year at a junior high school. All other courses were taught in English, even though he could not understand the material being presented. He had little comprehension of what was going on in school, lost interest, an eventually dropped out sometime during the tenth grade. He made one abortive attempt at high school, but after 2 weeks, dropped out because of the difficulty of the material, lack of understanding, loss of interest, and the necessity of having to attend evening classes.*

*José, who speaks Spanish fluently, reports that he has no difficulty understanding instructions or materials that are presented in Spanish. The language is spoken exclusively in his parent's home and predominantly in his own home, even though his wife and her parents are equally conversant in English. José reports he feels more comfortable conversing in Spanish and therefore uses it whenever possible. His use of English is primarily confined to rather simple words and phrases and is spoken somewhat haltingly. His ability to comprehend English tends to decrease rapidly with the increase of rate, word complexity, and level of word abstraction.*

*Although José has been working for approximately 4 years, his experience is essentially circumscribed by the types of jobs he has held and negative circumstances. His first job, which he reports began sometime in 1974, was as a dishwasher/kitchen helper at a large hotel. He eventually* *advanced to the pantry, where he learned to prepare many different kinds of salads. He reports liking this type of work but he had to quit because he was unable to subsist on minimum wage. José reports his second job was as an apprentice roofer. According to him, he began this job in October, 1978 at a reported rate of $4.25 per hour; but, in November, 1980, he suffered a burn accident to the right forearm, which required being off the job for approximately 3 months. During this time, skin graft surgery was performed, which, according to the medical report, was successful, leaving no residual complications or disabilities. Four months after returning to work from the previous recuperative accident, José suffered a second accident, which resulted in his present disabilities.*

*While working for his company at a large construction site, José reportedly drove a skiploader and cart loaded with gravel off a two-story building under construction. According to the report, "He fell free of the vehicle and landed on the ground on both ankles." Multiple injuries were sustained, primarily: 1) severe multiple fractures of the right leg and foot; 2) comminuted fracture and dislocation of the left foot; and 3) fracture of the right navicular in the right wrist area.*

*Since this accident, José claims that he has been almost continually in pain in his right foot and that prolonged walking, extended standing, walking on inclined surfaces, or climbing causes almost immediate pain and swelling. José tends to see his disability as something that will pass with time. This is not surprising because, in retrospect, he has seen himself become progressively better, especially viewed from the day of the accident to now. Yet, the medical report reveals that on examination of the right lower extremities, there is roughly 50% limitation on eversion and inversion of the right forefoot as compared to the left.*

*During the initial interview, José indicated that although he tends to possess a positive outlook toward future employability, he is very diffuse as to how this is to be accomplished. However, he seems to have unrealistic concepts concerning what kind of work he can do and seems to be unaware of the training and job demands appropriate to these jobs. Although he verbalizes the necessity for training so that he can return to work, he nonetheless displays (primarily by his manner) some hesitation to become involved in an extensive training program. At times, he shows a high level of responsibility, seeing the need for training in order to take care of his family, but occasionally he becomes confused over how this is to be achieved.*

With this information, please answer the following questions:

1.  What do you perceive as "employability" capabilities and limitations of this client?

2. What type of vocational assessment would you conduct with José? What problems do you foresee could arise during the evaluation with José?
3. What do you believe are the particular placement problems with this client? What would you look for in determining placeability?

## REFERENCES

Bitter, J.A. 1969. Toward a concept of job readiness. *Rehab. Lit.* 28:201–203.

Bolton, B. (ed.). 1982. Vocational Adjustment of Disabled Persons. University Park Press, Baltimore.

Forrest, J.W. 1963. Evaluating job readiness. Paper presented at the Bi-Regional Institute on Placement, March 29, Oklahoma State University, Stillwater.

Ginzberg, E. 1972. Restatement of the theory of occupational choice. Voc. Guid. Q. 20:169–176.

Hoppock, R. 1976. Occupational Information, (4th Ed.). McGraw-Hill Book Co., New York.

Knefelkamp, L.L. and Slepitza, R. 1976. A cognitive-developmental model of career development—an adaptation of the Perry scheme. Couns. Psychol. 6:53–58.

Lofquist, L., and Dawes, R. 1969. Adjustment to Work. Appleton-Century-Crofts, New York.

Sinick, D. 1969. Training, placement and follow-up. In: D. Molikin and H. Rusalem (eds.), Vocational Rehabilitation of the Disabled. New York University Press, New York.

Super, D.E. 1957. The Psychology of Careers. Harper and Row Pubs., Inc. New York.

Tiedeman, D.V. 1961. Decision and vocational development: a paradigm and its implications. Pers. Guid. J., 40:15–20.

Vandergoot, D. 1982. Work readiness assessment. Rehab. Counsel. Bull., November:84–87.

Vandergoot, D., Jacobsen, R.J., and Worral, J.D. 1979. New direction for placement practice in vocational rehabilitation. In: D. Vandergoot and J.D. Worrall (eds), Placement in Rehabilitation. University Park Press, Baltimore.

Walker, R.A. 1966. "Evaluation." Paper presented at the Institute on Professional Services, sponsored by the Pennsylvania Association of Sheltered Workshops, April, Harrisburg.

Walls, R.T., Zane, T., and Werner, T.J. 1979. The Vocational Behavior Checklist (Experimental Ed., 2nd Printing). West Virginia Research and Training Center, Cunbar, W.V.

Zytowski, D.G. 1965. Avoidance behavior in vocational motivation. Pers. Guid. J., 43:746–750.

chapter 2
# SELECTED ISSUES FOR
# DEVELOPING EFFECTIVE
# VOCATIONAL ASSESSMENT

The following issues are important to the task of rehabilitation assessment:
1) the particular role of the rehabilitation professional in vocational evaluation;
2) the varied ethical and legal issues in vocational assessment; 3) the needed
considerations when preparing the client for the evaluation process; 4) the
relationship between disability effects and the selection, administration, and
interpretation of different tests; and 5) an assessment battery for rehabilitation
professionals. These issues are presented in this chapter as building stones that
comprise a foundation for effective assessment.

## THE ROLE OF THE
## REHABILITATION PROFESSIONAL IN ASSESSMENT

As stated in the Introduction, this book is directed mainly to students in human
services or rehabilitation professionals to help them develop many basic
vocational/rehabilitation skills or enhance or update their already existing
knowledge of client evaluation. Although many practitioners may believe that
an early diagnosis of client strengths and work-related limitations is necessary,
unless they have been specifically trained as vocational evaluators, assessment
does not comprise a large part of their job duties. Fortunately, many allied
health professionals are trained in diagnostic skills, which can be applied to
exploring vocational goals.

The utilization of evaluation skills is based on the belief in early diagnosis,
the available time to perform such an exploration, and the assessment knowledge of approaches and measures that can generate relevant information. The
usual practice in most rehabilitation agencies is to purchase vocational diagnostic services. The waiting period for obtaining such information is often very
long, and clients can lose interest in the rehabilitation process. Or, other

evaluation resources may not be available. Roessler and Rubin (1980) explained that other assessment opportunities should be considered because many clients have a positive work history that does not require intensive vocational evaluation. If a person is not returning to his or her previous job, a brief vocational analysis can be conducted to identify other employment options. Also, understanding the client's productive-related strengths early and providing him or her with this information can often strongly motivate the client to achieve rehabilitation goals.

In rehabilitation, particularly in state vocational rehabilitation agencies, many cases are reopened after services in the rehabilitation process have been interrupted. Frequently, these clients do not have to go through another extended vocational evaluation (depending on the circumstances), but an update of client employable strengths can be most useful. When the counselor has the ability to conduct such an exploration, this assessment may expedite the achievement of rehabilitation goals.

The National Seminar on Competency-Based Rehabilitation Education in Atlanta in July, 1978 (Rubin and Porter, 1979) indicated that rehabilitation counselors as well as vocational evaluators must be capable of developing a systematic evaluation plan and writing useful evaluation reports on clients. Roessler and Rubin (1982) believed that counselors must be able to ''manage'' a comprehensive medical, psychologic and vocational evaluation of the client. An implication of this management is that the counselor must at least be able to understand the process of obtaining assessment data; recognize the diagnostic instruments used; and organize all of this information for client planning purposes.

The independent living movement in rehabilitation suggests a more active role for the rehabilitation counselor in evaluation functions. Although counseling is usually the only direct service provided in local rehabilitation offices, many assessment measures have been devised for use by rehabilitation professionals who work with the severely disabled (Bolton, 1982). The Functional Assessment Inventory (Crewe and Athelstan, 1978), the Vocational Behavior Checklist (Walls et al, 1978), and the Rehabilitation Initial Diagnosis and Assessment of Clients (RIDAC) are a few examples (Bolton, 1982). Boland and Alonso (1982) explained that in order to meet the demands of clients in independent living, counselors must have the knowledge and skills to develop and carry out highly individualized rehabilitation plans. They also have to continually reassess their clients in order to determine new areas of need and then change their rehabilitation plans accordingly. Wright (1980) believed that rehabilitation professionals who work with the severely disabled often confront the demands of a basic evaluation. Their assessment includes determining functional limitations and capacities. The intake interview with the severely disabled necessitates the responsibility for knowing what specific independent living services are needed for the particular client. But such a task presumes an ability to understand client capabilities and then actually evaluating rehabilitation potential and goals.

Consequently, for varied reasons, rehabilitation professionals should help their clients acquire some useful knowledge related to productive, rehabilitation related capabilities. For many years, the opportunity to do this has been given primarily to those specially trained in vocational assessment. Although psychologists or vocational evaluators are credibly performing a very needed job, still other rehabilitation professionals could perform many vocationally related, diagnostic activities. But these assessment duties cannot be performed without adequate knowledge of basic evaluation situations, particular approaches, and developed methods. Even then, the extent of the professional's assessment tasks will be limited. For example, many areas of personality functioning or disabilities that relate to brain impairment demand specialized training and should only be evaluated by professionals who are expert in these areas.

For the rehabilitation counselor, the amount of time that can be devoted to this task of evaluation is uncertain. Other case management functions are quite time-consuming. For professional, philosophical reasons that impact on job responsibilities, counselors may hesitate to become involved in assessment tasks. Arguments about the role and function of the rehabilitation counselor have been going on for many, many years. Roessler and Rubin (1982) identified several studies that describe how rehabilitation counselors spend their time or view their jobs. The majority of time seems to be spent either in recording, report writing, clerical work, counseling, and guidance (Rubin and Emener, 1979; Zadny and James, 1977). All the research reports suggest that the rehabilitation counselor has a diverse job role (Rubin and Emener, 1980; Wright and Fraser, 1976).

Although all of these considerations suggest a variation in thought and research on the role and functions of many rehabilitation professionals, they do not eliminate the opportunity and necessity for helping the client to acquire important information for eventual rehabilitation planning. An understanding of productive- and work-related capabilities is an integral part of this knowledge. These client goals bring not only a challenge but in many instances, also a responsibility for the rehabilitation professional. Whether the professional is a physical or occupational therapist working in a hospital or clinic; a rehabilitation nurse or counselor pursuing private practice or employed by a state agency, private firm, or a large institution; or a social worker who is also assisting clients back to work, he or she can conduct many vocational assessment tasks with the training and motivation to perform the beginning evaluation. This book presumes the presence of motivation and is written to provide both basic and selected rehabilitation assessment skills.

## LEGAL AND ETHICAL ISSUES IN VOCATIONAL ASSESSMENT

Matkin (1980) identified many important issues concerning the provision of evaluation services. He explained that:

> Problems with test use can be avoided or substantially reduced if care is taken to select devices which reportedly measure those traits to be evaluated. The evaluator should also be aware of the intended use for which the instrument was designed and avoid interpreting results in areas beyond the capabilities of the device.

Other significant guidelines (Matkin, 1980) are as follows:

1.  Caution must be exercised when depending on test instruments to provide information about client needs and traits. The client's evaluation program should be carefully planned to avoid the overuse or indiscriminate use of testing. For example, instrument selection should be tailored to the needs of the client, and tests designed specifically for certain disability groups should be used to ensure the accuracy of outcome scores.

2.  Vocational assessment may be used as both a descriptive measure of client functioning and as an indicator of potential. When exploring client capability, the rehabilitation professional must examine the appropriateness of the testing instrument with regard to reliability, validity, and norming populations. Matkin (1980) wrote: "The vocational evaluator is ethically obliged when reporting outcomes to indicate the reasons why clients fail to perform at average or above levels and ways for remediating the deficiency." (p. 59).

3.  The privacy of the client must be respected and all information and materials obtained during the assessment process should be safeguarded. The Code of Ethics of the Vocational Evaluation and Work Adjustment Association states that confidentiality of information and materials should be maintained, and the client should be informed as to whom the assessment information will be transmitted and under what circumstances it will be released. Test scores, moreover, should be released only to those persons qualified to interpret them.

4.  The clients' needs and reaction to the assessment process should be carefully considered. Environmental influences (e.g., room temperature, ventilation, restricted movement, or inappropriate language in the instructions) and client traits (e.g., sensory defects, inability to read, motivation level, lighting, or test-taking strategies) demand attention to ensure that "outcome measures reflect an accurate assessment of the evaluated traits." (p. 60).

5.  Although a relatively long period of intensive training and supervised experience is required for the proper use of individual intelligence tests and most personality measures, a minimum of specialized psychologic training is needed for educational achievement or vocational proficiency tests.

6.  When there is a need to modify tests to accomodate certain disability groups, the appropriateness of the reported normative data must be determined, and, when warranted, validation studies should be conducted.
7.  Testing should only be used when necessary, and the rehabilitation professional should be aware of the proper use of testing and the specific instruments from which to choose. Also, testing material should be stored in a secure place.
8.  The client should be involved in the selection of testing and the interpretation of results.
9.  Rehabilitation professionals involved in assessment should demonstrate competencies not only in the understanding and interpretation acquired during the assessment and rehabilitation process but also knowledge of the world of work, familiarity with studies of human behavior, and an awareness of the limitations of test interpretation.
10. Rehabilitation professionals involved in assessment should periodically reexamine their own competencies, as well as keep abreast of current labor market trends, employment requirements for assorted occupations, and work modification techniques.

## CLIENT PREPARATION IN ASSESSMENT

Building upon the assumptions that rehabilitation workers perform some evaluation with their clients and also communicate effectively with them, a necessary step in the assessment process is to prepare the client for this involvement. (Preparing clients who are referred to "outside" agencies for vocational evaluation is discussed in Chapter 10.) Because the interview itself can be a valuable assessment resource (as explained in Chapter 4), no specific client preparation for the interview is needed.

After the professional decides to utilize standardized measures in order to gain more information for rehabilitation planning, he or she should prepare the client for this opportunity. The professional should: 1) create a relaxed, nonthreatening atmosphere; and 2) solicit the client's input for the particular goals of assessment. In other words, explaining the purpose of assessment and how it fits into the development of effective rehabilitation planning frequently helps the client to identify some personal goals for evaluation. The importance of learning more about and, especially, becoming aware of personal strengths should be stressed. Such questions as: "How do you feel about identifying your capabilities and interests?" and "What particular information about yourself would you like to have?" could encourage the client's input. It is necessary to be aware of the client's level of understanding or what obstacles might block the client's comprehension of these questions and the assessment process itself.

Speech and hearing limitations, intellectual deficits, and the side effects of medication can all present barriers to effective communication.

With client input, a decision must be made about the sequence of tests that should be taken. This choice should not be made, however, until the rehabilitation worker decides what further information must be obtained after the initial interview, especially one used for diagnostic purposes. This author's priority for providing standardized measures is for interest tests to begin the formal evaluation process. A number of these tests, appropriate for a wide variety of clients are discussed in Chapter 9. Frequently, the client can take home an interest test after the initial interview, but the professional must be very careful about reliability and related test-taking issues, discussed in Chapter 5.

Regardless of the sequence in which tests are administered, precautions should be taken. During testing, all possible distractions should be reduced and client fatigue minimized. Also, the client should realize that every effort must be exerted in order to do as well as possible. Of course, all clients experience anxiety and apprehension when taking any test. However, when the nature of the test, background information concerning the norm group, and how the particular measure fits in with assessment goals are all communicated, this tension can be reduced. When confidential issues with assessment are explained and clients are told that when taking an interest or personality measure, they are actually describing themselves *to* themselves, often they feel better about the evaluation. Also, questions from clients about a particular assessment measure should be solicited.

Client preparation is based on timely and knowledgeable communication from the rehabilitation professional. Understanding client needs and disability-related limitations, how the particular test will be used, and those factors that enhance the reliability of the client's involvement (such as rest, minimal distractions, control of anxiety, and best possible effort) can contribute to developing a relaxed, nonthreatening atmosphere. Such an evaluation environment can help to make the assessment experience a valuable one for the client.

## RELATIONSHIP OF DISABILITY EFFECTS
## TO THE SELECTION, ADMINISTRATION,
## AND INTERPRETATION OF ASSESSMENT MEASURES

Even with careful preparation of the client, further considerations must be attended to when developing assessment plans. There is the ever-present possibility that evaluation, especially psychometric testing, may do more harm than good. Unless particular attention is directed to the choice of an appropriate test, the prudent use of administration procedures, and the enlightened interpretation of assessment results, the client and rehabilitation professional will have a decidedly negative experience.

Clients bring to rehabilitation opportunities a variety of individual traits, competencies, and limitations. Frequently, factors like motivation, interests, and work tolerance may be just as important for reaching rehabilitation goals as qualities like intelligence and learning-related aptitudes. Using standardized test instruments is not necessarily the best way for evaluating many of these client characteristics. Observation of the client in different settings, trial experiences in a job situation, and behavioral techniques could be better methods for understanding the disabled person's rehabilitation potential. For example, a client who has a congenital disability may have had different life experiences from those of the populations on whom the standardized tests were normed. The use of standardized, psychologic measures, therefore, may not be appropriate for him or her, and other assessment approaches should be explored.

The inappropriateness of standardized tests for certain populations in rehabilitation is especially true when such measures are used only for exploring the person's potential for learning. The test performances of the severely disabled are often affected by emotional issues and sensory and motor limitations. Comparing the disabled person's performance on a particular test to the norm group used to standardize the measure when the norm group did not have comparable limitations is discriminatory.

When the purpose of evaluation is to understand the client's level of current functioning, the use of standardized measures may be justified. The rehabilitation professional wants to know how the client scores on the measure and how this compares with nondisabled persons. The careful use of tests, particularly aptitude and achievement measures, is warranted because specific knowledge of how a client's abilities or competencies compare with those of nondisabled persons may be necessary for rehabilitation planning to be relevant. After all, the client may work with the nondisabled population, their production demands may have to be met. Information on how the client compares with these demands and what will be needed in order to compete in a training or work situation is most useful when developing rehabilitation plans.

If the rehabilitation professional is aware of these issues and pays special attention to disability effects and their impact on the vocational assessment process, then evaluation can become a valuable opportunity for the client. In this perspective of awareness, the following factors should be considered when exploring evaluation approaches for a particular client:

1. Age of disability onset
2. Nature of physical and emotional limitations
3. Medication effects
4. Relationship of the client's life experiences to the content of the proposed evaluation measures

5. Educational experiences
6. Physical tolerance
7. The extent to which rehabilitation procedures have assisted the client in compensating for physical limitations

This exploration presumes, of course, that the rehabilitation professional is knowledgeable about particular tests and measures used in vocational assessment, especially the nature of test items and what effects the reliability of the testing situation. (These issues are discussed in Chapter 5.) But with the seven factors identified above, particular concerns relating to disability effects (physical, emotional, and intellectual) must be addressed when considering the selection, administration, and interpretation of evaluation measures.

## Physical Disability Effects

Physical disability effects include communication difficulties, such as visual and hearing impairments, and motor and orthopedic problems.

### Selection

What is the verbal level of the test and the difficulty of the concepts involved?
How has the nature of the disability affected the range of life experiences to which the disabled person has been exposed?
With the visually impaired, do they have vision of some use in handling large objects, locating test pieces in a work space, or following the hand movements of the rehabilitation professional? Also, can those persons read ink print effectively although they may need large type?
What is the extent of impaired manual ability?

### Administration

To minimize client anxiety, the less involved and performance type tests should be administered first.
When possible, tests should be administered individually and in small blocks of time rather than in concentrated periods. Many clients with neurologic impairments, for example, may have a high level of distractibility. Also, many of the physically disabled, especially those with severe impairments, tire easily. Fatigue is often facilitated by attempts to deal with a variety of communication difficulties during the testing process.
Particular attention must be given to those with visual or auditory impairments. The professional should consider the absence of flickering lights; where light is provided; the establishment of rapport so that the client feels free to tell the professional that he or she is tiring; and the possible adjustment of

time limits, realizing that such a change will affect the standardized scoring.

For many of the severely disabled, the manner of recording answers may have to be changed. For example, a client may have no use of either hand or, even with use of one hand, have great difficulty in correctly marking the answer space. The use of another person to record the answers or a specially designed answer sheet may have to be utilized.

### *Interpretation*
(This subject is discussed in greater detail in Chapter 10)

Always communicate test results at the client's level of understanding.

Give special concern to how the client's disability relates to influences on the test-taking process, such as transient emotional states, the deviation from the normative response and why there is a deviation. Is there a deviation because, for example, of special disability factors, or, is it because of developmental factors? In other words, the disabled person's current functioning, as well as past experiences, are considered in the process of test interpretation.

## Emotional and Intellectual Disability Effects

Emotional and intellectual disability effects can include organically based mental deficiencies; emotional states of long duration, such as grief and mourning; anger, depression, and denial; and emotional behaviors resulting from chronic mental conditions, such as varied forms of schizophrenia.

### *Selection*

Attention should be given to the selection of assessment measures that are appropriate to the client's level of understanding, particularly his or her reading ability.

Tests that are particularly long or assessment measures that require a long period of time to complete, should be avoided. Most clients with serious emotional and cognitive problems have low attention spans and shorter tasks are certainly more appropriate.

### *Administration*

If possible, administer the assessment measures individually. Group testing may provide too many distractions for the emotionally disturbed, who may have difficulty understanding the test-taking procedures unless they are explained slowly, carefully, and individually.

Particular attention should be given to whether the client understands the directions for taking a particular assessment measure. It is helpful if the professional asks the client to explain these directions after they have been communicated to this disabled person.

*Interpretation*    As explained earlier, interpretation issues are discussed in Chapter 10. Feedback regarding test results is critical in vocational evaluation. The rehabilitation professional should make every effort to report information so that it is understood by the client. Disabled persons must also be given a chance to express their feelings about this information. Frequently, the clients' rehabilitation expectations exceed their measured abilities, and the professional will have to spend some time dealing with this discrepancy.

The preceding materials identify many selected issues that arise when clients with either a physical or mental disability approach the rehabilitation assessment situation. If the professional is aware that special problems (usually arising from disability-related limitations) could occur during evaluation, he or she can take a beginning step toward ensuring the credibility of the client's vocational assessment.

## AN ASSESSMENT BATTERY

Table 2.1 outlines assessment tools that can be utilized when exploring rehabilitation goals with the client. Most of these measures or approaches are explained in later chapters of this book, but they are introduced here to give an overview of the varied ways in which information about a person with a mental or physical disability can be gained.

## CONCLUSION

If the professional acknowledges the opportunity to gain needed information about a client's vocational capabilities and understands how disability limitations affect the evaluation process, a timely, relevant diagnostic experience for the disabled client can be facilitated. Vocational assessment, of course, is done to obtain needed information. It is part of the overall rehabilitation process, and as an integral factor in the client's development towards rehabilitation goals, presents an invaluable chance for self-awareness and effective decision-making. To achieve this effectiveness, the professional and client must work together. When the disabled person is intimately involved in vocational evaluation and the professional is knowledgeable about the different ways to gain information about a client, the process will be meaningful. The following chapters of this book discuss how this evaluation experience becomes an important, unique step for the client to reach rehabilitation goals.

Table 2.1.    Assessment tools for exploring rehabilitation goals

| Information needed about the person | Measures/Approaches | Type of handicap |
|---|---|---|
| *Physical functioning* Current level of performance in strength, walking, stooping, reaching, talking and seeing; Current level of response to work location, cold, heat, humidity, noise, hazards, and atmospheric conditions | Medical records Interview information and self description Crawford Small Parts Dexterity Test | Learning disability, emotionally disturbed, mentally retarded, hearing impaired, and some cerebral palsy and orthopedically handicapped |
| | Pennsylvania Bi-Manual Worksample | All handicaps |
| | Purdue Pegboard | All handicaps, but special modifications needed for visually and hearing impaired and orthopedically handicapped. |
| *Intellectual and aptitude functioning* Current level of reasoning, mathematics, and language development; specific capacities and aptitudes | Educational experience and records Interview information and self-description Weschler Adult Intelligence Scale (WAIS) | All handicaps, but limited use with visual and hearing impaired. |
| | Slosson Intelligence Test; Peabody Picture Vocabulary Test (PPVT); Revised Beta Examination; Raven Progressive Matrices; Quick Test; Shipley-Hartford; Otis Quick Scoring Mental Ability Tests | All handicaps, but limited use with visual and hearing impaired; Peabody is more for MR |
| | Haptic Intelligence Scale for the Adult Blind; Standford Kohs Tactile Block Design | Designed more for the visually impaired. |

*(continued)*

Table 2.1.    *(Continued)*

| Information needed about the person | Measures/Approaches | Type of handicap |
|---|---|---|
| | Wide Range Achievement Test; Adult Basic Learning Examination (ABLE); Peabody Individual Achievement Test | All handicaps except the hearing-impaired and visually impaired. |
| | General Aptitude Test Battery; Nonreading Aptitude Test Battery; Differential Aptitude Tests; Flanagan Aptitude Classification Tests; Bennett Mechanical Comprehension Test; Minnesota Clerical Test | All handicaps except the visually impaired; GATB might require modifications for the cerebral palsied, orthopedically handicapped, mentally retarded, and hearing impaired |
| | Work samples | All handicaps, but some modifications of each work sample may be necessary for some disabilities |
| *Emotional functioning* Adjustment to different types of occupational situations | Verified work history Interview information and self-description | |
| | Edwards Personnel Preference Schedule | Learning-disabled; cerebral palsied; orthopedically handicapped; hearing impaired |
| | Sixteen Personality Factor Questionnaire, (16 PF), Form E | All handicaps except the mentally retarded and visually impaired |
| | AAMD Adaptive Behavior Scales | Mentally retarded |
| | The Psychological Screening Inventory | All handicaps except the mentally retarded and visually impaired |
| | Tennessee Self-Concept Scale | All handicaps except the mentally retarded and visually impaired; some modification for the mentally ill |

*(continued)*

Table 2.1.   *(Continued)*

| Information needed about the person | Measures/Approaches | Type of handicap |
|---|---|---|
| *Interest exploration* | | |
| Preference for certain types of work activities | Picture Interest Inventory | All but visually impaired |
| | Wide Range Interest Opinion Test | All handicaps |
| | Geist Picture Interest Inventory (Revised) | All but visually impaired |
| | Minnesota Importance Questionnaire | All handicaps; fifth-grade reading level is required |
| | Vocational Interest and Sophistication Assessment Survey | All handicaps except visually impaired and mentally retarded |
| | Minnesota Vocational Interest Inventory | All handicaps except visually impaired and mentally retarded |
| | Gordon Occupational Checklist | All handicaps, if verbally presented |
| | Strong Vocational Interest Blank for Men and Women | All handicaps except visually impaired and mentally retarded |
| | Kuder Occupational Interest Survey | All handicaps except visually impaired and mentally retarded |
| | The Self-Directed Search | All handicaps except visually impaired and mentally retarded |
| *Functioning in particular areas (employability and placeability)* | | |
| Job readiness | Previous work experience | Much of this information |
| | Employability Evaluation | obtained by a supervisor, |
| | Employability Information Sheet | if the client takes the particular measure, then |
| | Placement Readiness Checklist | all handicaps except the visually impaired |
| | Service Outcome Measurement Form | and mentally retarded |
| | Interview information and self-description | |
| | Employability Plan | |
| | Job Readiness Scale | |
| | Job Readiness Test | |
| | Readiness Planning Checklist | |

*(continued)*

Table 2.1.  *(Continued)*

| Information needed about the person | Measures/Approaches | Type of handicap |
|---|---|---|
| *Environmental (family situation and financial resources)* | | |
| Influence of significant others | Interview information and self-description | |

## CASE STUDY

The following case study emphasizes the importance of both preparing a client for the evaluation opportunity and understanding how emotional and physical factors influence the way assessment is pursued with him or her.

*Bruce presents himself for vocational rehabilitation opportunities. He is age 26, married for 5 years, and has two children. He played professional football for 3 years. He was injured in a car accident 10 months ago, immediately after the conclusion of the football season. Because of permanent injury to his legs, he has been told that he can no longer consider "contact" sports as an employment possibility. Bruce uses a cane when walking and is unable to stand for prolonged periods of time.*

*After graduating from high school with a C average, he went into the army for 2 years and then enrolled in college at a state university. After the first year, he was awarded a football scholarship. Although he left college before completing a degree program, he was only 16 credits short of receiving a Bachelor of Science degree in Business Administration. Bruce has not returned to college to complete the degree requirements, and during the "off" season worked for a car dealer as a salesman. In his spare time, he would be with his family or go to the gym for physical conditioning. He now believes that he would not like to return to selling cars but is interested in something else. Yet, he has no idea what that is. Also, Bruce's father was killed in an automobile accident 3 years ago, and his mother lives with his brother and wife. There are no other relatives.*

With this information, answer the following questions:

1.  As a rehabilitation worker, what opportunity would you have to perform any vocational assessment with this client? Could you use any standardized tests?
2.  Presuming that Bruce will return for some vocational assessment with you, how would you want to prepare Bruce for this experience?

3. Considering Bruce's disability, and related factors, what must you keep in mind as possible influences (physical, emotional, and intellectual) on the evaluation process?

## REFERENCES

Boland, J.M. and Alonso, G. 1982. A comparison: Independent living rehabilitation and vocational rehabilitation. J. Rehab. 48:50–59.

Bolton, B. (ed.). 1982. Vocational Adjustment of Disabled Persons. University Park Press, Baltimore.

Crewe, N.M., and Athelstan, G.T. 1978. Functional Assessment Inventory. University of Minnesota Department of Physical Medicine and Rehabilitation, Minneapolis, MN. (Reprinted in: B. Bolton and D.W. Cook (eds.), Rehabilitation Client Assessment, pp. 389–399, University Park Press, Baltimore.

Emener, W.G., and Rubin, S.E. 1980. Rehabilitation counselor role and functions and sources of role strain. J. Appl. Rehabil. Counsel. 11:57–59.

Matkin, R. 1980. Legal and ethical issues in vocational assessment. Voc. Eval. Work Adj. Bull. 13:57–60.

Roessler, R.T. and Rubin, S.E. 1982. Case Management and Rehabilitation Counseling. University Park Press, Baltimore.

Rubin, S.E. and Emener, W.G. 1979. Recent rehabilitation counselor role changes and role strain—a pilot investigation. J. Appl. Rehabil. Counsel. 10:142–147.

Rubin, S.E., and Porter, T. 1979. Rehabilitation counselor and vocational evaluator competencies. J. Rehab. 45:42–45.

Walls, R.T., Zane, T., and Werner, T.J. 1978. The vocational behavior checklist (Experimental Edition). West Virginia Research and Training Center, Dunbar, WV.

Wright, G. 1980. Total Rehabilitation, Little, Brown, and Co., Boston.

Wright, G.N., and Fraser, R.T. 1976. Improving manpower utilization: The "Rehabilitation Task Performance Evaluation Scale." Regional Rehabilitation Research Institute, University of Wisconsin, Madison.

Zadny, J., and James, L. 1977. Time spent on placement. Rehabil. Counsel. Bull. 21:31–35.

# chapter 3

# UNDERSTANDING THE CLIENT
## Characteristics of Clients Most Frequently Seen in Evaluation

There are a number of vital considerations when preparing vocational rehabilitation plans for clients. Among them are: 1) the results of vocational assessment; 2) employment opportunities; 3) existing training resources in the geographical area; 4) the feasibility of alternative goals when a full-time job is not possible because of physical or mental limitations; and 5) the need for client input to the plan itself. One of the most important ingredients in effective planning is *the professional's awareness of specific client dynamics that can facilitate or impede the achievement of rehabilitation goals*. A client's vocational rehabilitation, for example, is influenced by personality (DeNour and Czaczkes, 1975). Clients come for assessment with a wide assortment of distinctive vocational assets and problems, including certain emotional difficulties that represent barriers to productivity. Recognizing all of these factors is important in identifying what vocational evaluation approaches should be used for a particular client. This chapter explains such problems, assets, and emotional issues by describing typical clients in rehabilitation assessment. Client categories have been identified mainly by the author's experience in working with rehabilitation clients throughout the years.

### THE RESTORER-ACHIEVER

Restorer-achievers have usually incurred a disability after years of satisfying work. Generally, they are younger (ages 30 through 45), have a strong work ethic, and through working, have gained both a sense of stability and identity in their lives. Importantly, these persons believe they possess many work-related skills. Although they harbor feelings of loss because of disability-related limitations, they are anxious to return to work and are usually open to many job alternatives. They perceive their disabilities as a fact of life, an inconvenience, and/or a cause of frustration.

These clients can manage their own affairs, and come to a state or private rehabilitation agency for training or other remedial help, e.g., prosthetics or job leads. Unaware of the different resources that can assist them in their rehabilitation efforts, they seek information on how to reenter the job market. Although they are often suspicious about the kind of help the agency can offer, they are task-oriented, show much energy and motivation, and possess a positive attitude shaped by past experiences. They need and want the help that rehabilitation agencies can provide. These clients have many of the employable traits that are necessary to hold a job, e.g., psychologic readiness, a work personality previously shaped by conscientiousness and competitiveness, and transferable job skills. What they particularly need from assessment is an awareness of transferable skills and abilities that can help them to regain employment.

## Case Example

*Bradley, who worked for 24 years as a machinist, was injured on the job. He is a high school graduate, married for 16 years and has three children. He had risen slowly in his plant until an accident he suffered while moving some heavy machinery. After hospitalization and entering outpatient status for back and leg injuries, he learned that the entire factory was moving to the South for economic reasons. He and his family, were against such a move; but work in his skill was scarce in his geographic area, and he decided to apply for vocational services at a state rehabilitation agency. During assessment, he was eager to learn new tasks; although still sad about seeking another line of work, he was anxious to begin employment. His family depended on him for support. Disability-related benefits were being paid and continually available and he still saw himself as the main family provider. He viewed evaluation as an opportunity to learn new job-related capabilities.*

Assessment approaches for Bradley and similar clients, while identifying transferable skills, should also be challenging enough to explore optimal capabilities. The client's input should be solicited frequently during the evaluation, especially regarding personal feelings about performance on evaluative tasks. Soliciting such feedback conveys the professional's respect for the opinion of clients, helping them to become more involved in the assessment process. Such involvement might alleviate feelings of suspicion about the agency, and leads to a greater independence and sense of control.

## THE AMBIVALENT

Clients who have mixed feelings about returning to work represent one of the lingering thorns in the side of the rehabilitation professional. Because of a long period of medical recuperation, many individuals become accustomed to an inactive life-style, which gradually minimizes vocational responsibility. Ambivalent clients want to go back to work and believe they can return to their former job; deep down, however, they harbor the strong suspicion that it is not going to be possible. Many ambivalent clients are receiving workman's compensation payments. Often, paid employment provides these clients with little gain of income over insurance payments, and rehabilitation offers little incentive for renouncing secure, steady, and dependable payment (Schlenoff, 1979). Yet, these persons are frequently required to seek rehabilitation services. They are afraid of losing their newly gained benefits if they find a job, and such monetary compensation often fosters a dependence upon these benefits. They view themselves as suffering individuals. They feel inept and unable to meet the standards of being productive. They are afraid to take risks and are particularly uncomfortable if their considerations about returning to work include competing for available jobs. Competition involves too many risks of failure. Generally, they show repeated expressions of an approach/avoidance conflict about employment and independence.

Ambivalent clients usually have attitudinal problems, including a pessimistic view about their occupational future. Surprisingly, however, when they are involved in the assessment process, they are usually cooperative and are often willing to please the agency staff. These clients also actively pursue many assessment tasks and are anxious to learn about the evaluation results. At the same time, their actual job outlook is characterized by extreme caution, suspiciousness, and a reluctance to learn about their own capabilities.

What often maintains this ambivalence is not only a suspiciousness of accepting employment, but also the realization of little, continued satisfaction from previous work experiences. Work has never been viewed as a desirable goal in life, and when rehabilitation opportunities are presented, they become very uncertain, defensive, and confused. Disability gives them a convenient and socially acceptable excuse for their continued hesitation to work.

There are some occasions when clients who present themselves as having mixed feelings about rehabilitation actually are only being very cautious or suspicious of the evaluation process itself. They may associate assessment primarily with "testing," but they have poorly developed test-taking skills or failed many tests in school. Consequently, they feel reluctant about going into a situation where they might "look bad" or "more inadequate" than they really are. For many of the disadvantaged, for example, the most difficult part of any assessment is not in content (such as achievement tests or work samples) but the very fact they are being tested. Ambivalence can be caused by fear of failure; many past, negative reinforcing experiences; or a hostile attitude of the

vocational evaluation staff toward minority or handicapped clients. Clients
may perceive that the rehabilitation professional already has a negative expectation toward them or really does not expect too much. In approaching an
assessment situation, then, the client has a tendency to "freeze" as his or her
values and way of life are challenged.

## Case Example

*Angela, a salesclerk in a leading department store, broke her arm
and severely injured her knee in a fall while working. She always had a
difficult time with school and usually did poorly in examinations because
of her extreme anxiety in a testing situation. She found her present job
after 7 months of an employment search. She had been working with the
store for 11 years and during her convalescence was referred to vocational
rehabilitation because she told her social worker that she was too embar-
rassed to return to her former employment. She states that her accident
made her feel like an irresponsible person, and she was extremely afraid
that her co-workers would be talking about her. Even though she had re-
cuperated nicely, Angela was no longer able to stand for prolonged periods of time as her former job required.*

*In assessment, she had conflictual feelings about returning to work.
She was quite anxious during evaluation, and the evaluator had to spend
much time before each evaluation task to relieve her test anxiety. She mentioned that she had spent many years becoming a good, highly productive
salesperson, and "now that is gone." Her disability payments were
enough to sustain her close to her previous level of living because she is
unmarried and has no unusual financial demands. But during assessment,
she often expressed to the agency staff, "I really wonder whether there is
anything I can do that would bring me as much satisfaction as my previous
job in the store."*

Generally, clients who have mixed feelings about whether or not to work
need information about their capabilities, support in facing the unknown,
clarification about their medical condition, and assurance that renewed opportunities can bring personal satisfaction. Alternatives to a life of dependency on
disability-related benefits or opportunities for newly discovered self-esteem
through work accomplishment should be indicated. This exploration of choice
is usually more successful with younger clients because the older, disabled
worker tends to find disability payments a much better alternative to the
tediousness of employment, especially if his or her job brought little emotional
gain. Also, short experiences during assessment that will give immediate,
positive feedback to the client are necessary. Situational assessment, explored
later in this book, is often the most valuable evaluative method to provide this
feedback.

## THE SECONDARY GAINER

Secondary-gainers are clients who make no pretense about their desire to return to work. They usually will go through an assessment experience because they are required to do so in order to receive continued disability-related benefits. Unlike the ambivalent client, secondary-gainers are not even willing to cautiously try to find new work opportunities. They maximize the extent of work limitations resulting from a chronic condition, and many of these limitations are self-imposed.

The concept of secondary gain proves to be of particular concern with regard to clients who receive insurance payments. They generally have had little confidence in themselves as workers and now find a dependency role a preferred style of living. Disability even strengthens the dependency. Family members may also encourage this dependence because they may unwittingly contribute to the disabled person's helplessness and inactive life-style. Lowered family expectations regarding the performance of household responsibilities or an exaggerated attention to the person's needs may further contribute to this dependency. The family attempts to make the person's life easier and less burdensome, and in doing so not only meets the person's needs but at the same time may also remove responsibilities related to home and family goals. Dependency then becomes a way of life, and the disabled person is very comfortable in an existence where needs are easily met and demands are minimal.

In an interview session during vocational evaluation, secondary gainers are often manipulative. They try to present their current life situation in such a way to solicit sympathy for their disability. There are also difficulties in establishing plans of action to meet any life responsibilities. They convey a lack of definiteness about future plans or little willingness to meet scheduling demands for medical, training, and counselor appointments during the rehabilitation process. Furthermore, these clients focus more on the negative aspects of their life. The secondary-gainer may have had many negative experiences associated with work. Employment that is personally fulfilling has never been found, and now the disability provides an excuse for not working.

Many clients who have found a valuable secondary gain in dependency also have continued physical pain related to the disability. This is particularly true with workers who have injured their lower backs. These workers often display:

> . . . unusual postures, limps, patterns of inactivity, or a reliance on medication and prosthetic appliances to help control the pain. Ironically, reliance upon such methods often serves to maintain the disability process and in turn, reduces the probability of successful vocational rehabilitation (Lynch, 1979, p. 165).

Pain becomes a dominating reality in their lives and precipitates such behaviors as fear, chronic complaining, depression, and dependency.

Surprisingly, the person's self-esteem is often not lowered because of the continued gratification for dependency needs. The role of being disabled becomes satisfying because it may force others to care for the client. Compensation benefits accruing from an injury also increase the reinforcement value of the sick role.

### Case Example

*After discharge from the military service, Oscar obtained a job as a sorter with the post office. While coming to work one winter day, he slipped on ice, fell, and although proceeding to his "boring, dead-end job," went to his family doctor at the end of the day. During the examination, the doctor discovered other symptoms that eventually led, after specialized consultation, to the diagnosis of multiple sclerosis. Oscar was told that he could still work and generally maintain the pattern of his daily life. Instead, he decided to leave his job and seek compensation benefits to maintain an unmarried, very routine, and single life-style. After a few months, he obtained these benefits because of his medical condition, and for the next 26 years did not seek or have regular employment. When he married, his wife worked, for she was anxious to pursue her own career as an elementary-school teacher. Over the years, the compensation benefits grew. When he was eventually referred to evaluation for possible rehabilitation goals, he stated to the evaluator, "I never derived any pleasure from working." He went through the motions of assessment, but before its conclusion, called the evaluator to say that he felt his illness had become worse and he could not continue.*

Another form of secondary gain is expressed by clients who want to maintain the status quo of an inactive life-style. Usually middle-aged and with good work histories, they become injured and then resist any efforts for a return to the work sector. They are basically very angry at having disabilities, but the anger is suppressed and takes the form of reluctance. As the disability is perceived as a burdensome and unwelcomed disruption on what was a stable, conservative life-style, they claim "I've done my work already . . . I can't do anything more." Attempts to plan rehabilitation goals are resisted, and although they may come for assessment, they really do not want to be involved in evaluation and are most reluctant to follow through on any vocational plan formulated to begin after the assessment. During work evaluation, they cannot organize effectively, and because of slowness and hesitancy, their assessment productivity is below competitive standards. These clients often claim they lack the physical energy to meet the job expectations of others.

During assessment, it is important to help these clients acknowledge their own remaining work capabilities, and gradually to assist them in recognizing their life-styles of dependency and secondary gain. When reluctance to be involved in evaluative tasks is detected, the professional should communicate a concern and then explore the reasons for this hesitancy by reflecting the feelings of the client, interpreting the secondary gain to the client, and providing the client with an understanding, for example, that his or her reluctance to be involved or to return to work may be a fear of losing compensation or newly found family support. These clients should be involved in decisions for assessment planning and given as much responsibility as possible.

One of the assessment goals also should be to raise the client's level of expectations. Continued feedback on work-related strengths then becomes vitally important. Even with these efforts, however, the prognosis for return to employment is generally guarded.

## THE ANGRY RESISTER

Many clients who begin rehabilitation assessment with good work histories, motivation to work, and confidence in themselves as workers at the same time show a "you owe me something" attitude, or say "I will go back to work, but only on my terms." Often, they bring a history of personality disturbances (Lynch, 1979). Pre-disability life situations were often troubling times, and their personality structures made it almost impossible to cope with their life problems. The occurrence of disability brings another source for inadequate coping.

Overall, they are angry and disability represents the main source of this anger, causing disruption of a stable life-style. These clients usually want to return to their former place of employment; but they may have a job-related, handicapping accident, and the employer views the injured worker

> . . . as incapable of functioning productively not only in that person's former capacity but in any capacity involved in the employer's business or operations (Eaton, 1979, p. 61).

Such rejection affects the client's self-concept, and with this deterioration in self-esteem comes a hostility often projected toward others.

Another source of anger may be the perceived reality of different losses accruing from the disability situation. Because the onset of accidents is sudden, often many disabled clients are unprepared to handle the physical, social, psychologic, vocational, and financial implications of their injuries. They may no longer have control of their life situations and thus also have lost their self-determination (Lynch, 1979). For many disabled persons, lingering anger is a sign of unresolved grief; perhaps they have never been given the chance of coming to terms with their losses. These feelings of loss stimulate questions about their self-worth, and to counteract self-doubts, they develop grandiose plans. For example, they may want money to begin their own business, and often feel that this money is owed them because of their disability.

Other clients, who can be typified as angry resisters, are critical of rehabilitation possibilities, rigid in their own work expectations, and resistant to counselor suggestions. They express behavioral patterns that tend to turn people off, such as appearing late for counseling appointments or demanding too much of the counselor's time. During vocational assessment, they may ask for detailed reasons for every request that is made of them and are hesitant to cooperate with the counselor in reaching evaluation objectives unless such goals are in complete harmony with their own wishes. Consequently, what occurs during assessment is a conflict between the expectations of the client and those of the rehabilitation professional. Although this conflict may also occur with secondary gainers or those who are ambivalent about their own rehabilitation gain, angry clients are determined to have their vocational wishes followed.

## Case Example

*After operating his own plumbing business for 18 years, Mark became ill with a chronic disease. Depressed over the reality that he could become disabled, especially because his walking and bowel and bladder functions were affected, he sold the business and decided to sit at home and watch television. After 7 months of this behavior, his wife could no longer tolerate his inactivity and insisted that he seek vocational rehabilitation services. To please his wife, he made an appointment with a rehabilitation counselor.*

*During the interview, he stated that he could find a part-time job in a factory doing work similar to that of a plumber, but he said the job "does not meet my expectations." He wanted to set up his own business at home and requested a considerable sum of money from the state rehabilitation agency to finance its beginning. When the counselor tried to convince him that such an investment was not practical at the present time, he responded, "This money is owed to me, for I have paid taxes for a long time, and now I should be helped with what I want to do."*

The rehabilitation professional needs to deal with the client's anger before any assessment can provide a reliable estimate of vocationally related capabilities. These clients should have the opportunity to ventilate their feelings. When employee rejection or unresolved grief has been identified, understanding from the professional could facilitate the client's involvement in evaluation tasks.

After this expression of feelings, the angry client should have an opportunity during assessment for short-term reality experiences that provide immediate feedback about his or her work potential. Work samples are often effective in achieving this goal. Importantly, the professional should not raise work expectations to an unrealistic level, promising these clients that better job opportunities will be available when it may not be so. Such false hope will not only provoke anger and resentment from the client but will also further inhibit the assessment process.

## THE DEVELOPMENTALLY DISABLED

Many clients who present themselves for rehabilitation are functioning at a borderline or lower level of intelligence. They may have been in special education classes throughout their education, and when schooling formally concluded, remained at home. Overprotective parents or underdeveloped social skills become inhibiting factors to choosing opportunities that would bring job possibilities. There has been no transition to the world of work.

Because these clients have never learned about the behavioral demands of working, they usually approach the assessment situation cautiously and anxiously. These behaviors are more from ignorance than from rejection of work itself. With little self-confidence and unaware of their employment-related assets, they are passive at the beginning of the rehabilitation process. At the same time, however, the developmentally disabled want to work but they have no knowledge of their job usefulness. Also, when initially presenting themselves for vocational rehabilitation, they are cooperative but hesitant because of the unknown.

Their inexperience with work and the many years under close supervision of others have created dependency patterns and little self-initiating behavior. Although their energy level and motivation may be high, they have little capacity to solve their own problems. These clients are almost exclusively outer-directed, and they look to rehabilitation as a resource that will lead them by the hand to job opportunities.

### Case Example

*Following completion of her high school special education classes, Laura was awarded a special certificate. Like her classmates, she wanted to seek work in her community, but her parents insisted that she stay at home and babysit with her younger brother and sisters. Because she had been limited to only a few, parent-chaperoned dates during high school, her parents were afraid that she was not mature enough for daily interaction with men in a job situation.*

*Laura stayed at home for 3 years until a social worker finally insisted that her parents allow her to see a rehabilitation counselor. During the interview, Laura was quiet, speaking only to answer questions and ex-*

*pressing her wishes for a job in a soft, passive tone. Often during the interview, she mentioned that she had no idea of what would be expected of her in a job, yet said that she was very anxious to get out of the house and earn some money.*

The assessment situation becomes an important beginning for the developmentally disabled because it can provide them with necessary feedback about job-related capabilities. They have been tested many times, and their perception of assessment might be of another failure situation. What is often more appropriate is situational assessment, i.e., placement in an actual work environment, where disabled persons can realistically explore their abilities and limitations. (This form of assessment is explained in Chapter 10.) Such an opportunity also provides a chance for behavioral exploration. Many developmentally disabled individuals have difficulty reaching their maximum skill-functioning levels because of behavioral limitations, most of which are derived from an unawareness of what is expected in a work situation. Whether a client is aware of such work behaviors as sustained attention to a task or promptness in returning from work breaks should be explored. Many of these persons become more employable with an acquisition of important job-keeping behaviors. Consequently, rehabilitation professionals approaching assessment with the developmentally disabled, often find that a diagnostic picture obtained from an actual job situation can be more accurate than what is learned from paper-and-pencil measures. Through this assessment, the client gains a better understanding of his or her abilities and the demands of the working environment. Understanding establishes the groundwork for the worker's self-confidence and identity.

## THE ISOLATED WORKER

Many clients referred to vocational rehabilitation have been institutionalized for many years. The de-institutionalization movement in mental health has facilitated the return to community living of thousands of the mentally ill who otherwise would have remained in state hospitals. Yet, this movement brings distinct problems to rehabilitation. Usually, mentally ill people have not been taught the skills necessary to function appropriately in the community. Years of institutionalization have created dependency behaviors that inhibit the assessment process. Often combined with this passivity is a minimal amount of formal education, a feeling that opportunities for the future are quite bleak, and a lingering sense of inferiority. When confronted with an assessment situation, these clients usually do not say very much, often giving the impression that they have no demonstrated commitment to change and find it uncomfortable to take the risk of learning more about themselves and their abilities for work. During assessment, they generally give the impression of being bored.

## Case Example

*Evelyn, age 28, was placed in a state hospital after a severe nervous breakdown. Before her illness, she had worked successfully as a secretary but changed jobs every 2 years because she felt the job pressure was becoming too stressful. When her boyfriend of many years left her just before they were to get married, she began to experience hallucinations, delusions, and could not attend to her daily needs.*

*After 1 year of intense psychiatric treatment in the institution, Evelyn was referred to the hospital's workshop, where she worked 5 hours a day performing simple packaging tasks. For 6 months, she made sufficient progress to warrant the social worker to make arrangements for a community living situation. Upon settling into her new residence, she was referred for vocational rehabilitation. During the initial interview, she had difficulty establishing continued eye contact, never initiated any conversation, and with her hands folded on her lap, would briefly respond to questions, occasionally explaining: "I am very anxious to work." She referred to her rejection by her boyfriend almost 2 years earlier, and expressed doubt as to whether any employer would hire her.*

Many isolated workers want to work but are hesitant to take that first step to learn about themselves or understand realistic work demands. The assessment opportunity can be a valuable time to provide many of these clients with positive feedback about themselves. Assessment should be structured so that they can gain some helpful information about what they can do. Also during evaluation, they will need much support because their anxiety about meeting a new situation can seriously hinder personal effectiveness. Paper-and-pencil measures should be used minimally for diagnostic purposes, and more stress could be given to work samples and the initial interview as assessment tools. Moreover, a comprehensive assessment of the client should be acquired, namely, an understanding of the client's functioning in the living, learning, and working areas of his or her life. A client often needs to learn basic social living skills before employability can be explored. The client who is unable to talk appropriately with other people in a living environment is not going to be able to meet personal and social interaction demands in a job situation. Living skills impact on work responsibilities, and a comprehensive approach to assessment generates information that will show the relationship of performance in living to skills in working.

## THE MEDICATED CLIENT

Clients with mental or physical disabilities usually take some form of medication. Those with chronic conditions often receive a continued, regular dosage, either to alleviate pain or counteract harmful symptoms that threaten active responses to daily life demands. For example, the chronic pain patient or chronic schizophrenic must take daily medication to minimize symptoms so that he or she can assume necessary living responsibilities. However, taking these drugs constantly can facilitate the formation of a hypchondrically organized personality or produce harmful side effects during the assessment process.

Aside from the alleviation of pain, many drugs are taken by clients, especially the chronic mentally ill, to control systems that would inhibit overall life functioning. For example, certain drugs can help to keep disruptive behavior in check, minimize hallucinations, or prevent continued delusions. However, these drugs can also produce such side effects as drowsiness; confusion; a tendency toward confabulation, absurdity, and fluidity; and sometimes even a loss of a sense of distance.

Many clients who experience continued pain have become dependent on drugs to control their personal discomfort. Unfortunately, much of their attention focuses upon their symptoms, and they often become egocentric, demanding, and easily prone to irritability. They view their life through the pain experience, and they are psychologically dependent on their medication.

During assessment, the counselor should determine how much the client's pain experience and the resulting medication has influenced his or her energy, motivation to reach rehabilitation goals, and relationships to others. Many chronic pain patients enjoy talking about their symptoms and the various remedies they choose to assuage the discomfort. Moreover, because of their medical condition, they usually have a pessimistic outlook toward rehabilitation and are even predisposed toward failure. They self-impose limitations (many of which are unwarranted) on their daily performances.

The interview in particular should be utilized as an assessment tool to ascertain not only motivation and energy level but also mood and effect, coping resources, residual capabilities, and goal-directedness. How clients talk about themselves reveals much information about these aforementioned factors, and in turn, this information can be used to determine the clients willingness to be rehabilitated. The counselor should also discover when drugs were last taken, what they were, and how have they affected the client. If drugs have been consumed recently and a behavioral disturbance or change is noted, then the reliability of the assessment situation can be seriously compromised. The counselor may then have to delay assessment until a time when he or she can respond more appropriately to evaluation measures.

## CONCLUSION

These seven different types of clients represent many of the varieties of people who present themselves for rehabilitation. Categorizing is one way to identify the many behaviors that clients show; such behaviors can either facilitate or deter progress to rehabilitation goals. The categories often overlap because many disabled persons display, for example, both angry resister and secondary gainer traits. Regardless of the way the professional understands client behaviors, however, most disabled clients have strong inhibitions about going into an assessment situation where they might look bad. They feel that assessment might show them as more inadequate than they really are. Many clients also have negative expectations toward the counselor because they perceive that their counselors have negative expectations toward them. Professionals may have a low expectation for the rehabilitation success of their clients, and although such a feeling may be quite warranted, this attitude breeds distrust and apprehension.

For all clients who have a history of physical or mental disability, the most difficult part of the assessment phase of rehabilitation is not necessarily its content but the very fact that they must be evaluated. Fear of a strange situation, poor test-taking skills, inferior feelings, discouragement attributable to past failures relating to the disability, and perhaps a hostile attitude from the counselor might cause conflict and anxiety. Vocational evaluation could even be seen as a way of humiliation—a device for proving and exposing the client's limitations.

Client assessment, then, becomes an opportunity for professionals to ask themselves the following questions:

1.  *Will my characteristics as a helping professional make a difference in the client's assessment performance?*  The assessment process involves a complex interaction between the professional, the client, and situational variables. The manner in which rapport is established and maintained and how the evaluator responds to the client's attitudes and feelings have a bearing on how successful the professional is in attempting to elicit a client's best efforts.

2.  *How can I, as a professional, recognize and accept the client's fears, apprehensions, distrust, and skepticism?*  By recognizing and accepting these perceived behaviors, professionals can begin to acknowledge the emotional rewards needed to give stimulus or meaning to the rehabilitation experience. Support, approval, and encouragement are important professional responses and become more meaningful to clients as they progress through the steps in the rehabilitation program. These responses also can help to increase the client's self confidence.

3.  *What can I, as a professional, do to enhance the reliability of the assessment situation?*  In other words, what can be done to reduce anxiety and to generate mutual respect. The professional's beliefs about the expectations of the disabled can be the key to client trust and confidence. If the professional possesses high, positive expectations for clients, usually clients will respond accordingly and attempt to be open and provide as much energy as possible in the assessment situation. Attention

to the client's emotional needs and listening intently to the client are tools that can help to build mutual respect.

The answers to these questions will influence the effectiveness of client assessment. Such questions pervade the entire assessment process and demand attention as professionals attempt to learn more information about their clients. How they can respond to these issues in assessment as well as formulate a comprehensive assessment approach to the different behaviors of clients in the preceding pages, are discussed in the next 11 chapters.

## CASE STUDY

To assist the reader to become more aware of the different characteristics shown by clients with a physical and mental disability, the following case is presented with questions that may facilitate discussion.

*Mr. R. is a white, fair-complected male of average height who appears somewhat overweight. He was born December 18, 1952 in Wilmington, North Carolina. He is the youngest of three children—a brother is 6 years older and a sister 11 years older. The father worked for the post office.*

*Mr. R. graduated from high school in July of 1971, reporting that he received "average" grades during school with science and history as his best subjects. He played varsity football and during the last 2 years of high school, was part of the work study program. He went to school in the morning, was employed in the afternoon and took electronics courses in the evening. Mr. R. mentioned that when he was in grammar school, his father told him that the family only had enough money to send one of the children to college and he was going to send his older brother. The brother went to the University of South Carolina and after graduating, went to ministerial college and obtained a Master of Science degree in Counseling and another degree in Theology. According to Mr. R., the brother is presently a minister, in the largest Protestant Church in a capital city in the South.*

*Upon graduating from high school, the client enlisted in the army, because "I wanted an education and liked to travel." During boot camp, he attended night classes in medical science at the University of North Carolina. This continued for 10 weeks. The client was then notified that he had been selected for military intelligence school at Fort Davens. There, he was trained in espionage, surveillance, and investigative techniques. Mr. R. states that he was very happy to be selected for such work and enjoyed the school. He was then assigned to survelliance work in Vietnam, where he was selected as the "top man in a class of 30." He was then assigned to Officer's Candidate School, and upon graduating in 1973, was immediately assigned to Vietnam, where he was the intelligence officer for an artillery battalion. His duty was to direct support fire while in the field and direct B-52s to bomb enemy positions and villages where there were suspected Vietcong.*

*While on patrol during a late enemy offensive, the impact of an incoming shell blew Mr. R. off a bridge, and he landed in a gully 20 feet below. He remembers that upon awakening, he couldn't feel anything from his waist down, but that after 4 days, he was able to get up and return to base camp where he was placed in bed for a week. His injury was diagnosed as a back sprain. While recuperating at base camp, he was walking outside with two buddies when an enemy rocket attack occurred, killing both friends. Mr. R. sustained shoulder and hand injuries. These injuries were diagnosed as sprains, and he was returned to duty. Because of the patient's continued complaints of back pain, he was returned to the United States and was eventually assigned as an intelligence officer to an army unit in Tuscon, Arizona. Mr. R. still complained of back pain, and in September of 1975, was notified that he was going to be discharged. He left the military service in December of 1975 and upon discharge, started looking for work. He states that "I applied for 67 jobs, but was turned down because of my back." Finally, he obtained a position in Maine as an assistant juvenile officer. He is very unhappy in this job and has come for vocational evaluation. He is married and has two children.*

With this information, please answer the following questions:

1.  What behaviors is this person showing that could be detrimental to obtaining accurate information from the vocational evaluation process?
2.  According to the categories of clients identified in this chapter, to which category do you feel this client belongs?

## REFERENCES

DeNour, A.K., and Czaczkes, J.W. 1975. Personality factors influencing vocational rehabilitation. Arch. Gen. Psychiatry. 32:573–577.

Eaton, M. 1979. Obstacles to the vocational rehabilitation of individuals receiving worker's compensation. J. of Rehab. 45:56–58.

Lynch, R. 1979. Vocational rehabilitation of worker's compensation clients. J. of Applied Rehab. Counsel. 9:164–167.

Schlenoff, D. 1979. Obstacles to the rehabilitation of disability benefits recipients. J. of Rehab. 45:56–58.

chapter 4
# THE INTERVIEW
# AS AN EFFECTIVE
# ASSESSMENT TOOL

The preceding chapter identifies different clients who present particular behavior-related problems and concerns for vocational evaluation. As effective rehabilitation planning begins with a thorough evaluation of the disabled person's residual capacities, so an assessment approach should provide useful and reliable information for the rehabilitation professional. Unfortunately in vocational assessment, traditional evaluation approaches are still frequently used, and this can be unfair to the client. (Some of these issues are discussed in Chapter 2.) Many of the assessment instruments presently used are developed from theories that assume certain client traits are unalterable. However, many aptitudes, abilities, and other so-called traits are not static; rather, they are influenced by the situational variables that surround a person's evaluation or learning experiences. The pattern of failure in the lives of many disabled people, the negative influence of family members, or the stereotypic expectation from many rehabilitation professionals that certain clients cannot do well in evaluation can decidedly influence how a client will respond to evaluation. These attitudes can also inhibit a disabled person's motivation or performance.

Because of the difficulty in using much of the standardized data to develop interventions that can make a significant difference in the disabled individual's reaching rehabilitation goals, the author utilizes the interview as an evaluation tool. An *intake interview*, of course, is required in all rehabilitation agencies. Farley and Rubin (1982) defined this interview ''as a conversation between a counselor and a client with a definite mutually acceptable purpose'' (p. 39). The purpose of the intake interview can differ according to the agency, but usually it:

1. *Develops rapport between the professional and client (Farley and Rubin, 1982)*
2. *Gives the client necessary information about the role and function of the*

*agency, available services, and client responsibilities (Farley and Rubin, 1982)*

3.  *Helps clients to identify their own strengths and weaknesses, as well as to recognize and be aware of personality traits, abilities, and aptitudes that may facilitate achieving rehabilitation goals.* Self-understanding is a necessary goal for the rehabilitation process, and more so for disabled clients who need to appreciate their residual physical, intellectual, and emotional assets. During medical treatment, attention usually focuses on the impairment or illness. Patients grow accustomed to focusing upon what they cannot do. Interview feedback can help clients move away from these perceptions to a more helpful knowledge about themselves.

4.  *Helps the client to feel more comfortable about the rehabilitation process and helps him or her to begin to gain a feeling of self-confidence.* As mentioned in the previous chapter, many disabled persons harbor anxiety or tension over the possibility of reaching rehabilitation goals. Dependency patterns might already have been developed or an assessment situation during vocational rehabilitation could revive memories of previous failures in testing. This memory only stimulates added anxiety. The interview creates an opportunity for the professional to begin to ease the anxiety as well as provides a chance for the client to discuss particular fears that can arise from the rehabilitation experience.

5.  *Provides the counselor with beginning information for rehabilitation training, intervention planning, and effective programming.* Also, the interview helps the rehabilitation professional to gain an appraisal of the disabled individual's life history, pattern of behavior, and potential for acquiring knowledge and skills suitable for entry into possible training or eventual employment. The acquisition of this information is basic to the interview process.

Apart from relationship-building and provision of information, the intake interview can be a valuable opportunity to generate necessary facts for rehabilitation planning. Much of this knowledge is identified when clients discuss their social/vocational/educational histories. What is needed is an interview structure to organize this information for rehabilitation purposes.

This chapter presents such a structure that, in turn, gives the intake interview more of a diagnostic perspective. There are occasions when more than one interview meeting is needed in order to obtain the necessary information for planning purposes. Time considerations or the initial reticence of a client to disclose information can extend the interview beyond one session. Regardless of the time it takes to learn more about the client, the time itself (namely, the interview) is more evaluation-based (Rubin and Roessler, 1982). In utilizing the intake interview as a diagnostic resource, there are two general steps, each of which depends upon the other: 1) conducting the interview itself;

and 2) using a structure to collect the information gained from this interview. Certain dynamics generate an effective interview. Also, if the interview is to be a valuable opportunity for a beginning evaluation of the client, a structure for organizing the facts must be identified. All of these issues are discussed in this chapter.

## CONDUCTING THE INTERVIEW

There are many ways to conduct an interview. Each method depends upon what type of information is to be gained, the circumstances in which it is to be obtained, and the individual conducting the interview. What follows is an approach that the author has used with disabled clients, especially those with severe handicaps. If these clients are to be assisted in feeling better about themselves, recognizing their productive capabilities, and controlling their own fears about future training or other rehabilitation opportunities, a relationship must develop between the rehabilitation professional and the disabled client. The process for developing this relationship basically includes two components: 1) contextual interviewing; and 2) personal interviewing. Both of these concepts, described at length by Carkhuff (1969, 1979) and Anthony (1972, 1979), apply to the vocational evaluation process.

### Contextual Interviewing

This part of interviewing is concerned with both the environment in which the interview is conducted and how the rehabilitation professional physically relates to the disabled client. For example, it considers 1) the location of the professional's office; 2) privacy and confidentiality factors; 3) where the professional sits while interviewing; and 4) the number of distractions that could be present in an office. For example, many interviews are conducted while the professional sits behind the desk, with the client in front. The desk represents a barrier to communication, a ''distancing'' factor between two people. Clients usually feel very strange with this arrangement, and often feel more comfortable if the professional moves away from the desk. If this is not possible, then having the client sit beside the desk reduces some of this communication difficulty.

Also, too many posters in the professional's office can be very distracting. A few posters, if appropriately placed, can have a calming effect on the client and convey a personal dimension about the professional. However, if the office is a mini-museum (even if there is an interesting assortment of collectibles), the client might feel overwhelmed.

Another facet of contextual interviewing is whether the rehabilitation professional takes notes or uses an agency's standard interview form to write comments while talking with a client. If possible, the client should complete this form before the interview itself, and if this is not possible because of some functional limitation, the agency should assist the client. Before the interview begins, the professional should scan the form to discover any needed information that might be missing and to learn basic demographic facts about the individual. The professional should tell the client in advance if notes are to be taken during the interview. Clients often become cautious about revealing information if they do not understand how it is going to be used by the interviewer.

Contextual interviewing establishes a mood by creating an atmosphere in which people feel more comfortable and are reassured that they are receiving direct attention. The rehabilitation professional's office can be a form of communication that helps both to reduce the client's anxiety and to develop a good relationship during the interview. The warmth that is expressed by the office decor, where the professional sits in relation to the client, and the privacy and confidentiality that is maintained during the interview can promote communication between the interviewer and the disabled person. Good interviewing is not only the result of the complex interplay of the rehabilitation professional, the client, and the purpose of the interview, but also is achieved by the setting in which it is conducted.

### Personal Interviewing

If the interview is to be utilized as an assessment approach, the rehabilitation professional must not only establish and maintain a good relationship with the client, but also stimulate the disabled person to participate productively in the interview. Also, the conversation must keep moving productively in order to achieve needed information. This entails communication, flexibility, control of the interview situation, organization of the information embedded in much of the interview conversation, and processing this data according to interview goals.

Carkhuff and Anthony (1979) identified four communicative skills that, when utilized by the rehabilitation professional, can considerably enhance the effectiveness of the interview situation. These skills, attending, observing, listening, and responding, are fundamental and should be used throughout the entire interview session to help the client to become involved.

*Attending*   This skill refers to the physical positioning of rehabilitation professionals as they talk with clients. It implies eye contact and sitting in such a way that both interest and attention are communicated to the client. Eye contact should be natural, direct without constituting a stare, and generally constant because frequent breaks in eye contact suggest inattention.

*Observing*    This means that the interviewer first watches for specific aspects of the client's appearance and behavior and then uses this information to draw some careful inferences concerning the client's functioning (Carkhuff and Anthony, 1979). For example, when observing the client's use of eyes, grooming, changes in posture, and, in particular, changes in the positioning of the head and shoulders during the interview, the rehabilitation professional gains a beginning, tentative understanding of the client's interest and motivation in the assessment situation.

*Listening*    Like observing, listening can promote the client's participation in the interview and facilitate the disclosure of information important for rehabilitation planning. Listening implies attention not only to the client's verbal expression but also to the accompanying tone of voice, such as loudness, softness, and rapidity of speech. Listening also means that possible judgments about the client's behavior are suspended. It is very easy to formulate attitudes about the client as the interview proceeds. At this stage of rehabilitation involvement, these perceptions can become obstacles to a genuine and reliable understanding of the client's functioning. By actively listening to what the client is saying, the professional communicates continued concern which, in turn, often prompts the client to discuss valuable information needed for rehabilitation planning.

*Responding*    In responding to the client's verbal messages during the interview, the rehabilitation professional is attempting both to help the client become aware of his or her feelings and to understand how the client is experiencing the disability situation. The professional initially responds to verbal content as the client expresses specifics relating to his or her immediate situation. The professional then responds to the meaning that is inherent in the client's statements and nonverbal behavior. Finally, as clients express the immediate feelings that each aspect of the disability arouses in them, the professional promotes continued exploration of those feelings by responding to them (Carkhuff and Anthony, 1979). The following is suggested format for this development of responding:

*Responding to the content of the client's expression:*
"So you're saying_____," or "You're saying that_____"
*Client*:   "My family ignores me most of the time."
*Interviewer*:   "You're saying that members of your family leave you alone."

*Responding to the immediate meaning:*
"You mean_____."
*Client*:   "I am very upset because my disability prevents me from enjoying life."

*Interviewer*:   "You mean that you don't understand all your disability still allows you to do."

*Responding to the immediate feelings:*
   "You feel_____," or
   "That can really make you feel_____."
   *Client*:   "I have tried many times to return to work but I just can't bring myself to face my employer again."
   *Interviewer*:   "You feel anxious about what the employer might say to you."

The interviewer's responses during the interview should be frequently interspersed with feeling words. The most direct way in which to introduce a response to feeling is to use the opening, "You feel_____." The rehabilitation professional can vary the form of the response as long as there is the inclusion of a specific feeling word or phrase that the client recognizes as interchangeable with the feeling expressed in his or her own verbal statements.

To promote further a positive relationship between the client and interviewer and to convey to clients that they are respected as persons, other techniques may have to be used. One approach is for the professional to immediately introduce himself or herself and then briefly explain the particular job of a rehabilitation professional. (Many disabled persons are confused about job functions of rehabilitation counselors or vocational evaluators. They may believe that the professional's only responsibility is to get the person a job.) Following this introduction and to help the client feel initially comfortable about the interview situation, the professional can ask, "Could you tell me why you feel you are here at this agency today?" Most clients usually respond to that question, and a small exchange helps both professional and client to understand the purposes of the interview. During the beginning of the interview, therefore, there should be time both for relationship-building and for clarification.

With an awareness of these interpersonal skills and approaches, the rehabilitation professional also needs to determine at the beginning of the interview what topics should be emphasized and which areas are most critical to explore for eventual rehabilitation planning. Again, before the interview, the agency application form should be scanned to identify these areas. At times, however, the interview as an assessment resource might have to be conducted over several sessions. Such client disability factors as poor attention span or poorly developed communication skills may dictate a slower interviewing pace. Or, some topics, such as a past criminal record or a sporadic employment history may be too sensitive for the client to introduce immediately. The professional may want to proceed cautiously, helping the client to discuss initially those topics about which he or she seems to be most comfortable. When the client believes that the interviewer can be trusted, these more sensitive but necessary areas for rehabilitation assessment may be revealed. Often, this takes more than one session.

## ISSUES ARISING DURING THE INTERVIEW

Many other issues should be attended to during the interview if this dialogue is to be successful and provide the necessary information for rehabilitation planning. The following issues are particularly important: 1) the role of questions during the interview; 2) the timing of reinforcement; 3) effective confrontations; 4) the use of silence; and 5) being aware of certain "processes" that reveal information.

### The Role of Questions

Unfortunately, many interviews are conducted by a question-and-answer format with the client replying to the repeated inquiries from the professional. In order to gather needed information, broader responsiveness must be encouraged. Questions should be framed to invite exploration rather than a single "yes" or "no" response from the client. They should relate as closely as possible to the topic being discussed and flow from the immediate dialogue between the client and professional. Too often, questions are asked in order to change the subject when the helping professional becomes uncomfortable with the client's responses. Timing is also vitally important, for often questions can inhibit a client from pursuing a subject further, especially if he or she discusses the more negative aspects of his or her work history or disability experience. Also, comments such as "That sounds very interesting," or "It does take a lot of courage to look honestly at a person's background" are usually more helpful than questions in soliciting information.

However, using adroit, appropriate questioning can draw out the client so that perceived strengths or assets can be revealed. Open-ended, indirect questions encourage the expression of ideas and information that might never be obtained by a direct approach. For example:

*Direct Question*

*Interviewer*:   "Did you like that job?"
*Client*:   "Yes" or "No."

*Indirect Question*

*Interviewer*:   "What things did you like most about the job?"
*Client*:   "I thought the attitude of the supervisor toward his workers helped me to do the job better."

The professional may receive several responses that will contribute to understanding the applicant's motivation and interests. In probing for information, the use of such beginning words as "how" or "why" can provide the client with a chance to be more flexible in his or her response. A tactful use of the word "what" can also solicit information, but the professional must then try to employ a reassuring manner and tone. An abrasive tone of voice immediately inhibits clients from talking. Many questions may be asked too directly causing the client some reluctance in revealing needed information. For example, "Why did you leave that job?" might be too direct. Instead, a more appropriate inquiry would be: "How did you happen to leave that job?"

## The Timing of Reinforcement

One of the purposes of the interview is to facilitate responsiveness from the client. There are several ways to accomplish this goal, some of which have previously been discussed in this chapter and concern relationship-building through effective communication skills. Other approaches focus on helping the client to talk more readily about the negative aspects of his or her background. Persons with a disability usually have encountered many personal failures or rejecting attitudes. Their self-concepts are often low, and they are understandably hesitant to talk about areas that might convey a negative impression. Low marks in school, the inability to hold a permanent job, and slowness in motivating themselves to explore productive opportunities are frequently difficult to reveal in an interview situation, but at the same time should be discussed in order for the professional to identify possible obstacles for reaching rehabilitation goals.

The professional can attempt to make it as easy as possible for clients to talk about negative aspects of their backgrounds by playing down the importance of that information by some casual, understanding remark. For example, when the client begins to mention that he or she received low marks in school, the professional can compliment the person for having been able to recognize this difficulty and then face up to it. Rehabilitation professionals who give the slightest indication that their judgments are adversely influenced by unfavorable information will get no further information of this kind.

A skillful professional gives frequent "pats on the back," or verbal reinforcement, never openly disagreeing with a client on any point or giving the appearance of cross-examining. The technique of expressing agreement places heavy demands upon facial expressions and general interview manners, including watching the use of words that convey a negative meaning. For example, words like "weaknesses," "faults," or "liabilities" could be replaced by "shortcomings."

Spontaneous comments by the professional further help to create a favorable climate for conversation. These remarks provide some continuity to the client's verbal expression, as well as assist the client in revealing negative information. In fact, comments can often be used in place of questions. For example, the comment, "I can imagine there were some really tough problems in a job like that one" can be used instead of the question, "What were some of the most difficult problems you faced on that job?"

Also, by using such words or expressions as "and then" "ummhmm" and "right," the interviewer provides at least minimal encouragement and at the same time helps the client feel more at ease during the interview.

## Effective Confrontation

During the interview, the rehabilitation worker should identify contradictions in what the client is saying. The client might be setting very unrealistic goals in relation to his or her abilities or past experiences or be employing defensive strategies that could block appropriate rehabilitation planning, such as denial or projecting onto others his or her own anger. The professional wants to help the client identify and resolve these discrepancies.

Confrontation should only be used after a good client relationship has been established. There are many ways to confront a client. Comments should not include accusations, judgments, or solutions to problems. Carkhuff and Anthony (1979) suggested that using a format such as: "On the one hand you say/feel/do_____, and on the other hand you say/feel/do_____" is only minimally threatening to the client because it focuses on an element of contrast that comes entirely from the client's own frame of reference.

## The Use of Silence

Silences often occur during the interview, perhaps because clients are nervous, shy, or anxious about revealing information relevant to their disabilities. Silence is also a form of reluctance, which is discussed in a later section of this chapter. However, silences are often a positive form of communication, telling the professional that a certain subject is probably quite difficult to discuss. Or, a client may simply have exhausted a particular subject and is waiting for the professional to suggest another topic area. Silences themselves should not become too long without an interviewer response. The following are some examples of responses in a silent situation:

"You feel uncomfortable to discuss this subject further."
"Perhaps we should change the subject . . . "
"It is difficult to talk about those areas of your life that remind you of failure and pain."

Many clients are silent during the interview because their verbal skills are very low, the result of functional limitations. In these instances, the interviewer has to be more directive in the interview situation, providing reinforcing statements like, "This is your first time in this agency and I can understand that it would be difficult to talk about yourself." The low-verbal client frequently finds it hard to elaborate on any topic suggested by the professional. Appendix A (p. 241) suggests a format to facilitate both interview conversation and the disclosure of needed information.

## Certain Interview "Processes"

During the interview, certain processes that occur between the rehabilitation professional and client can reveal information about the latter's mental and emotional functioning. There are four areas that the professional should especially look for:

*Association of Ideas*    A client may be discussing some of the difficulties in finding a job and then switch suddenly to talking about his or her disability benefits and how they have alleviated many adjustmental problems. Thus, the client has probably indicated that the problem in finding a job is not isolated but is actually connected to receiving entitlement payments.

*Shifts in Conversation*    A sudden shift in conversation could indicate that clients feel that they are telling too much and do not want to reveal more information about that particular subject. Or, perhaps the client was beginning to talk about material that was becoming too painful to pursue, and decided to avoid further discussion. A sudden shift in topics during the interview should be responded to by the rehabilitation professional. Statements like: "On the one hand you were talking about . . . and now you are discussing . . . This is confusing to me and I wonder if you would clarify it" could encourage a response from the client.

*Recurrent References*    A client may repeatedly return to a certain subject. Such repetition often indicates a main focus of reference or how the client really feels about a disability situation. Someone who continually mentions that his or her family is pleased that more time is now spent with family members than pre-disability onset could be suggesting that it is really more rewarding to be at home then to return to employment. Frequent references should be explored by the professional for they usually contain valuable information related to the client's motivation and expectations for rehabilitation evaluation involvement.

*Inconsistencies or Gaps*    A client may tell a straightforward story but with unexpected gaps. For example, the disabled person may carefully neglect to give any reasons for leaving the last job. In being alert to the possibility of such a gap, the professional can mildly confront the client with a statement exploring the reason for such inconsistency, e.g., "As you were talking I noticed that something seemed to be left out . . . Could you give me some idea of what this is?''

## CONCLUDING THE INTERVIEW

When the interview is to conclude because of time considerations or the rehabilitation professional's realization that needed information has been obtained, the client should be asked to indicate what has been learned during this particular interview session. Because the client may have difficulty reviewing this information, the discussion should be stimulated by pointing out one or more strengths that have been observed, for example, "Well, I have learned that you seem to get along unusually well with people, and this, of course, is a tremendous asset in any job situation."

It is important for the client to leave the interview feeling positive about the experience and understanding what is needed for successful achievement of rehabilitation goals. Some of this feeling can be achieved through summarizing the information that has been gained from the session. The review focus again should be on the client's identified strengths. With this emphasis, the interview represents a beginning for the client, a new awareness of identified strengths, and a knowledge of the opportunities that rehabilitation offers. Also, the end of the interview is an important time to clarify any questions and discuss vocational evaluation arrangements.

## A STRUCTURE FOR THE
## COLLECTION OF INTERVIEW INFORMATION

As the client talks about personal history, the disability, and its implications for his or her immediate life, the information that is generated is most important for rehabilitation planning. The key to using this information effectively is to have a structure for organizing interview facts (see Figure 4.1). This structure can be like an interview guide, which the rehabilitation professional completes immediately following the interview, or like a mental outline, which the professional follows while talking with the client. (This author has used the structure both ways.) After gathering the interview information in this framework, the professional can then begin to make rehabilitation plans.

The structure is comprised of 13 items or needs of client functioning as they relate to rehabilitation goals. Each item should be explored during the interview. How each relates to training or employment is listed in the right-hand column. Importantly, approaches for gaining this information from the client are suggested in the middle column.

| Items/needs of client functioning | Approaches for gaining information about areas of client functioning | Relationship to training and/or employment |
|---|---|---|
| 1. General appearance and behavior | Observe | Personal habits Appropriateness Work behaviors Neatness Relationship to co-workers |
| 2. Principal way of communicating | List to the way in which client talks about problems and himself or herself | Attention Comprehension and retenion of instructions Reality contact |
| 3. Mental processes and content | Observe how the individual verbally constructs his or her life's experiences; listen to the association of ideas; shifts in conversation; and inconsistencies and gaps in the conversation | Realistic expectations Judgment and problem-solving ability Reality contact Potential to learn work demands |
| 4. Mood and affect | Observe nonverbal behaviors; listen to the client's affect as he or she talks; Ask: "How are you feeling now?" | Response to pressure Adaptability Emotional reaction to disability |
| 5. Coping resources | Ask such questions as: What do you think you do best? What are the most difficult problems you have faced...How were they handled? Have you experienced a recent stress? How did you manage? How do you handled pressure on the job or at home? What is your present living situation? | Independent functioning Frustration tolerance Handling failure or setbacks Response to pressure Confidence/self-concept Adjustment and maturity |
| 6. Orientation toward other people | Ask the client to describe the relationship with his or her co-workers. As such questions as: How do you feel when you are in social situations? Whose opinion do you see as valuable to you in your life planning? | Interpersonal skills Job-keeping behaviors Relationship with supervisor and co-workers Socially acceptable |
| 7. Capacity for facing problems | Explore with the client: What are the most difficult problems you have faced? How were they handled? What is your reaction to your disability? How do you handle unpleasant situations? | Job-getting behaviors Seeks training opportunities Adjustment and maturity |
| 8. Energy level | Ask: How do you think things can be different for you? What can you do about it? Are you willing to take risks to make changes? I would like to hear how you spend your time each day. Also watch for recurrent references in the interview. | Motivation Identification with productive role Job-seeking behaviors Job-keeping behaviors Attends work regularly, Promptness Work production Does not waste time |
| 9. Goal-directedness | Ask: What type of work do you see yourself doing 5 years from now? What are you looking for in a career...a job? | Growth and development Job objective behaviors Seeks a vocational goal Has an appropriate work objective |
| 10. Strengths of client | Ask What do you do well? What do you like about yourself? What do you feel are your strong points? What have you learned from your work experience? | Compensatory skills Confidence Job-keeping behaviors Relevance for work Sufficiency of work |
| 11. Interests of client | Explore educational experience Competencies Particular difficulties What was liked best Explore work experience Special areas of interest Special areas of competence Major duties and responsibilities Leisure time/general interests What would be the ideal job for you? | Training goals Job objective behaviors Job alternatives Readiness for work |
| 12. Work history | Ask: What kind of work have you performed in the past? | Skill/competence Adaptability/adjustment Stability |
| 13. Disability factors | Ask: Describe your present disability. How does it limit you? Are there any medications? What are the effects? | Performance Training selection and disability Transfer of skills |

*Figure 4.1.  A structure for organizing interview facts.*

| | Comments | Training goals |
|---|---|---|
| Work history and experience | | |
| Vocational goals | | |
| Education and training experience | | |
| Social factors | | |
| Disability factors | | |
| Principal way of communicating | | |
| General appearance and behavior | | |
| Mental processes and content | | |
| Mood and affect | | |
| Coping resources | | |
| Orientation toward other people | | |
| Capacity for facing problems | | |
| Energy level | | |
| Goal-directedness | | |
| Strengths of client | | |
| Interests of client | | |

*Figure 4.2.    Client intake interview form.*

Figure 4.2 shows the form used by the author during the client intake interview. Some of the items listed follow those already identified in Figure 4.1. As mentioned, the author completes this form after the intake interview or other needed sessions with the client. Then, this form is utilized when rehabilitation plans are developed (as discussed in Chapter 14 of this book). Relevant planning necessitates the use of this information, and it becomes an important step in rehabilitation planning.

## CONCLUSION

What is suggested in this chapter are ways for the interviewer to gain information about a client, especially when traditional assessment approaches are perceived as quite limited in providing the necessary data. For the interview to be used as an effective diagnostic tool means fundamentally that a positive helping relationship between the client and interviewer must be established. When this is achieved, both the interviewer and the client can begin to gain feedback that is crucial for rehabilitation planning.

One system, moreover, that also utilizes the interview as a principal resource for gaining information is called the Preliminary Diagnostic Questionnaire. Developed and copyrighted by Joseph B. Moriarity and the West Virginia Research and Training Center, its use is restricted to those persons who have completed the required training. It is highly recommended, as the system goes beyond the collection and recording of data to help the rehabilitation professional process information and develop hypotheses. The PDQ can be used as an organizer of information, as a pre-screening device, or as a way of documenting decisions. It is published by West Virginia Research and Training Center, One Dunbar Plaza, Suite E, Dunbar, West Virginia—(304) 348-6340.

## CASE STUDY

The personal history of Ms. B. illustrates how the interview can be used effectively in vocational assessment when either a specific structure or certain guidelines for obtaining information is followed. These guidelines are identified after the description of Ms. B. The following information was presented during the interview. Particular inferences can be made from it.

*Ms. B., age 25, was born in Newark, New Jersey. She moved to Long Island at age 5 to live in what she called a better neighborhood. She is the oldest of four siblings. Her sister, age 21, is a dental assistant, married 2 years. Ms. B. says she and her sister are opposites (the sister is never serious), but since her sister's marriage, they have become closer. Ms. B. also has a sister, age 14, whom she describes as easy to get along with, and a brother, age 19, who has school phobias, asthma, and slow learning and needs a lot of help. The mother, age 45, had a nervous breakdown following the birth of the youngest sister. Ms. B. feels that she had a lot of feelings resulting from this; she was asked to be good so that her mother would not get sick again. At the same time, she felt that she had a lot of responsibility because her mother was in and out of the hospital so often. She is quite certain that the mother got shock treatments, and the illness was described to her as post-natal depression. She said that the mother is still very unstable.*

*Ms. B.'s. father, age 49, is described as someone who always failed in business on his own. She feels that she was closer to him, in that she was a "son" to him (when he didn't have one) as well as his favorite daughter.*

*Ms. B. believes that she can always remember periods of depression, but the most difficult time for her began after she met her husband. They met while undergraduates at City College in New York, where she was majoring in Math and he in Economics. They knew each other for a year, and then decided to get married. Following the marriage, the husband got an opportunity to go for his Ph.D. in Economics at Harvard, and the patient transferred to finish up undergraduate work with a major in Math and Economics. She feels that her marriage was very difficult from the beginning and that her husband was unable to relate to people. He did not like children, and she began to feel that he didn't like any women, possibly including her. During this time, they were having sexual difficulties.*

*She urged that they both see a psychiatrist about their problem, but he refused. The marriage went on like this as her husband became more withdrawn under the pressure of his work. At this point, she became much more depressed, and she explains this was because she was trying very hard to help him, and now he was becoming more isolated. Ms. B. then became torn with guilt about leaving him, but finally she decided to get the marriage annulled. The marriage was annulled on the grounds of his refusal to have children, and she retook her maiden name.*

*During the year when the annulment became a reality, Ms. B. decided she would leave New York and go back to Boston to get her Master's degree in Economics. She felt she wanted to get away from her parents. Since that breakup, the patient has had relationships with two men, both of whom she considers destructive. She has also suffered severe bouts of depression and has been hospitalized for brief periods. Ms. B. is now on medication, has an apartment, and would like to find a suitable job. She comes for vocational exploration.*

## Guidelines/areas of client functioning

1. *Mental processes and content*
2. *Mood and affect*
3. *Coping resources*
4. *Orientation toward other people*
5. *Capacity for facing problems*
6. *Presumed energy level*
7. *Goal-directedness*

8.  *Strengths of client*
9.  *Interests of client*
10. *Work history*
11. *Disability factors*

What further vocational assessment measures are needed?


## REFERENCES

Anthony, W. A. 1979. The Principles of Psychiatric Rehabilitation. Human Resource
  Development Press, Amherst, MA.
Anthony, W. A., Duell, G. J., Sharratt, S., and Althoff, M. E. 1972. Efficacy of
  psychiatric rehabilitation, Psychol. Bull. 78:447–456.
Carkhuff, R. R. 1969. Helping and Human Relations. Holt, Rinehart and Winston,
  Inc., New York.
Carkhuff, R. R., and Anthony, W. A. 1979. The Skills of Helping. Human Resource
  Development Press, Amherst, MA.
Farley, R. C., and Rubin, S. E. 1982. The intake interview. In: R. T. Roessler, and S.
  E. Rubin. Case Management and Rehabilitation Counseling. University Park Press,
  Baltimore.
Rubin, S. E., and Roessler, R. T. 1982. Foundations of the Vocational Rehabilitation
  Process, University Park Press, Baltimore.

# chapter 5
# UNDERSTANDING SELECTED CONCEPTS IN VOCATIONAL ASSESSMENT

Rehabilitation professionals have an excellent opportunity to perform vocational assessment when their clients are first seen in an intake interview. The previous chapter suggests one structure for such an assessment. When the interview is utilized as an approach for obtaining important facts relevant to rehabilitation planning, the outcome of other evaluation procedures can be carefully weighed against this newly gained information. Most clients involved in the rehabilitation process usually go through further assessment procedures. There are many reasons for this practice. Work samples can furnish backup information and a further understanding of the client already gained during the interview. When paper-and-pencil tests are selected appropriately, they often introduce a reliable, solid, and objective dimension into rehabilitation assessment. The paper-and-pencil approach has been used in rehabilitation to provide a sample of a person's intellectual functioning, developed abilities, and emotional behavior.

For many years, procedures for testing handicapped people have left much to be desired (Sherman and Robinson, 1982). Even when assessment measures are appropriately modified, the meaning of the scores is uncertain. Unfortunately, fully developed test modifications suitable for all handicapped individuals do not currently exist, and there is no information about the comparability of available tests for handicapped and nonhandicapped groups (Sherman and Robinson, 1982).

Two important functions of tests are *selection* and *diagnosis*. This book focuses on the use of selected tests to explore and identify the client's independent living and work-related strengths and limitations. Yet, test results that reflect a person's disability do not provide an unbiased estimate of his or her potential. The issue of what tests are appropriate for handicapped individuals is a crucial one in rehabilitation assessment.

Paper-and-pencil tests are classified in many ways including: 1) individual or group; 2) verbal or nonverbal; 3) highly structured or unstructured; 4) closed choice or open ended; 5) objective or subjective; and 6) machine-scored or scored by judgment. Psychometric tests may also vary a great deal in the degree of quality of their standardization and how much interpretive information they furnish. Consequently, when utilizing tests for vocational evaluation, the helping professional has to decide a test's appropriateness for particular clients. In other words, certain standards for evaluating tests should be employed in order to choose the most appropriate and available measure.

When evaluating a paper-and-pencil test, the rehabilitation practitioner should become acquainted with the test manual, the situation in which the test is to be used, and the requirements and training required to administer the test. Other standards determine the relevance of an assessment approach and the accuracy of the test data. This chapter discusses these issues and explains the guidelines for interpreting test scores.

## APPROPRIATE NORMS AND THE CRITERIA PROBLEM

A norm refers to that group of people on whom an assessment procedure has been standardized and from whom the scores on a particular test have been obtained to determine level performance. In rehabilitation, many of the assessment procedures have not been standardized on a representative sample. This is true, for example, of most paper-and-pencil tests. Also, vocational evaluation involves prediction. A predictive assessment measure that cannot be used in exactly the same surroundings as the behavior that is to be predicted is definitely limited. For this reason, assessment procedures other than paper-and-pencil tests are frequently used in vocational evaluation. The best prediction of what persons will do in a given situation is usually what they did the last time in that situation. Consequently, the approaches of work samples or situational assessment (which are explained in later chapters of this book) are frequently used for predictive purposes because they can tap a person's previous experience.

Rehabilitation agencies have conducted much research and development on assessment procedures. But norms are available on only some of the tests used by rehabilitation agencies, and rarely is there an interest in comparing test scores for handicapped and nonhandicapped people (Sherman and Robinson, 1982).

Because of these norm-referenced difficulties many of the measures used in rehabilitation assessment should determine what a client can do and not how he or she stands in comparison to others. Initially, the rehabilitation professional would determine the skills necessary to accomplish satisfactorily tasks in an employment situation or consult manuals that identify these demands. Then the assessment will provide an estimate of whether or not a client has the capability to perform, with training, the necessary skills.

## VALIDITY

Although Section 504 of the Rehabilitation Act of 1973 specifies many requirements, one in particular has important relevance for rehabilitation assessment:

> ". . . shall assure itself that tests are selected and administered so as to best ensure that the test results reflect the handicapped applicant's aptitude or achievement level or whatever other factor the test purports to measure, rather than reflecting the applicant's impaired sensory, manual, or speaking skills (except where those skills are the factors that the test purports to measure) (Sec 104.42 (b) 37).

In other words, the concept of validity is important in considering the appropriateness of any use of a test. Validity provides an estimate of how well a test measures what it purports to measure, and the concept is central to the 504 regulations of the Rehabilitation Act of 1973.

Rehabilitation professionals should always refer to the validity of a particular use of a test. It is the use and not the test itself that has validity (Sherman and Robinson, 1982). Validity is not an either/or attribute of a use of a test; it exists in varying degrees in various situations. Conducting validity studies by no means ensures that a particular application of a test is appropriate (Sherman and Robinson, 1982). But validation of tests for handicapped populations has been rare. Few, if any, validation studies have given any attention to the applicability of the test producer's validation to local conditions. Differential validation research on testing handicapped people is virtually nonexistent in the private sector. Such studies are considered unfeasible because of the small numbers of handicapped employees in similar jobs (Sherman and Robinson, 1982).

The 504 regulations relevant to testing imply that a handicapping condition should have no effect whatsoever on test scores unless the test is explicitly designed to measure an ability directly related to the handicap. This implication rests on the assumption that the use of modified tests and test administration procedures is in itself sufficient to ensure that a test will reflect abilities that are unaffected by a client's handicap. A Panel on Testing of Handicapped People, developed in 1979 by the National Research Council in Washington, D.C., rejected this implication as a safe working assumption. The panel stated that "Although the goal of constructing measures that are unaffected by a handicapping condition is generally accepted as the ideal, most test developers believe that it is largely unattainable in the near future in many if not most instances" (p. 108). The panel also believed that "Psychology and psychometrics are not yet fully capable of ensuring that tests for handicapped people measure skills independent of handicapping conditions'' (p. 110).

Considering the relatively large testing programs in existence, this same panel considered predictive validity to offer the greatest promise for comparability of test results between the handicapped and nonhandicapped. Predictive validity gives an estimate of the strength of the association between test scores and a measure of performance on the criterion to be predicted (Sherman and Robinson, 1982). Consequently, one of the major recommendations of this important panel was '' . . . for sponsors of large testing programs to modify tests to accomodate most kinds of sensory and motor handicaps and to conduct predictive validity studies in order to ascertain whether the modified tests have a predictive power near that of the standard test used with the general population'' (p. 126). The panel felt that this is an achievable form of comparability, although empirical studies will have to be conducted in order to determine the actual feasibility of the approach (Sherman and Robinson, 1982). At the end of the research, it should be possible to determine whether modified and standard forms of a test actually have comparable predictive power.

Traditional validation methods assume that there are four types of validity: *content, construct, concurrent* or *predictive,* and *face.*

## Content Validity

Content validity refers to the representativeness of the test items. One way to estimate it is to determine carefully what items make up the domain or content of some specific behavior. Then, a sample of items are pooled together to represent different levels of the behavior. When the items are pooled together, it is thought that the resulting test will discriminate between individuals at different levels of mastery. A statistical procedure called *factor analysis* is sometimes used to assess content validity. This procedure groups test items together into different factors, suggesting that the items in a factor relate to some specific content or knowledge base. Content validity is most likely to be reported for achievement tests. Also, content validity for work evaluation procedures exists when the duties and tasks of the work sample or situational assessment are highly similar to those of the job itself.

## Construct Validity

Construct validity is more theoretical than the other types of validity and refers to the degree to which a test measures any hypothetical construct. It is most likely to be used in measuring psychologic traits and characteristics. For example, anger is a hypothetical construct that can exist in different forms. What anger is, where, and when it is likely to be experienced is linked to psychologic theory. In construct validity, it is suggested that something like anger exists; next, the anger is related to a theory concerning the phenomena; and then a test, in measuring the construct of anger, attempts to predict how anger would differentiate people in terms of the construct. In vocational rehabilitation, a convenient starting place in determining construct validity of evaluation procedures is to examine the worker functions required in successful performance of the job. These functions are identified very clearly through job analysis techniques. Construct validation emphasizes the analysis of the job in terms of standard definitions of the constructs underlying successful performance of the duties and tasks of the job. Examples of such constructs may be speed in performing the task, eye/hand coordination, and finger dexterity.

## Predictive Validity

This refers to the relationship between a test and some criteria. It can be established by giving a test to a group of persons and then assessing the eventual outcomes for the group. Most commonly, in determining predictive validity a test is administered to a group of persons who are then placed into a training program or job. At some later time, data is collected on training or job success criteria, and this is correlated with the initial scores. These predictive validity procedures have an advantage in that they can show the capability of the evaluation device to differentiate between persons who are successful on the job and those who are not.

## Face Validity

This is a subjective appraisal of the degree to which a test seems to measure what it is designed to measure. A test that measures anger should have items that look like they measure anger. Although face validity is a very crude technique, it is often necessary in order to ensure that a test is acceptable to potential users or test-takers. For example, if a test used to predict job performance has no obvious relationship to the job itself, rehabilitation professionals may be less likely to use it. However, face validity is not the same thing as content validity. Face validity concerns judgments about a test after it has been constructed; content validity implies that although the test is being constructed, the selected test items are a reflection of an adequate sampling of a defined domain of content that bears a relationship to the trait being measured. Face validity can establish "rapport" between the test-taker and the test administrator.

Issues pertaining to validity are particularly important to the rehabilitation professional when conducting vocational assessment. For example, if a written test is employed to make decisions about individuals or groups, all the available evidence should be studied before any attempt is made to interpret the scores. Also, a test that is going to be used for prediction or selection should be validated in the specific situation in which it is going to be used. Validity awareness further implies that the professional will be up-to-date not only on new knowledge about assessment procedures but also about the qualities or individual traits they measure.

Another issue with validity revolves around the term "validity coefficient." This is a correlation between a test score and a criterion measure and is expressed by a number, such as 0.51, 0.36, or 0.2. A measure may be used, for example, to select personnel for long-term training or to predict success in school. Anastasi (1976) explained that the validity coefficient ". . . provides a single numerical index of test validity, and is commonly used in test manuals to report the validity of a test against each criterion for which data are available. . ." (p. 163). However, validity coefficients may change over time because of changing selection standards. But the interpretation of a validity coefficient must take into account a number of concomitant circumstances (Anastasi, 1976). While the correlation should be high enough to be statistically significant at some acceptable level, such as the 0.01 or 0.05 levels, the rehabilitation professional needs to evaluate the size of the correlation in the light of the uses to be made of the test.

As an example of the use of the validity coefficient, Bolton (1979) reported that the validity coefficients for the Workshop Scale of Employability (with 500 clients of the Chicago Workshop) were 0.23, 0.23, and 0.26 for the three criteria of early placement, long-term placement, and maintenance. He continued to say that the corresponding validity coefficients for a sample of 100 clients of the Indianapolis Goodwill Workshop were 0.43, 0.43, and 0.31. Consequently, Bolton (1979) concluded correctly that placement in employment was clearly more predictable using the Workshop Scale in Indianapolis than in Chicago. The rehabilitation professional can then attempt to identify the factors that may have accounted for the difference, such as economic conditions or differences among the sample groups. But the question remains: "How good is a coefficient of 0.43?" (Bolton, 1979).

An answer may be obtained by asking "What is the use of a particular measure?" Is it for prediction (i.e., employment), for selection of clients, or to support the validity of the instrument? Bolton (1979) believed, however, that a validity coefficient of 0.43 is about average, and seldom do coefficients exceed 0.60.

Validity concerns are also important when the rehabilitation professional refers a client to an evaluation resource or agency to determine vocational potential. Questions pertaining to validity include:

1.  Does the vocational evaluation program have competently trained personnel?
2.  Are there clearly specified objectives to the assessment program, and do they have the particular resources to accomplish the vocational evaluation?
3.  Can my client, despite physical and emotional limitations, meet the demands of the particular vocational evaluation experience?

Thoughtful consideration of these questions can enhance the credibility of the assessment phase of the rehabilitation process.

## RELIABILITY

Reliability refers to the dependability, consistency, and precision of an assessment procedure. A reliable procedure is one that produces similar results when repeated. An assessment task is reliable when clients who are involved in the evaluation process receive the same or similar score results if the evaluation measures are repeated.

Reliability is usually expressed by the coefficient *r*. It is a convenient statistical index for estimating indices of the relationship between distributions of test scores when a test (or some equivalent form) is administered to a single representative sample of subjects or clients on two or more occasions. The coefficient is expressed as a ratio, ranging from zero to one and represents the degree to which a group's test scores fluctuate from test to retest. If test scores are reliable, the test/retest correlation coefficient should be high. For example, high scores on one occasion should be matched by high scores on a second, and low scores should relate to low scores. The following is an identification of some correlation coefficients:

0.80 to 1.00 Very high correlation
0.60 to 0.79 Substantial correlation
0.40 to 0.59 Moderate correlation
0.20 to 0.39 Little correlation
0.01 to 0.19 Practically no correlation

There are three traditional ways of estimating this coefficient:

1. *Test/retest* The test or other assessment procedure is readministered to the same people after a one or two week interval. The scores on the first administration are co-related with the scores on the second administration, and a correlation coefficient is obtained.
2. *Alternate or parallel forms* Although not employed as frequently as the test/retest method, the use of two or more parallel forms of the same assessment instrument can provide the best estimate of reliability. These parallel forms are administered to the same subjects within a 1-to 2-week interval.
3. *Split-half* In this approach, the items within a written test, for example, are assigned arbitrarily to two forms. For example, even-numbered items may comprise one set and odd-numbered the other set. Yet, item pairs or test-halves must be equal in terms of difficulty and content, and individuals taking the particular measure must have the opportunity to complete the entire test. Then, each client receives two scores on the same instrument,

and the two sets of scores are intercorrelated. Both halves, of course, are administered at the same time.

Unfortunately, the reliability data provided for most tests are incomplete (Shertzer and Linden, 1979). Both the labor required and the cost involved prohibit the evaluation of the reliability of any measure for all people on whom the measure may be used. Rehabilitation professionals are then faced with the problem of searching among reliability data provided for a particular test or another appraisal measure in order to find the population that corresponds as closely as possible to the clients with whom they intend to work.

A question frequently raised is "What constitutes practical, minimal reliability?" The answer depends on the type of measurement instrument used (i.e., intelligence, personality, aptitude, or interest), the purpose for using the instrument, and the degree of accepted reliability. Different types of published tests show different ranges of reliability. Personality inventories, for example, tend to be less reliable than achievement tests. Importantly, the purpose for using a measurement instrument influences what is considered an acceptable level of reliability. If an instrument is used to make diagnostic decisions, such as the determination of what level of academic training the client should begin, then the test should have a reliability coefficient from 0.80-1.00.

Inherent in the reliability of assessment approaches, however, is the possibility of *error variance*. This can relate to random fluctuations in the behavior of the individual when responding to the measurement procedure, or situational variables, or to random flaws in the test, itself (Shertzer and Linden, 1979). Client characteristics and behaviors that could influence reliability include fatigue, health, motivation, understanding the mechanism of testing, the ability to comprehend test instructions, overall level of ability, and emotional strains. Situational variables refer to: external conditions of heat, light, ventilation; freedom from distractions; and clarity of instructions. Factors in the test itself that could influence reliability are the possible ambiguity of the test items, length of the test, and the level of difficulty. (The test may be so difficult for the less adept clients that their scores will be influenced unduly by guessing. Consequently, the reliability will be lowered).

To enhance the reliability of the assessment situation, the rehabilitation professional should explore not only the clients' history in taking tests or other evaluation procedures but also: 1) their motivation for the vocational assessment process; 2) any emotional pressure they might be under, 3) the possible effects of their disability on test-taking performance; and 4) the difficulty of the different assessment tasks usually given and whether they are appropriate to the level of the clients' current capabilities. Furthermore, the rehabilitation professional should be familiar with the environment in which the vocational assessment will take place. The situational variables mentioned previously can have a decided effect on a client's performance.

Reliability issues are also important when tests are considered for persons who are severely disabled. Such factors as test instructions, item content and format, and methods for answering the test items are designed to make a particular test useful for a specific population. When a different population with different characteristics is introduced, the test procedures might have to be changed.

Most of these changes involve the medium in which test instructions and questions are presented to clients. For many of the severely disabled, a variety of modifications may be needed. Despite the history of attempts to modify tests for handicapped people, there have been few investigations of the effects of such test accommodations on the reliability and validity of the resulting scores. (Sherman and Robinson, 1982). In adapting or modifying a test or evaluation measure, the rehabilitation professional must be very careful not to make changes that can alter the nature of the task. Useful guides for modifying tests for administration to handicapped people are available (Bolton, 1976; Heaton et al., 1980).

The following items pertaining to test administration may be modified to apply the tests to the severely disabled:

## Time Limit

When evaluation procedures have to be administered within time limits, many of the severely disabled may not be able to follow or complete these guidelines within the alloted time. Allowances for the time limits will have to be made. The effects of increasing the length of time have not been studied fully, and only a few studies of the time needed by handicapped individuals to complete a modified test are available (Sherman and Robinson, 1982). Studies of the appropriate time limits for modified tests have been undertaken by the U.S. Office of Personnel Management (Nester and Sapinkopf, 1981). Speed tests, moreover, are considered inappropriate for test-takers with visual impairments.

Many assessment measures were developed for specific time limits. To change the time frame would distort the credibility and value of the test. A decision to follow the time limits should be based upon the type of test and the purpose for giving the test. If the rehabilitation professional wishes to compare the client's performance, for example, with a particular group of people used for "norming" the test, then the time limits should be strictly followed. But if he or she is interested in obtaining only maximum performance, the client could be given extra time.

## Length of Test

Many evaluation procedures are long, and fatigue can considerably reduce optimal performance. The professional could suggest that the test be given in the morning or, if possible, a long test could be divided into several parts and each part administered at a different time.

## Test Content

Before administering a test, its items should be checked for content because they can often be discriminatory toward clients with physical disabilities. Changes in test content are often required for clients with visual or hearing impairments. Many personality tests that are designed to explore certain traits in nonhandicapped persons could result in a different interpretation for a blind or deaf person. Such test items as ''I sometimes avoid people . . . I feel people look at me as if I were different'' should be looked at carefully, for the responses of many disabled people might be wrongly interpreted to indicate a severe neurotic problem. But the disabled often have atyptical experiences and many of their responses do not indicate behavioral pathology but different life experiences.

## Individual or Group Administration

Tests are often administered in group sessions, and many persons seem to perform better with this format. The severely disabled can also experience vocational evaluation with small groups, such as three or four persons. The test should be appropriate for each person in the group. But when the client is extremely anxious or fearful of the testing situation or adaptation in testing procedures is necessary because of severe sensory impairment or motor disability, then individual administration should be done. The reasons for having an individual administration include the existence of no convenient and practical way to use a group administration; the desire not to interfere with others in a group taking a test; and further consideration for handicapped clients, such as wanting to reduce their anxiety over the test (Sherman and Robinson, 1982). For example, the use of a Braille version of an assessment procedure should be used for blind clients and also be individually administered.

When considering individual administration over group test-taking, the rehabilitation professional should be cautious of the interaction effect between himself or herself and the client. Such interaction might negatively influence the client's assessment experience. For example, the professional may be uncomfortable with a particular disability or inexperienced in the administration of a specific measure. These problems could cause him or her to become irritated or impatient, which, in turn, might deflate the test score of the disabled client.

There are instances, of course, in which a handicapping condition has almost no effect on test performance, and consequently, modifications are not needed. Furthermore, some modifications will have no effect on the test results. Yet, very severe disabling conditions can have a great impact on test performance, and their influence on test results could be considerable. Generally, when the disability imposes a language obstacle; interferes with understanding the test items, problems or materials; or prevents a person from making the responses required for indicating test answers, such as using a pencil or marking responses on answer sheets, then the evaluation measure will fall considerably short of evaluating those factors it is intended to assess. Also, many disabled people must take drugs that are antispasmodic, anxiety-reducing, or anti-convulsant. Many of these medications can easily lower the credibility of the assessment results. The rehabilitation professional should match the evaluation procedure to the particular limitations of the disability that affect assessment performance.

Consequently, when considering the use of different tests or evaluation procedures with the disabled, the rehabilitation practitioner should review the purpose, format, reading level, and length of the particular test. Also, the manual of instructions could be examined to determine whether it contains special information for disabled persons. An affirmative answer to such questions as: "Has the assessment procedure been 'normed' with a disabled population?" and "Has it been successfully used with various disability groups?" could considerably enhance the value of the assessment results.

## INTERPRETING TEST SCORES

When reading assessment reports from an evaluation resource or explaining test scores to a client, the rehabilitation professional should understand how to interpret various types of test scores. Raw scores derived from psychologic tests and inventories are converted to some form of standard scores that indicate a relative position in a distribution of scores obtained by the norm group. Norms are the bridge for converting raw scores into standard scores and percentiles. Test norms, usually found in the particular test manual, enable the rehabilitation practitioner to compare a client's performance to an appropriate reference group. Comparisons must frequently be made in order to obtain specific information for predicting a client's performance level in various educational and vocational areas.

Some examples of scores that appear in client evaluation reports are as follows:

1. *Stanine scores*   range from one to nine
2. *T-scores*   transformed standard scores with a mean of 50 and a standard deviation (SD) of 10.
3. *Percentiles*   not to be confused with percentage scores; express what proportion of the group falls below the score obtained by the client. For

example, a percentile rank of 55 means that 54 out of 100 of the scores in the normative sample were lower than the client's.

Figure 5.1 shows the relationships among different types of test scores in a normal distribution. It identifies, for example, that a $t$-score of 60 is one SD unit above the mean, corresponds to a stanine score of 7, and is approximately equivalent to the 84th percentile. The figure is a useful guide when interpreting test scores, especially when explaining $t$- and stanine scores in terms of the corresponding percentile score. Frequently, percentiles are more readily understood by clients.

## CONCLUSION

When a client attempts to carry out a task during rehabilitation assessment, whether a paper-and-pencil test, work sample, or job tryout situation, his or her performance will be a complex function of: 1) the capacity to carry out the task; 2) effort; and 3) directing the efforts appropriately. With disabled clients, the

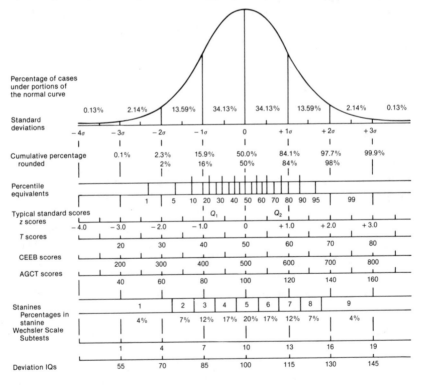

*Figure 5.1.    Relationships among different types of test scores.*

factor of capacity must be cautiously measured, considering the issues of appropriate norms, the testing environment, and the possible mental and physical limitations of the client. Motivation and energy present particular concerns because there are no specialized techniques to measure them. A careful exploration of the client's capacity, motivation, and energy can lead to more accurate predictions in rehabilitation assessment.

Prediction is an integral part of rehabilitation evaluation. It involves finding out what the client can do. His or her capacities can be evaluated by many approaches, assuming that the rehabilitation professional is aware of validity and reliability issues. But evaluating available drive and energy resources and the appropriateness of the direction in which that energy is applied call for assessment strategies that go beyond psychometric measures. Among many options, situational assessment embraces a variety of evaluation paths and approaches. These assessment methods are explained in the following chapters.

## CASE STUDY

The case study of Mr. T. will help the understanding of the relevance of reliability issues in vocational assessment.

*Mr. T. was discharged 2 weeks ago from the rehabilitation hospital, where he received treatment for injuries caused by a motorcycle accident. The injuries were mainly to his head, shoulder, and back. During rehabilitation, he met a vocational rehabilitation counselor who interviewed him to determine eligibility for services and begin the rehabilitation process.*

*During the initial interview, Mr. T. states that 10 years ago (at age 16), he dropped out of high school to work for a construction company. He has been employed with this company for 10 years and performed jobs associated with running the heavy motorized equipment. Because of his injuries, he will be unable to continue this work. He further states that he takes "many pills a day" for continual back pain and since leaving the hospital, has been watching television for most of the day.*

As a vocational evaluator, you realize that your agency requires a few paper-and-pencil tests. Although you will be careful to select those that would be appropriate to Mr. T.'s level of functioning, you still want to keep the following issues in mind.

1. From what Mr. T. has stated in the initial interview, what factors would affect the reliability of the "testing situation?"
2. What steps could you take to minimize these factors?

## REFERENCES

Anastasi, A. 1976. Psychological Testing, 4th Ed. Macmillan Publishing Co., New York.

Bolton, B. (ed.). 1976. Handbook of Measurement and Evaluation in Rehabilitation. University Park Press, Baltimore.

Bolton, B. 1979. Rehabilitation Counseling Research. University Park Press, Baltimore.

Heaton, S. M., Nelson, A. V., and Nester, M. A. 1980. Guide for Administering Examinations to Handicapped Individuals for Employment Purposes. Personnel Research and Development Center. PRR 80–16, U.S. Office of Personnel Management, DC.

Nester, M. S., and Sapinkopf, R. 1981. Statistical Characteristics of the Written Test for the Professional and Administrative Career Examination (PACE) for Deaf Applicants. U.S. Office of Personnel Management, DC.

Sapinkopf, R. 1978. Statistical Characteristics of the Written Test for the Professional and Administrative Career Examination (PACE) for Visually Handicapped Clients. U.S. Civil Service Commission, Personnel Research and Development Center TM 78–1, DC.

Sherman, S. and Robinson, N. (eds.). 1982. Ability Testing of Handicapped People: Dilemma for Government, Science, and the Public. National Academy Press, DC.

Shertzer, B. and Linden, J. 1979. Fundamentals of Individual Appraisal. Houghton Mifflin Co., Boston.

chapter 6
# INTELLIGENCE TESTING

An important area of rehabilitation assessment is the exploration of a client's capability to solve problems, adapt to new situations, and show competence when confronted with new learning demands. Competence itself is both ability-oriented, emphasizing positive, coping skills, and situation-oriented, because it relates to a person's ability to function in environmental interactions (Sundberg, 1977). One of the approaches to measure competence is the assessment of intelligence.

Intelligence tests represent a highly specialized field with a vast body of literature and research surrounding their use. Intelligent behavior is as much a function of drive and incentive as the more traditionally conceived components of intellectual ability, such as abstract and logical thinking, reasoning, judging, and retaining knowledge (Shertzer and Linden, 1979). Intelligence is not a single, unitary ability, but rather a composite of several functions. It is the global capacity of the individual to act purposefully, think rationally, and deal effectively with the environment (Wechsler, 1981). Intelligence is a function of the total personality, and personality characteristics generally affect the direction and extent of the individual's intellectual development. Affective life and cognitive life, although distinct, are inseparable. (Shertzer and Linden, 1979).

Precisely what intelligence tests measure has been the subject of dispute since their origin. Wechsler believed that they measure . . . "the capacity of an individual to understand the world about him and his resourcefulness to cope with its challenges" (Shertzer and Linden, 1979, p. 123). But no intelligence test available today measures innate ability (Shertzer and Linden, 1979). Rather, such tests measure the extent to which an individual's innate potential has been modified or developed within his or her environment. Many factors other than intelligence (like creativity, exploratory interests, economic supports, and environmental opportunities) may influence success in intelligence testing. Measured intelligence has been found to both reflect past schooling and predict future school success. The IQ score resulting from such tests could be viewed as "measured intelligence, not necessarily the adaptive intelligence used in everyday living" (Sundberg, 1977, p. 245). The concept of intelligence common to all intelligence tests, however, is the *ability to learn*.

The ability to learn is also shared by *aptitude*. Although learning ability may be narrow or wide and specific or general in importance, intelligence is considered more as a wide-scope aptitude, comprised of a variety of closely related mental abilities that are most useful for predicting general achievement. Verbal and numerical abilities, which are essential in some degree to nearly all forms of achievement, have become the main ingredients of many intelligence tests. Verbal intelligence tests are most like achievement tests and in that respect, are better suited for predictions of success at the next higher level of learning than for assessing the full range of trainability. Also, the great majority of intelligence tests include appraisal of the reasoning factor. These tests are especially useful for differential appraisal of past learning versus present capacity. Intelligence testing, therefore, does not provide a comprehensive measure of all aspects of intelligence. Because the concept of intelligence is so complex, any test or assessment procedure attempting to measure all of its theoretical aspects would be too lengthy to be practical. What is measured is the client's performance on a series of tasks, and from this performance the amount of ''intelligence'' that a client possesses is inferred. Consequently, intelligence should be regarded as a descriptive, rather than explanatory, concept. It is an expression of an individual's ability at a given point in time in relation to age norms.

Because of the norm concept discussed in the previous chapter, the interpretation of intelligence test results in rehabilitation assessment must be done cautiously. Most intelligence tests do not include handicapped people in their standardization sample. Unfortunately, IQ and intelligence have become so value-laden in society that persons are labeled on the basis of a small amount of evidence.

Is intelligence related to employment success? People tend, insofar as circumstances permit, to gravitate toward jobs in which they have the ability to compete successfully with others. In turn, having capabilities considerably in excess of those required by a job often causes dissatisfaction because of the lack of challenge and consequent loss of interest in the work. Correlation between intelligence test scores and job success may actually be an artifact, the product of their joint association with class status (McClelland, 1973). Although many employers select some employees who have gone to the ''right'' schools because they do better, intelligence does not necessarily make people proficient at their jobs. Among college students, there is no consistent relationship between their scholastic aptitude scores and their actual accomplishments, whether in social leadership, the arts, science, music, writing, or speech and drama (McClelland, 1973). Likewise, in routine occupations that require speed and accuracy (whether clerical or semi-skilled factory jobs), intelligence measured by an alertness factor rather than standard time-powered tests is more related to success in the learning period.

For the rehabilitation practitioner, it is important to remember that the reliability of most well-known intelligence tests is high (usually in the 0.80s or 0.90s), but even these figures allow for variation (Sundberg, 1977). Some people change markedly from time to time, especially if they have gone through periods of maladjustment. Also, the attainment of physical growth does not mean that mental, emotional, and psychologic growth have ended. An adult, age 40, can learn new things almost as well as a young person, age 13. In fact, an adult who is motivated strongly enough to make up some slight loss in alertness and adaptability may learn better than the young person. The greatest difference in mental ability between younger and older persons may be in speed rather than accuracy or power (Shertzer and Linden, 1979).

The most commonly used tests of mental ability are highly reliable, with reliability coefficients in the low to mid 0.90s (Shertzer and Linden, 1979). In developing the validity of their tests, the authors usually correlated them with criteria such as the Stanford-Binet performances, grades, academic averages, or ratings of teachers and supervisors. Predictive validity coefficients usually fall in the 0.40 to 0.60 ranges, with grades as the criteria.

Because of the multitude of abilities and the complexity of mental activities, it is important not to base decisions for rehabilitation planning on any single measure of ability. Several different kinds of evaluation tasks, such as the interview or the job tryout, should be utilized. Sundberg (1977) believed that any one IQ should be treated as a range rather than as a single score, keeping in mind the reliability or accuracy of the instrument. Also, it is necessary to ask: "How and where does my client want to use a certain capability?" Many training environments, for example, do not demand a high level of abilities.

Intelligence is a complex concept. Although an intelligence test does not give a comprehensive measure of all aspects of intelligence, it can still evaluate a person's general ability more quickly and economically than many other procedures. Also, its appraisal of ability is usually more accurate than subjective methods and can provide the professional with a beginning understanding of the client's ability to learn in a training situation.

## FACTORS WHEN CONSIDERING INTELLIGENCE TESTS

When considering the use of intelligence tests with disabled people, certain factors should be kept in mind:

### Factor 1

*Who should administer and interpret these tests?* Unless the rehabilitation professional has had specialized training, ordinarily a psychologist or psychologic examiner should give the measure and interpret the results. This is particularly true of two of the tests suggested in this chapter: the Wechsler Adult Intelligence Scale-Revised (WAIS-R) and the Haptic Intelligence Scale for the Adult Blind.

Yet, the rehabilitation professional should still be familiar with these measures, specifically regarding their strengths and deficiencies, as well as the meaning of the test results. These scores frequently come from other sources, and the helping professional should understand their relevance to a particular client. This is especially true concerning the validity of scores with regard to the client's disability, socioeconomic state, and other variables in the testing process. Many intelligence measures, for example, rely heavily on the client's verbal ability, which is not a well-developed trait in many disabled persons.

The other measures suggested in this chapter can be administered and interpreted by rehabilitation professionals with a graduate degree or training in standardized instruments. The manuals of these tests contain clear instructions on administration and interpretation, and the tests, themselves, take a relatively short time for completion. Their results can be valuable in determining what occupations or training possibilities would not be appropriate for an individual as well as any intellectual strengths or competencies for eventual vocational programming.

**Factor 2**

*Particular attention should be given to the selection of tests relevant to a specific disability.* As Table 2.1 in this volume indicates, the WAIS-R is appropriate for all handicaps but has limited use with the visually and hearing-impaired. The Haptic Intelligence Scale for the Adult Blind is really useful only for the visually impaired. The Peabody Picture Vocabulary Test is applicable for the mentally retarded. The Quick Test is a valuable instrument for identifying a general range of intelligence functioning, although it is not applicable for the visually impaired. The Shipley-Hartford Test is really more useful for those clients who have at least some high school education. The Slosson Intelligence Test, Raven Progressive Matrices, and Otis Quick Scoring Mental Ability Tests are appropriate for all handicaps, although they have limited use with the visually and hearing-impaired.

An IQ test should be chosen according to the client's educational and life experiences as well as his or her disability-related limitations. Also, when administering an intelligence measure, the rehabilitation professional should consider how long it has been since the client took such a test. Records may state that many years have elapsed since the original identification of measured intelligence functioning. But mental growth can be a continuing process, although not an even one. The creative process, for example, can continue through adulthood and into old age. Or, deterioration of basic functioning may be suspected because of the presence of head trauma or chronic disease.

Consequently, an update of the client's intelligence functioning should be considered.

## Factor 3

*When evaluating the vocational potential of the severely disabled, many of the problems found in intelligence testing are magnified.* If a physical disability limits a client's capacity to perform in the areas of social competence or psychomotor functioning, do the results of the test, then, reflect intelligence or simply the degree of physical impairment (Schlenoff, 1974)? Each disability has specific and characteristically limiting effects, and disabled clients reflect adaptive and learning behavior aspects of intelligence differently. Consequently, it is necessary that the rehabilitation professional be aware of the problems and limitations characteristic of the client's disability. The initial interview can identify these concerns. Exploring the client's physical, social, educational, and occupational history can provide further information on the best possible ways to evaluate intelligence functioning.

When exploring intelligence levels with clients, it is often useful to utilize at least two intelligence measures. This can provide more comprehensive information for rehabilitation planning. For the severely disabled, the assessment of intelligence is not really a process that is different in "kind" from traditional evaluation, but rather is different in "extent". At the same time, this testing process can be overwhelming to clients, particularly to those who are unaccustomed anyway to testing. To alleviate client anxieties, time should be spent on explaining the goals of assessment and the purpose of each IQ test to be used. After the preparation, and when two or more IQ measures are to be utilized, the following sequence is recommended:

For clients whose records contain no recent information on intelligence functioning, and whose educational background and reading ability are apparently poor:
  1.   Peabody Picture Vocabulary Test
or
      Revised Beta Examination
or
      Raven Progressive Matrices
or
      Slosson Intelligence Test
  Then:
  2.   WAIS-R

For clients whose records also contain no recent information on intelligence functioning and who have had no education training in the past 5 years but whose records indicate some high school education:

    1.  any one of the measures identified previously in (1), but at least the Quick Test

Then:

    2.  WAIS-R

For rehabilitation professionals who want an update on intelligence functioning for a client who has graduated from high school when interview information suggests a well-developed reading ability or recent educational training:

    1.  Shipley-Hartford Test

                or

        Otis Quick Scoring Mental Ability Tests

Then:

    2.  WAIS-R

## Vocational Implications

With the exception of the WAIS-R, all of the IQ measures explained in this chapter can be administered by a rehabilitation professional who has had some training in assessment and has access to qualified supervisors. These tests also suggest a general estimate of intelligence competencies, although the WAIS-R provides more precise information. The tests further suggest levels of possible training, language development, and with certain test results, levels of reasoning.

## IQ CLASSIFICATION CHART

The following table, with information provided by Wechsler (1981), can be used when interpreting scores on intelligence tests:

| IQ | Classification |
| --- | --- |
| 130 and above | Very superior |
| 120–129 | Superior |
| 110–119 | High average |
| 90–109 | Average |
| 80–89 | Low average |
| 70–79 | Borderline |
| 69 and below | Mentally retarded |

    The following section gives more detailed information on the different measures of intelligence functioning that are useful when evaluating disabled clients. These tests emphasize developed general ability (achievement) more than the raw aptitude for such development. Except for the WAIS-R, which identifies particular abilities, all the suggested tests provide a general estimate of intellectual functioning.

## WECHSLER ADULT INTELLIGENCE SCALE-REVISED EDITION (WAIS-R)

The WAIS-R assesses general and specific intellectual abilities of ages 16 to 74. Wechsler (1981) believed that:

> Intelligence is a function of the personality as a whole and is responsive to other factors besides those included under the concept of cognitive abilities. Intelligence tests inevitably measure these factors as well (p. 8).

The WAIS-R consists of 11 subtests, grouped under Verbal Scale and Performance Scale. Each scale explores particular dimensions of intelligence functioning, and the verbal and nonverbal group may be administered separately or together to yield, respectively, a Verbal, Performance, and Full-Scale IQ.

In the WAIS-R, about 80% of the items are retained from the 1955 WAIS. The administration of the current test has been changed so that Verbal and Performance tests are systematically alternated. For the development of the WAIS-R norms, a stratified sampling plan was adopted to ensure that representative proportions of various classes of adults would be included in the standardization sample. The sample was specified using 1970 census data and was updated as more current population figures became available. There were sixty occupational groups, including professional and technical workers, managers and administrators, clerical and sales workers, craftsmen and foremen, operatives, service workers, farmers, laborers, farm laborers, farm foremen, and those not in the labor force. The sample did not include individuals with known brain damage, severe behavioral or emotional problems, institutionalized persons with mental retardation, and individuals with physical defects whose ability to respond to test items would be restricted. Standardization cases were tested between May, 1976 and May, 1980, and the revised version of the WAIS was published in 1981.

The Verbal, Performance, and Full-Scale IQ distributions were constructed to have means of 100 and standard deviations of 15 IQ points. On any of the scales for a given age, an IQ of 100 defines the performance of the average adult at that age. About two-thirds of all adults obtain IQs between 85 and 118 (Wechsler, 1981).

The WAIS-R has demonstrated high reliability coefficients across all age groups (16 to 74). Validity studies have been reported mainly on the original WAIS and have been investigated primarily through correlations between test scores and scholastic achievement. However, Silverstein (1982) conducted a principal-factor analysis and a two-factor solution for the WAIS-R and the original WAIS. The stability of the two factors, identified as Verbal Comprehension and Perceptual Organization, was very high both within and between scales.

Although not normed with the disabled population, the WAIS-R is perhaps the best general adult intelligence test available. With a trained examiner and careful test preparation, this measure can provide very useful information in many areas of client functioning. The results allow the client to be compared to the normal population in "intelligence" areas. The different scales of the WAIS-R are as follows:

## Verbal Scales

*Information*   Twenty-nine questions cover a wide variety of information that adults in the American culture should presumably acquire. An effort was made to avoid specialized or academic knowledge.

*Comprehension*   Sixteen items require the subject to explain what should be done under certain circumstances, the meaning of proverbs, and why specific practices are followed. The items are designed to measure practical judgment and common sense.

*Arithmetic*   Fourteen problems are similar to those encountered in elementary-school arithmetic. Each problem is to be solved without the use of paper and pencil and is orally presented.

*Similarities*   Fourteen items require the subject to say how two things are alike.

*Digit Span*   Orally presented lists of three to nine digits are to be reproduced orally. In the second part, the subject must reproduce backwards lists of two to eight digits.

*Vocabulary*   Thirty-five words of increasing difficulty are presented both orally and visually. The subject is asked what each word means.

## Performance Scales

*Digit Symbol*   This is a version of a familiar code-substitution test that dates to the early Woodworth-Wells Association Test and often has been included in nonlanguage intelligence scales. The key contains nine symbols paired with nine digits. The subject's score is the number of symbols correctly written within 1½ minutes.

*Picture Completion*   Twenty cards each contain a picture with some part missing. The subject must tell what is missing from each picture.

***Block Design***     This test consists of increasingly complex designs made from four to nine cubes, or blocks. The cubes have red, white, and red-and-white sides.

***Picture Arrangement***     Each item consists of a set of cards containing pictures to be rearranged in proper sequence to tell a story. The new pictures of the WAIS-R depict people of both sexes and different races.

***Object Assembly***     A number of pieces are to be assembled much in the manner of a jigsaw puzzle. The subtest includes four pictures to be reproduced, including those of a mannequin, hand, profile of a face, and side view of an elephant.

## SLOSSON INTELLIGENCE TEST

The Slosson Intelligence Test[1] is an individually administered, oral test that can be used for initial screening purposes. The test is brief, and scoring is fairly objective. Because the test is oral, it can be used with those who are blind, have reading handicaps, are physically disabled, cannot respond to paper-and-pencil tests, or cannot work effectively under the pressures of a time test, e.g., those who are on heavy medication or are "test anxious."

Siders and Wharton (1982) explained that when providing educational services to mildly handicapped children, the Slosson Test, as well as the Peabody Picture Vocabulary Test, may be used as a quick screening device. Also, if these tests do not rule out a disabling condition, such as mental retardation, they may be followed by a more in-depth exam.

Although no research is available on its use with the adult disabled, it can be utilized with the disabled population as a screening instrument. The examiner should give particular attention to the capability of the client to respond to the test items. The Slosson can be administered in from 10 to 30 minutes. Because of the brevity of the test, it should not be relied on without other supporting information, particularly in situations where important diagnostic decisions are required.

## PEABODY PICTURE VOCABULARY TEST (PPVT)

The PPVT[2] is an untimed individual intelligence test, orally administered in 15 minutes or less. No reading is required by the client, and scoring is rapid and

---

[1]The Slosson Intelligence Test is available from McGraw-Hill Publishers Test Service, 2500 Garden Rd., Monterey, CA 93940. 800-538-9547.

[2]The PPVT is available from the American Guidance Service, Inc., Publisher's Building, Circle Pines, MI 55014. 612-786-4343

objective. The total score can be converted to a percentile rank, mental age, or a standard deviation IQ score. No special training is required to administer, score, or interpret the PPVT.

This test was standardized on a national sample of 4,000 children and adolescents between the ages of 2½ and 18 years (Anastasi, 1982). Additional adult norms were obtained on 828 persons ages 19 to 40 and were selected to be nationally representative of geographical regions and major occupational groups (Anastasi, 1982). No handicapped people were included in the norm population.

PPVT provides an estimate of the client's verbal intelligence and has been administered to groups who had reading or speech problems, were mentally retarded, or were emotionally withdrawn. Because the manner of the client's response to stimulus vocabulary is to point in any fashion to one or four pictures that best fits the stimulus word, these tests also apply to rehabilitation clients who have multiple physical handicaps but whose hearing and vision is intact. The test also has high interest value, and this can establish good rapport with the client. For its administration, the examiner presents a series of pictures to each client. There are four pictures to a page, and each is numbered. The examiner states a word describing one of the pictures and asks the client to point to or tell the number of the picture that the word describes.

The test is not useful in its present form for the blind and deaf, but is very useful for the mentally retarded, for whom no modifications in instructions or format are needed. The only possible problem is that the illustrations for about the first 50 items often use children. These may not be acceptable to the adult mentally retarded person.

## REVISED BETA EXAMINATION (BETA)

This test [3] is designed to serve as a measure of general intellectual ability of persons who are relatively illiterate or non-English speaking. A nonverbal estimate of intelligence is given as a single IQ score. This group test, including instructions, can be administered in about 30 minutes. Subtests are timed from 1½ to 4 minutes. The test is also designed to be given individually, when necessary.

The test contains six subtests. The first requires completion of mazes; the second test—number/picture substitution; the third and fifth tests—finding the wrong drawing in a series of illustrations; the fourth test—form perception; and the sixth test—identifying sameness of objects.

No reading is required for this test; it is mainly designed for illiterate

---

[3]The Revised Beta Examination is available from The Psychological Corporation, 757 Third Ave., New York 10017. 212-888-3500

clients. All responses are recorded in a nonreusable booklet. The ability to hold a pencil, print numbers, and the dexterity to trace mazes are required for recording the responses. Each subtest includes several demonstration items and at least three practice items. The Beta includes several practice items for each subtest, together with instructions that the examiner carefully check the client's performance on each.

Most of the norms are based on British samples, and the normative data is sketchy at best (Thorndike and Hagen, 1969). Thorndike and Hagen also explained that although the test is claimed by some to be "culture fair," there is little evidence to support the claim.

For the blind, this test is not usable in its present form. It can, however, be used effectively with mentally retarded clients. The only problem that may arise is with the abstractness of some of the items in several of the subtests. With modifications, the test can also be used with the deaf, because of visual content as well as the fact that the test can be individually administered. The problem is in giving the instructions, which could be signed or placed on cards for the client to read. The client who cannot understand signing and who cannot read could be administered the Beta if the examiner carefully goes over each practice exercise.

## RAVEN PROGRESSIVE MATRICES

The Raven Progressive Matrices[4] are designed to measure general ability, especially the ability to perceive and utilize relationships between nonverbal materials. It taps such qualities of the intellect as spatial aptitude, inductive reasoning, and perceptual accuracy. The tasks or matrices consist of designs that are incomplete. The individual being tested chooses from several designs or patterns and selects the pattern that best completes the matrix.

The Raven Progressive Matrices are available at three levels and can be used with ages 5 and older. The test can be administered individually or in groups, and is hand-scored. It is easy to administer and relatively brief. Although not useful for the visually impaired, the test is helpful with the physically handicapped and emotionally disturbed. There is no time limit to the test, and this is a favorable feature for many disabled.

A literature review indicates no research on its use or standardization with the disabled population. This test should be used in conjunction with a vocabulary test, which will provide an index of the general information a client has acquired up to the present as well as his or her command of the English language.

---

[4]The Raven Progressive Matrices is available from The Psychological Corporation, 757 Third Ave., New York 10017. 212-888-3500

## OTIS QUICK SCORING MENTAL ABILITY TESTS

These tests[5] have been among the most widely used tests in public schools (Thorndike and Hagen, 1969). The Otis can be administered individually or in a group and can be hand-scored in a few minutes. The Gamma Form for grades 9 through 16 consists of 80 items, which tap functions such as Word Meaning, Verbal Analogies, Proverb Interpretation, Logical Reasoning, and Arithmetic Reasoning. The test requires little or no training to administer and yields a single IQ score. The Otis can be used either to obtain a rough estimate of the client's general learning ability or as a quick check to verify questionable test data. The test requires an approximate sixth-grade reading level.

There is no available research evidence that the Otis Tests included the disabled population in their standardization sample, and reports of its use with the disabled population are very sketchy indeed. However, because the tests are extremely easy to administer and score they are helpful in rehabilitation. Because of their brevity, major vocational or diagnostic decisions should not be made on the basis of these tests alone.

There are three Otis tests: Alpha (grades 1 through 4); Beta (grades 4 through 9); and Gamma (grades 9 through 16).

## THE QUICK TEST (QT)

This test[6] is a carefully standardized, individual intelligence test in three forms and is based on perceptual/verbal performance. It takes 3 to 10 minutes to administer. Anyone who can see the drawings, hear or read the word items, and signal yes/no can receive this assessment instrument. The client is not required to read, write, or speak, and with adequate administration, scoring is quick and objective. Item responses are easily scored during the administration of the test. Summary scores, mental ages, tentative IQs, and percentile ranks can be quickly computed or read from tables on the record form and in the manual.

This test is most helpful for gaining a general understanding of a client's perceptual/verbal functioning. The measure should be followed by a more comprehensive test, like the WAIS, after an estimate of the client's functioning has been achieved, although many rehabilitation practitioners use the results of this test to move into an assessment exploration of aptitude and abilities functions.

The QT can be used with the hearing-impaired, but it is not suitable for the blind. The test can also be used to build rapport in the testing situation, to test

---

[5]The Otis Quick Scoring Mental Ability Tests are available from the Psychological Corporation, 757 Third Ave., New York 10017. 212-888-3500

[6]The QT is available from the Psychological Test Specialists, Box 1441, Missoula, MT. 59801.

persons with a short attention span, and to estimate the intelligence of severely physically handicapped persons for whom larger and more complicated tests may not be appropriate. Reported reliabilities of single forms of the QT have been high, from a range of 0.78 to 0.97. The QT is designed for quick, efficient estimations of general levels of intellectual ability when circumstances are less than optimum and time is at a premium.

## SHIPLEY-HARTFORD

This test[7] consists of a 40-item multiple choice Vocabulary Subtest and a 20-item Abstract Thinking Subtest. The Shipley-Hartford has the advantage of being a short, easily administered, and easily scored objective test, adaptable to group or individual testing and requiring little training for nonpsychologic personnel to administer, score, and interpret. The scale was devised to provide a quick, objective, self-administering measure of mental deterioration. It is based on the clinical, experimental observation that in mental deterioration, vocabulary level tends to be affected only slightly while the ability to see abstract relationships declines rapidly. These facts suggest using the differential between vocabulary and abstract thinking levels as a possible index of deterioration. Besides providing an estimate of mental deterioration, it is a good instrument to assess whether clients have at least average intelligence before they begin training or employment.

The test cannot be used with the visually impaired but is suitable for those with hearing deficits. As mentioned earlier in this chapter, the test is more applicable for those who have at least a sixth-grade reading level. Yet, the results have more use when the client has at least a tenth-grade education.

Each subtest has a 10-minute time limit. Reliability coefficients are 0.87 for the vocabulary test, 0.89 for the abstract thinking test, and 0.92 for the two combined.

## HAPTIC INTELLIGENCE SCALE FOR THE ADULT BLIND

A timed, individual test requiring 90 to 120 minutes, the Haptic Intelligence Scale for the Adult Blind[8] should be administered in two sessions because of its length. The test explores how the client compensates for loss of sight and his or her flexibility in dealing with nonvisual materials. It consists of such subtests as Digit Symbol, Object Assembly, Block Design, and Object Completion—all

---

[7]The Shipley-Hartford is available from The Institute of Living, The Neuropsychiatric Institute of the Hartford Retreat, Hartford, CT 203-241-8000

[8]The Haptic Intelligence Scale for the Adult Blind is available from the Psychological Research Technology Center, Chicago, IL.

of which were modified from the WAIS. Bead Arithmetic and the Pattern Board are two other sub-tests that have been added.

This test was developed as a nonverbal test to be used in conjunction with the Verbal Scale of the WAIS (Anastasi, 1982). Both tests utilize a completely tactile approach and if given to the partially blind, requires wearing a blindfold. The standardization procedures closely follow those employed with the WAIS. Blind subjects tested in the standardization sample included a proportional number of nonwhites and were distributed over the major geographical regions of the country (Anastasi, 1982). Split-half reliability for the entire test was found to be 0.95.

The Haptic should be interpreted with caution. The client's degree of disability, age at loss of vision, special schools attended, and knowledge of Braille and abacus should all be considered before administering this test. Some of its disadvantages are that it is costly, requires a lengthy administration time, and the client must be readily available over a period of several days.


## CONCLUSION

In rehabilitation, assessment of the client's ability to learn or his or her competence in handling everyday situations can be most valuable. This information can help clients to appreciate their remaining capacities after a serious trauma has brought extensive physical limitations. Also, many clients may have no idea about their general range of intellectual functioning because they have received no feedback about this capacity for several years or even decades. An awareness of this information can be a stimulus to a more realistic, individually oriented rehabilitation plan. All the evaluation data should lead to effective, individualized, rehabilitation programming.

The measures suggested in this chapter have all been utilized by the author in different circumstances. The choice of test often depends upon the training of the rehabilitation professional and the purpose for obtaining information in intelligence functioning.

But assessment cannot end with an understanding of the client's intelligence potential. More information on other areas of client functioning, such as achievement, personality, and interest, is needed. The following chapters identify and describe these assessment tools.


## CASE STUDY

*Mr. L., age 51, is a black male who injured his left leg in an industrial accident. He has a brace on this leg and walks with a cane. Before his accident, he was employed as a bricklayer for 26 years and has re-*

*cently been told by his physician that in the future, he will only be able to perform sedentary work. Prior work experience includes brief periods of employment as a pipelayer, a construction laborer, and a farm worker.*

*Mr. L. reports that he had to leave school in the third grade because of economic reasons. Although he claims to enjoy "reading" history books, he states that one of his daughters helps him to interpret written material. He is married and has six children, is an active church member, and has social ties with his family and neighborhood companions.*

*During the initial interview, Mr. L. mentioned that he is very willing to learn a new trade. He was well-dressed for this session, and appeared enthusiastic for vocational evaluation.*

Considering this information, please answer the following questions:

1. Because of the client's life history, what are some special concerns when selecting a measure of intelligence?
2. From the list of intelligence tests described in this chapter, which ones do you feel would be appropriate for this client?

## REFERENCES

Adams, G. S. 1964. Measurement and Evaluation in Education, Psychology, and Guidance. Holt, Rinehart, and Winston, New York.

Anastasi, A. 1982. Psychological Testing. MacMillan Publishing Co., New York.

Guertin, W. H., Frank, G., Ladd, C., and Rabin, A. 1966. Research with the Wechsler Intelligence Scale for Adults. Psychol. Bull. 66:385–409.

McClelland, D. 1973. Testing for competence rather than for intelligence. Am. Psychol. January. 28:1–14.

Schlenoff, D. 1974. Considerations in administering intelligence tests to the physically disabled. Rehab. Lit., 35:362–363.

Shertzer, B., and Linden, J. 1979. Fundamentals of Individual Appraisal. Houghton Mifflin Co., Boston.

Siders, J., and Wharton, J. 1982. The relationship of individual ability and IEP goal statements. Elem. Sch. Guid. Couns. 16:187–192.

Silverstein, A. 1982. Factor structure of the Wechsler Adult Intelligence Scale-Revised. J. Consult. Clin. Psychol. 50:661–664.

Sundberg, N. 1977. Assessment of Persons. Prentice-Hall, Inc. Englewood Cliffs, N.J.

Thorndike, R., and Hagen, E. 1969. Measurement and Evaluation in Psychology and Education. John Wiley and Sons, Inc., New York.

Wechsler, D. 1981. WAIS-R Manual. Harcourt Brace Jovanovich, New York.

# chapter 7
# UNDERSTANDING ACHIEVEMENT AND APTITUDE ASSESSMENT

One of the objectives of vocational assessment is to assist clients in understanding both their own strengths and weaknesses in relation to the world of work and the usual demands flowing from most employment opportunities. These demands include reading, writing, perceptual abililties, and the capability to understand and follow directions. Whether or not a client either actually possesses such skills or has the capability to acquire them is determined through two traditional approaches—achievement tests and aptitude tests.

Achievement tests are designed to provide an evaluation of what individuals have learned from their education and experience. These tests can also be used both to explore the changes in what a client has or has not learned since leaving school or other formal training and to assess competencies needed for many occupational opportunities. From this information, a client can begin to explore both appropriate occupational choices and the amount of training that might be needed to enter a particular field. Also, the two achievement areas that a rehabilitation worker should especially consider are the client's verbal and numerical skills. Verbal achievement is demonstrated in reading and spelling. In numerical achievement, such factors as counting, reading number symbols, and performing written computations are necessary for efficiency in related jobs.

Aptitude tests, however, attempt to identify an ability or characteristic, mental or physical, native or acquired, that is believed or known to indicate a client's capacity or potential for learning a particular skill or knowledge. As achievement tests attempt to measure the outcome of specific training, education, and experience, so aptitude tests focus on performance capabilities that have been developed without conscious effort. Anastasi (1982) believed that achievement tests measure the outcomes of standardized school experiences, such as courses in mathematics or social studies, while aptitude tests measure the cumulative influence of a multiplicity of daily experiences. Also, aptitude tests can be used to determine the extent to which clients will profit from training.

Although aptitude cannot be directly measured, it can be inferred from the client's performance on an evaluation instrument. Frequently, there are multiple aptitudes required for successful performance in a particular vocational area, and the matching of an individual's aptitudes with the abilities needed for the vocational area are indicators for potential or possible success in this area. With the information gained from aptitude assessment, the professional has a better opportunity to assist clients in making appropriate choices among training or occupation possibilities.

The reliabilities for aptitude and achievement tests tend to cluster in the high 0.80s and low 0.90s. The validity of these tests is also relatively high. For occupations that are clerical, service, trades and crafts, and industrial, the client's potential for successful training at different levels is predicted rather well by tests of intellectual abilities, spatial and mechanical abilities, and perceptual accuracy. But prediction of job proficiency for these occupational groups is much more tenuous. For example, a client might take a mechanical aptitude test and score at the 75th percentile. If the group that was used to standardize these scores in this test, called the norm group, were successful auto mechanics, it might be predicted that this client would also be successful as an auto mechanic. This kind of prediction would still involve a subjective judgment because there is no conclusive research evidence that a score at the 75th percentile ensures a high probability of success in auto mechanics. Norms are not predictive devices. Aptitude and achievement tests can indicate whether a client has the potential or capacity to meet the training or occupational demands. They do not necessarily predict success.

Unfortunately, the norms for these tests often are inappropriate for comparison purposes when used with handicapped individuals, and this should be considered when interpreting results. They can be useful, however, if certain minimum acceptable performance levels are established for various training opportunities or placements into local area workshop situations. There are many types of achievement and aptitude tests, and this chapter identifies those that the rehabilitation professional may find useful. Following each test description is a brief section on the vocational implications of the particular measure for rehabilitation planning purposes.

## ACHIEVEMENT TESTS

### Wide Range Achievement Test (WRAT)

The WRAT[1] is one of the most frequently used achievement tests. It is primarily an individually administered test, but the sections on spelling and arithmetic

---

[1] The WRAT is available from Jastak Association, Inc., 1526 Gilpin Ave., Wilmington, DE 19806. Phone: 800-538-9547.

can be given in a small group. This is a brief measure that can provide a rough indication of a client's academic achievement. The achievement factors measured by the test include: 1) Reading—the ability to recognize and name letters and pronounce words; 2) Spelling—copying marks resembling letters, writing the name, and writing single words to dictation; and 3) Arithmetic—counting, reading number symbols, solving oral problems, and performing written computations.

For many years, the WRAT has found widespread use in rehabilitation facilities. The findings of Moore et al. (1981) supported the validity of using the WRAT to assess achievement among such workshop populations of clients 16 years and older who have vocational handicaps that limit their employment opportunities. These populations included developmentally disabled, emotionally disturbed, and physically handicapped individuals. The directions for administration are clear in the manual, and it can be given by someone who has at least a 2-year college degree. The test is not appropriate for the visually impaired. Also, the emphasis on hearing the examiner and the necessity of having to pronounce words correctly on certain parts of the test place the deaf at a disadvantage. The WRAT, however, is particularly helpful in assessing academic achievement when the client has not had recent educational experience and the rehabilitation professional wants to determine basic reading and arithmetic capabilities for possible training. The items in each part of the test are arranged in order of difficulty. For the mentally retarded or other clients for whom many items may be too difficult, an oral section with easier questions is provided with each test.

*Vocational Implications*   Explores adequate level of basic educational skills and development; provides suggestions for level of possible training

## Adult Basic Learning Examinatioin (ABLE)

The major purposes of ABLE[2] are to determine the general educational level of adults who have not completed a formal eighth-grade education, diagnose individual strengths, and assist in the development of educational plans. ABLE provides scores in five areas: vocabulary, reading, spelling, computation, and problem solving (math). This paper-and-pencil test contains three levels: Level I—grades 1 through 4; Level II—grades 5 through 8; and Level III—grades 9 through 12. Each level has two alternate forms. There are five subtests at each level: Vocabulary, Reading, Spelling, Arithmetic, and Computation and Problem Solving. Each test consists of multiple-choice items as well as items requiring the writing of a word or the answer to an arithmetic problem.

ABLE was designed to be adult-oriented in content, and was specifically designed for use in connection with adult education classes or job-training

---

[2]The Adult Basic Learning Examination is available from The Psychological Corporation, 757 Third Ave., Newark 10017. Phone: 212-888-3500.

programs (Anastasi, 1982). Vocabulary, reading, spelling, and arithmetic are related to the everyday life of adults. The test is administered in group form and can be hand- or machine-scored. Machine scoring is somewhat impractical because all math problems must first be hand-tallied before machine scoring. Total testing time for Levels I and II is about 2½ hours; Level III takes about 3 hours.

Anastasi (1982) indicated that split-half and Kuder Richardson reliabilities of each test in the ABLE range from 0.80 to 0.96. Correlations between corresponding tests of ABLE and the Stanford Achievement Test in the elementary and high school samples range from the 0.60s to the 0.80s.

Regarding the utilization of the test for the handicapped, the reading level for each of the three tests gets progressively more difficult. There is no information on the disabled in the test manual. For the severely visually or hearing-impaired, the test is not usable in its present form. However, it can be used without modifications for the mentally retarded. The parts of the ABLE that are administered orally can be used with the blind if responses are recorded using a Braille answer sheet, typewriter, or in the case of individual administration, given aloud for the test administrator to record. The major problem with the test is the arithmetic parts; although some of the arithmetic problems could be presented orally, many problems require computation using paper and pencil. For the deaf, major modifications are needed in the orally administered parts. The items read by the examiner could be printed together with multiple-choice answers found in the test booklets. Clients who are unusually proficient in signing and/or lipreading could have the test administered to them by these methods. Although no modifications are necessary, individual administration may be considered for the mentally retarded. Extra practice items may also be necessary.

***Vocational Implications***   Explores adequate level of basic educational skills and current levels of reasoning, mathematics, and reading development; assists in the determination of basic job-getting behaviors, such as completing the interview form

## Peabody Individual Achievement Test (PIAT)

The purpose of the PIAT[3] is to provide a wide-range, screening measure of achievement in the areas of mathematics, reading, spelling, and general information. The test yields six final scores: mathematics, reading recognition, reading comprehension, spelling, general information, and a total score. The PIAT is individually administered, and none of the five subtests are timed. All items are presented orally, and the examinee responds by selecting the appropriate number or illustration from four alternatives. The items are contained in two booklets. Results are given in grade scores, percentile ranks, age scores, and standard scores. The length of the test varies with the individual. The

---

[3]The PIAT is available from the American Guidance Services, Inc., Publisher's Building, Circle Pines, MN 55014. Phone: 612-786-4343.

manual states, however, that this untimed test usually requires between 30 and 40 minutes to administer and score.

No information is given on the disabled in the test manual. It is not useful in its present form for the blind and deaf, although for the mentally retarded, it is very useful in its present form. The usefulness of this test for the blind depends upon the extent of the person's visual disability. The high contrast black-and-white drawings may be perceived accurately enough to permit the use of the test with partially blind clients. Such clients should try a few practice items in each section to determine if they can accurately perceive them. Those that cannot should not be given the PIAT.

The emphasis on hearing the examiner and the necessity of having to pronounce words correctly on certain parts of the test place the deaf at a severe disadvantage on the PIAT. However, the visual content of the test has much to offer this group. The questions could be signed or printed on separate cards and presented one at a time. The deaf person who does not speak very well could easily point to the correct answer or respond by signing.

No modification of this test is necessary for the mentally retarded, although it is helpful for the rehabilitation worker to know that the Mathematics Subtest requires the client to know numbers and some symbols and the Reading Recognition requires knowing letters, identifying words and then reading and pronouncing the words aloud. In the Reading Comprehensive Subtest, the client reads a sentence silently and then matches it with the appropriate illustration.

*Vocational Implications*    Explores adequate level of basic educational skills; provides client pool of learned skills that can be drawn upon and used; suggests educational skill readiness for training


## APTITUDE TESTS


### General Aptitude Test Battery (GATB)

The GATB[4] is a group test designed for use in the vocational and occupational counseling program of the United States Training and Employment Service and is provided for use through the local state employment service. The traditional procedure for testing students with the GATB is through referral to the local state employment service. However, several agencies have entered into a cooperative agreement with their state employment service for use of the GATB by the agency staff.

This battery is administered to applicants who have not yet chosen a field of work or who are uncertain as to the appropriateness of their choice. Among

---

[4]The GATB can be obtained from the U.S. Employment Service.

the groups usually tested are: 1) high school graduates with no specialized training; 2) young people who are uncertain as to their abilities; 3) experienced workers who want to or must change their field of work; 4) applicants who have not discovered their aptitudes through training or experience; 5) any applicant suspected of having untapped abilities; and 6) those with a number of interests who have difficulty in choosing among a number of seemingly suitable fields. In other words, a counselor suggests the GATB for all applicants where vocational choice is involved if it is felt that a further exploration of aptitudes will be of assistance to them in the process of making a vocational decision. There are nine aptitudes measured by the GATB.[5]

*General Learning Ability (G)*    Ability to "catch on" or understand instructions and underlying principles; ability to reason and make judgments closely relates to doing well in school

*Verbal (V)*    Ability to understand meanings of words and ideas associated with them and to use them effectively; to comprehend language, understand relationships between words, understand meanings of whole sentences and paragraphs; and present information or ideas clearly

*Example in Work Situations*    Reading comprehension required to master books used in work process; presentation of understanding of oral or written instructions or specifications; mastery of technical terminology

*Numerical (N)*    Ability to perform arithmetic operations quickly and accurately

*Example in Work Situations*    Situations in which change is made, time or production records kept, geometric patterns laid out, things weighed, accurate measurements made, or numerical entries made or checked

*Spatial (S)*    Ability to comprehend forms in space and understand relationships of plane and solid objects; ability to "visualize" objects of two or three dimensions, or to think visually of geometric forms

*Examples in Work Situations*    Blueprint reading; activities such as laying out, positioning and aligning objects; observing movements of objects, such as vehicles in traffic or machines in operation and comprehending how the movements affect their spatial position; achieving balanced design; and understanding and anticipating the effects of stress in structural situations

*Form Perception (P)*    Ability to perceive pertinent detail in objects, in pictorial or graphic material; and to make visual comparisons and discriminations and see slight differences in shapes and shadings of figures

*Examples in Work Situations*    Inspecting surfaces for consistency in coloring, scratches, flaws, grain and texture; observing lint, dust, etc., on surfaces; determining if patterns match or are correct; and recognizing small parts.

---

[5]Adopted from the Counselor's Handbook, Bureau of Employment Security.

***Clerical Perceptions (Q)***    Ability to perceive pertinent detail in verbal or tabular material; to observe differences in copy, to proofread words and numbers, and to avoid perceptual errors in arithmetic computation

*Examples in Work Situations*    In trade and craft jobs when reading the work orders, specifications, dials, gauges, and measuring devices; proofreading words and numbers from the standpoint of perceiving individual characters

***Motor Coordination (K)***    Ability to coordinate eyes and hands or fingers rapidly and accurately in making precise movements with speed, ability to make a movement response accurately and quickly

*Examples in Work Situations*    Objects guided into position or parts assembled

***Finger Dexterity (F)***    Ability to move the fingers and manipulate small objects with the fingers rapidly and accurately

*Examples of Work Situations*    Handling bolts and screws, manipulating small tools or machine controls, playing musical instruments, and fine adjustments and alignments to instruments and machines

***Manual Dexterity (M)***    Ability to move the hands easily and skillfully and to work with the hands in placing and turning motions

*Examples in Work Situations*    Hand and wrist movements to place and turn in pushing and pulling activities

Certain limitations of the GATB should be noted. Anastasi (1982) explained that all the tests are highly speeded, the coverage of aptitudes is somewhat limited, and a comprehension test is not included nor are tests of reasoning and inventiveness well-represented. Anastasi (1982) believed that a more comprehensive investigation with a large sample and a wider variety of tests would provide more solid and useful information.

The test manual for the GATB, however, provides extensive standards on the occupational requirements of jobs. The evidence for many of the jobs upon which the determination of minimum scores and the assignments of jobs to patterns is based is rather limited; however, the information can still be quite helpful for the rehabilitation worker. Also, the GATB data available in the records at the U.S. Employment Service represent one of the major pools of data on the relation of tests to job success (Anastasi, 1982).

***Vocational Implications***    Explores current level of reasoning, mathematics, and language development; provides client pool of learned skills that can be drawn upon and used for skill transfer following onset of disability; suggests marketable job skills and necessary job-getting behaviors, such as completing the interview form; when appropriate, can assist clients in developing more realistic job expectations; can suggest level of possible training and training capabilities

## Non-Reading Aptitude Test Battery (NATB)

The NATB[6] is an adaptation of the GATB for nonreaders. Many of the mechanics and principles of test use and interpretation are the same for the two test batteries. Both batteries, for example, have the same norms; both use the same Occupational Aptitude Pattern format; and both use the same technique for matching the client's aptitude scores with occupational aptitude requirements. The NATB is not a nonverbal test, but a nonreading test. The NATB measures the same nine aptitudes as the GATB but adds the following nine subtests:

1. Picture-Word Matching Test: Examiner reads stimulus word and client chooses which of the five pictures offered best associates with examiner's word
2. Oral Vocabulary: Examinee decides whether two words read by examiner are the same, opposite, or different
3. Coin Matching: Examinee decides whether two groups of coins have the same value
4. Design Completion: Examinee completes 29 matrices
5. Tool Matching: Examinee indicates which of four black-and-white drawings of tools matches the stimulus drawing
6. Three-Dimensional Space: Examinee is presented with stimulus picture of sheet metal with lines indicating where it is to be bent or rolled; then chooses a picture that represents what the metal will look like after it has been reshaped
7. Form Matching: Examinee matches two identical line drawings
8. Coin Series: Examinee performs mental manipulations of coins as required
9. Name Comparison: Examinee decides whether two sets of names are the same or different
10. Mark Making, Placing, Turning, Assembling, and Disassembling: Examinee performs these subtests taken from sections of the GATB other than those listed earlier

The most important distinction between the two batteries is that the GATB is designed for use with a literate population and the NATB is designed for individuals with limited reading skills. The GATB Screening Exercises are used to determine which of the two batteries a client will take. The NATB makes it possible to test the vocational abilities of individuals with little or no reading skills, and to interpret these scores over a wide range of occupations.

The NATB was originally introduced on a trial basis, and although it has been subject to continuing research and revision, many believe that the NATB has proved disappointing (Anastasi, 1982). Apparently, it has not correlated

---

[6]The NATB is available from the U.S. Government Printing Office.

highly enough with the GATB to permit equivalent interpretations of scores. In the 1980s, alternative procedures for assessing this group are being explored, especially for those who are the educationally disadvantaged.

*Vocational Implications*  Explores level of possible training and the current levels of reasoning, mathematics, and language development

## Differential Aptitude Test (DAT)

The Differential Aptitude Tests[7] are designed for children in the eighth through twelfth grades and adults. The tests can be administered in groups and can be either hand- or machine-scored. The term "differential" implies not only that the tests measure different aptitudes, but also that differences in score levels within one person's profile are likely to be significant and interpretable. The DAT consists of 9 tests: Verbal Reasoning, Numerical Ability, Abstract Reasoning, Clerical Speed and Accuracy, Mechanical Reasoning, Space Relations, Language Usage I, Spelling, Language Usage II, and Grammar.

Mastie (1976) believed that the DAT offers a psychometrically sound and logistically convenient source of information for young people, particularly for the educational and vocational decision-making process. If the complete battery is given, test administration requires slightly over 3 hours. Also, Omizo (1980) believed from the research findings that several of the variables tested by the DAT series are valid predictors of performance in engineering, mathematics, and science courses. Moreover, reliability coefficients are high and permit interpretation of inter-test differences with considerable confidence (Anastasi, 1982). The manual provides both percentile and stanine norms.

There is no information in the manual on the use of the DAT with the disabled population. For the educationally deprived, the use of this test for an initial exploration of aptitude is really not appropriate. More basic measures should be utilized. The DAT is not applicable for the visually impaired. The tests, however, do provide valuable information for those disabled clients who have at least a tenth-grade education and are interested in occupations demanding such technical skills, for example, in science and math areas. Also, for those who have completed high school and are not going to college but are planning an occupational career in technical fields, the DAT can be most useful for assessment purposes.

*Vocational Implications*  Because of their level of difficulty, these tests can assist clients in developing more realistic occupational and training goals; also explores client pool of learned skills that can be drawn upon and used for possible skill transfer following onset disability; provides suggestions for

---

[7]The DAT are available from The Psychological Corporation, 757 Third Ave., New York 10017. Phone: 212-888-3500.

marketable job skills; explores current level of reasoning, mathematics, and language development; many DAT tests, such as Abstract Reasoning, Numerical Ability, Mechanical Reasoning, and Space Relations, can also be used to explore client capabilities in electronic-related occupations, i.e., computer technology and television repair

## Flanagan Aptitude Classification Tests (FACT)

FACT[8] is a multi-aptitude battery which may be administered in a group. It includes 16 paper-and-pencil tests covering the following aptitudes: inspection, coding, memory, precision, assembly, scales, coordination, judgment and comprehension, arithmetic, patterns, components, tables, mechanics, expression, reasoning, and ingenuity. The entire battery requires approximately 10 hours for administration.

The test battery is intended for use in counseling for the development of educational and vocational plans. Vocational guidance materials identify potential for success in 37 occupational areas, approximately one-half of which require college preparation. The applicability of these tests to a large number of job areas makes the Flanagan Tests especially valuable for select rehabilitation clients.

FACT requires an eighth-grade reading level and the ability to follow directions accurately. This is not a battery that the rehabilitation worker has the time to administer routinely; nor is it recommended for the general rehabilitation client. However, using the FACT when other aptitude batteries like the GATB are not avilable can provide vocational guidance data for specific rehabilitation clients. These clients included the more educated. Also in its present form, the test is not usable for the blind nor the deaf.

*Vocational Implications*    Like the DAT, these tests, because of their difficulty level, can assist clients in developing more realistic occupational and training goals; provides suggestions for marketable job skills as well as educational capabilities, particularly at the college level; gives information on client's ability to follow written instructions; explores sufficiency of client experience as related both to transfer of skills following onset of disability and identified occupational areas

## Bennett Mechanical Comprehension Test

This test[9] is designed, according to the manual, to "measure the ability to perceive and understand the relationship of physical forces and mechanical elements in practical situations." There is one final score in percentile form for

---

[8]FACT are available from Science Research Associates, 155 North Wacker Dr., Chicago 60606. Phone: 312-984-7000.

[9]The Bennett Mechanical Comprehension Test is available from The Psychological Corporation, 757 Third Ave., New York 10017. Phone: 212-888-3500.

mechanical comprehension. The test is group-administered with each examinee receiving a test booklet and separate answer sheet. Most of the 68 items contain two illustrations and a written question about each illustration dealing with mechanical principles or general physical concepts. Examinees have three choices for each answer.

Anastasi (1982) explained that the Bennett is a widely used test and is suitable for such groups as high school students, industrial and mechanical job applicants, and candidates for engineering programs. The manual provides percentile norms for several groups, including educational levels, specialized training, or prospective job categories. Odd/even reliabililty coefficients of each form have been reported from 0.81 to 0.93. For clients with limited reading skills, forms *S* and *L* may be administered with tape-recorded instructions and questions. Spanish versions are also available for both regular and oral administration.

The test can be completely administered in 40 minutes, including directions and questions. The test itself has a 30-minute time limit. When considering the test for the handicapped, the manual states that the test falls within the "fairly easy level of popular magazines." However, a sixth-grade reading level would probably be necessary. In the manual, no information on the disabled is given. Although not usable in its present form for the blind, this test should be appropriate for deaf clients who can read instructions. Also, the instructions are easy for the mentally retarded to comprehend, but the concepts evaluated by the test may be too difficult for many retarded persons to grasp. If the rehabilitation worker is planning to give the test to these clients, then individual administration and sufficient practice during the first two trials should be carefully followed.

*Vocational Implications*   Explores training capabilities in mechanical fields; is also recommended as an initial measure for clients who wish to pursue occupations in one of many technical areas, e.g., computer technology or electronic repair fields

## Minnesota Clerical Test

The Minnesota Clerical Test[10] was designed both to aid in the selection of clerical employees and to advise individuals interested in clerical training. The specific trait measured by the test is the client's ability to notice within a specified time period the differences between two items. The test consists of two parts: Number Checking and Name Scoring. Each part contains 200 items, with 100 identical and 100 dissimilar pairs. The client is to identify and check the identical pairs. No special training is needed to administer and score this

---

[10]The Minnesota Clerical Test is available from The Psychological Corporation, 757 Third Ave., New York 10017. Phone: 212-888-3500.

test, and the test is hand-scored. Although not suitable for the blind, this test can be adapted for the hearing-impaired.

Percentile norms have been reported in the manual for several large samples of clerical applicants and employed clerical workers as well as for boys and girls in the eighth through twelfth grade. Moderately high correlations have been found between scores on this test and ratings by office supervisors, and commercial teachers, and by performance records in clerical courses (Anastasi, 1982). Note that the test measures only one aspect of clerical work.

*Vocational Implications*    Suggests specific capacities in the clerical area (is a good beginning test for many clients whose stated occupational interest is clerical work)

### Crawford Small Parts Dexterity Test

This is a performance test[11] designed to measure fine eye/hand coordination involved in assembly and adjustment of such devices as clocks and watches. The test is administered in two parts. In Part I, tweezers are used to pick up a pin, insert it in a small hole in a metal plate, and then place a collar over the pin. Only the preferred hand is used. In Part 2, the individual starts a screw into a threaded hole with his fingers and then uses a small screwdriver to turn the screw through the threaded hole. Both hands are used.

The Crawford is used in many rehabilitation agencies, and provides assessment information for those tasks requiring fine eye/hand coordination. Split-half reliability coefficients reported for the two parts of this test have been between 0.80 and 0.95 (Anastasi, 1982). The test can be adapted for both the blind and the hearing impaired.

*Vocational Implications*    Suggests what the client can do in fine hand-eye coordination tasks; can help to provide information on appropriateness for occupations that demand such coordination

### Pennsylvania Bi-Manual Worksample

This performance test[12] departs from the usual procedure for measuring finger dexterity in that it deemphasizes the inserting of pegs into holes and the placing of washers around pegs. Instead, the test involves the simple operation of selecting a bolt with one hand and a nut with the other, assembling the nut and bolt, and placing the assembly in a receiving hole. The second part of the test consists of disassembling the nuts and bolts and returning them to the proper places.

---

[11]The Crawford Small Parts Dexterity Test is available from the Psychological Corporation, 757 Third Ave., New York 10017. Phone: 212-888-3500.

[12]The Pennsylvania Bi-Manual Worksample is available from the American Guidance Services, Inc., Publishers' Building, Circle Pines, MN 55014. Phone: 612-786-4343.

The test purports to measure a combination of finger dexterity of both hands, gross movements of both arms, eye/hand coordination, bi-manual coordination and the ability to use both hands in coordination. The task involved in the test demands putting a nut on a bolt and placing it in a board in front of the client. One hundred and five nuts and bolts are in separate trays on either side of the board, and the worker records the time that it takes to turn all the nuts onto bolts and place them in holes on the board. Disassembly is also a part of the timed test. One administrator is required for at least every five examinees. No more than 10 to 15 minutes is required to administer the test, including directions. Final scores are expressed as "transmuted" scores, which are derived from the total minutes and seconds required to assemble and disassemble the bolts.

When considering this test for the handicapped, no reading is required. This test has also been normed on blind and partially blind people.[13] Deaf clients should have few problems with taking this measure and it should also be useful with those clients with mental retardation, for it can explore their manual coordination.

*Vocational Implications*   Explores dexterity skills, especially those that are related to many basic tasks in industry or certain clerical occupations; identifies an individual's capacity to integrate a number of motor traits into a well-organized and smooth working pattern of performance

### Purdue Pegboard

According to its manual, the Purdue Pegboard[14] was designed to measure "dexterity for two types of activity: one involving gross movements of hands, fingers and arms, and the other involving primarily what could be called 'fingertip dexterity'." There are five separate final scores, given in percentile form: right hand, left hand, both hands, right plus left plus both hands, and assembly.

The Pegboard includes pins, collars, and washers, which are located in four cups at the top of the board. Each subtest involves a separate task. For example, the right-hand test involves placing pins into holes on the board for a 30-second period. The left-hand test involves the same process but with the opposite hand, while the both hands measure involves placing pins as fast as possible into holes with both hands. The right plus left plus both hands is obtained by adding the above three scores together. The assembly task consists of assembling pins, collars, and washers on the board for a speeded time of

[13]A special supplement, *Motor Skills Tests Adapted to the Blind*, contains directions for use of the Pennsylvania Bi-Manual Worksample with blind people and is available from the publisher.

[14]The Purdue Pegboard is available from the Science Research Associates, Inc., 259 East Erie St., Chicago, IL 60611. Phone: 312-984-7000.

1 minute. This test should not take more than 10 to 15 minutes to administer and score.

When considering this test for the handicapped, no reading is required. Although there is no information on the disabled in the manual, the deaf client can be given this test with no problem except for changing how the directions and timing are administered. The Purdue Pegboard can also be used with the retarded client.

*Vocational Implications*   Found in many rehabilitation agencies; explores a client's finger and hand dexterity; like the Pennsylvania Bi-Manual Worksample, helps a client to identify many of the physical capabilities needed for some basic tasks in industrial or clerical occupations

## Other Measures

Importantly, achievement tests can also occasionally be developed by rehabilitation workers in order to quickly evaluate a client's daily living and employment-related skills. Although such tests are of the "homemade" variety, they can be more criterion-referenced, containing test items that are closely associated with the client's daily life demands. These tests have not been standardized but can still provide much useful information for rehabilitation planning purposes. An example of such a test is found in Appendix B. Although modified by the author, it was basically developed by Mr. John O. Willis. The test has generated sufficient data to provide a beginning understanding of the client's reading and numerical skills.

## SUMMARY

When working with different clients in rehabilitation, the following batteries of achievement and aptitude tests are suggested. It is assumed that the General Aptitude Test Battery will be administered when resources are available.

## Clients Who Have No Recent
## Educational Experience and Little Formal Education

*Step 1*   WRAT or ABLE

*Step 2*   Bennett Mechanical Comprehension Test or Minnesota Clerical Test

*Step 3*   Purdue Pegboard, or Pennsylvania Bi-Manual Worksample, or Crawford Small Parts Dexterity Test

*Step 4*   DAT series, if appropriate for rehabilitation planning purposes

## Clients Who Have No Recent Educational Experience but Are High School Graduates

*Step 1* ABLE or PIAT

*Step 2* DAT series

*Step 3* Purdue Pegboard, or Pennsylvania Bi-Manual Work Sample, or Crawford Small Parts Dexterity Test

*Step 4* Flanagan series with individual test selection, appropriate for rehabilitation planning purposes

## CONCLUSION

Both achievement and aptitude assessment are needed approaches to help the client achieve a better knowledge of work-related strengths and weaknesses. Fortunately, many standardized tests are available to provide an evaluation of achievement- and aptitude-related skills. If the rehabilitation worker uses these measures according to their specific directions, they will produce information about the client that is invaluable for rehabilitation planning.

## CASE STUDY

Bill has repeatedly made requests to see a counselor. He would like to return to work, but feels he needs some help from a "professional" counselor.

*Bill was a sturdy, industrious, and dependable employee of the Southeastern Electric Company with specific responsibility for several repair crews. There is evidence that he was regarded highly by his employers. According to his wife he had always been vigorously healthy until, at age 42, he suffered a severe cerebrovascular accident. He was hospitalized for 5 months, beginning in July, 1977, under the medical supervision of a general practitioner engaged by his employer. Damage resulting from the stroke is right hemiplegia and occasional grand mal seizures, occurring about once a week. During his hospital stay, speech and physical rehabilitation potentials were evaluated, and therapy engaged. There was some response to these efforts, as now he has good use of his left side and some mobility in his right hand and right leg, although he must use a cane when walking and walks very slowly. He is unable to do any prolonged standing. There is only a slight, detectable slurring in his speech, but the speech therapist claims that this might improve.*

*Inquiry was made about Bill's interests and personality before the cerebral accident. His wife described him as a man who needed at all times to be going somewhere and doing something. His preferred diversions were hunting and fishing, which he liked his two sons, age 19 and 14, to share with him. There is one daughter, age 11. Before his illness he had, on the weekends, consumed at least a six-pack of beer on Saturdays and Sundays, and when intoxicated, he could become quite abusive, verbally, to his family. Bill has no intellectual interests and reads very little except the local newspapers and manuals related to his work. He graduated from high school, but has received no formal education since then. Social activity had been restricted to family get-togethers. Apparently, he was keenly conscious about his work, rarely missing time because of illness, and taking much satisfaction in participating with repair crew members in some of the dangerous activities required. Bill was described by his wife as a stern, demanding husband and parent, who expected instant response to his demands.*

*Bill has worked for Southeastern Electric for the past 12 years. Before his employment he was an electronic technologist for a small company for 5 years, and upon leaving high school, he joined the service (army) for 5 years, where he was a medical corpsman and achieved the rank of sergeant.*

1.  From the information presented in this chapter, what aptitude tests do you feel would be appropriate for this client?
2.  What difficulties do you identify with this client that would create obstacles for the client taking any achievement or aptitude tests?

### REFERENCES

Anastasi, A. (ed.). 1982. Psychological Testing. Macmillan Co., New York.
Mastie, M. 1976. Differential aptitude tests, Forms S & T with a career planning program. Meas. Eval. Guid., 9:87–95.
Moore, A., Gartin, B. and Carmack, P. 1981. WRAT or SIT: Tools for assessing handicapped adults. Voc. Eval. Work Adj. Bull. 14:60–64.
Omizo, M. 1980. The differential aptitude tests as predictors of success in a high school for engineering program. Ed Psych. Meas. 40:197–203.

chapter 8

# BEHAVIORAL AND PERSONALITY ASSESSMENT IN REHABILITATION

When clients are either referred for or independently seek rehabilitation services, the rehabilitation professional usually needs information on their social and vocational background as well as reports of rehabilitation services previously rendered (Matkin and Rice, 1979). The professional can use an interview structure as suggested in Chapter 4 to obtain further information on the client's interests, vocational goals, assets, and liabilities. All of this knowledge can then be used to determine what further services are necessary.

Using a problem-identification perspective (Akridge and Means, 1982) can considerably enhance the diagnostic effectiveness of the interview. The client brings this perspective to the initial interview. In other words, the rehabilitation professional utilizes behavioral assessment techniques, and these strategies can provide a more complete vocational picture (Matkin and Rice, 1979). This chapter discusses behavioral assessment in rehabilitation and the appropriate use of personality measures. The concept of personality includes behavior; both factors help an individual to meet necessary job demands.

## BEHAVIORAL ASSESSMENT

Akridge and Means (1982) stated:

> Human behavior refers to consistent patterns of change in the relationship between a person and the environment (p. 153).

The client's potential or existing work behaviors should be identified during the interview. These behaviors, according to Marr (1982) fall into three categories:

1. *Behavior assets—behaviors that the client already has and that would enhance employability* Such behaviors are strengths on which new skills

can be built, and information about them can be learned from records, the client, and direct observation during the interview.

2. *Behavior deficits—behaviors that are necessary to prepare for, obtain, or maintain work that the client does too infrequently* These behaviors include job-objective problems (e.g., does not seek information about work), job-seeking skill deficiencies (e.g. cartnot complete application form or describe skills to interviewer), and job-retention problems (e.g., arrives late for work, does not stay on task).

4. *Behavior surpluses—behaviors that should occur only infrequently or not at all* Examples include violating safety rules or annoying other workers.

Depending on the severity of the client's disability and life circumstances, other behaviors may also need to be identified during the interview. Such behaviors, which are particularly necessary for independent living considerations, include: 1) self-help behaviors, such as dressing, eating, toileting, and personal hygiene and grooming; 2) social and interpersonal behaviors, such as basic interaction skills, group participation, play activities, social amenities, sexual behaviors, and responsibility; 3) domestic behaviors, such as kitchen skills, household cleaning, household management, and laundering and clothing care; and 4) health-care behaviors, such as the ability to establish preventative health measures and behaviors related to personal and emotional adjustment, which can include varied coping skills. (All behaviors will be discussed in Chapter 11.)

During the interview, the rehabilitation professional should specify the general type of problem and area of difficulty, and then further specify the particular skill deficit. For example, the client may be easily distracted or seem unmotivated. Translated into particular skill deficits for the purposes of rehabilitation planning, both behaviors can be termed: "Will not be able to attend with concentration to a work task," and "Work production may be considerably slower than what are average work demands." Rehabilitation planning may then include intervention strategies to alleviate these problems.

To assist in the identification of client problems, problem checklists can be a helpful supplement to the interview. They can help the rehabilitation professional review the behavioral domain and the client's particular vocation-related problems (Sundberg, 1977). The *Moody Problem Checklist* covers many of the possible problems brought by clients to the initial interview.

Behavior Rating Scales are also very valuable for exploring client behaviors. They can be used not only to guide and systematize observations during the interview, but also for other observation opportunities, such as in situational assessment or job tryout opportunities. These assessment tools offer both a methodology to observe, measure, and change behavior as well as a tool to determine overall vocational abilities (Matkin and Rice, 1979). If the rehabilitation professional is sensitive to structuring the initial interview, it is possible to observe the client's behavior in a rather standard situation (Akridge and Means, 1982).

The following are examples of Behavior Rating Scales that could be used by the rehabilitation professional. Most of the information on these scales is from Halpern et al. (1982) or from the manual of the particular scale.

## Vocational Behavior Checklist (VBC)

Rehabilitation professionals can use VBC[1] for a variety of purposes, including: 1) the evaluation of individual examinee skills; 2) the provision of input for individual program planning; 3) the specification of curriculum/training objectives; and 4) the broad-level evaluation of rehabilitation program effectiveness. No specific disability group is targeted.

The VBC contains 339 items organized into seven categories: prevocational; job-seeking; interview; job-related; work performance; on-the-job skills; and union/financial/security. The authors define VBC items as "vocational skill objectives." Each item in the VBC is a behavioral statement that includes condition, instruction, behavior, and standard for performance.

More than half (188) of the items are identified as "prevocational" skills, which include knowledge items, perceptual/motor tasks, and domestic skills. The range of skill objective sophistication is great. Later items deal with knowledge-testing of such areas as the function of unions, filling out income tax forms, and the identification of the duties of the supervisor.

Examinees can be evaluated from general knowledge of their functioning, from observation on the job or training setting, or by setting up assessment activities in a simulated environment. Checklist items may be modified by the evaluator in three ways: 1) by deleting inappropriate skill objectives; 2) by adding appropriate additional objectives (blanks are left at the end of each chart for that purpose); and 3) by modifying skill objectives by adapting conditions, instructions, behaviors, or standards to suit the particular needs and handicapping conditions of the client.

The checklist is described by the authors as "criterion-referenced." This means that the standard to which VBC results are compared should be set by the user. For some purposes, a 50% mastery of a skill category might prove sufficient. For another job setting, a supervisor may require 95% mastery. The criterion for evaluation is set individually, rather than as a comparison with some larger population.

Two hundred previously developed behavior checklists were obtained from rehabilitation facilities and schools throughout the United States and other

---

[1]The VBC is available from Walls, Zane, and Werner, West Virginia Rehabilitation Research and Training Center, Allen Hall, Room 806, Morgantown, WV 26056. 304-293-5313.

countries. Thirty-nine of the checklists contained vocational or occupational items. Of these 39, the authors found 21 constructed well enough to suggest objective ways to assess vocational behaviors. The items were sorted into the seven categories that make up the major divisions of the VBC. Overlapping or duplicate items were eliminated, and extensive rewriting and modification of the remaining items was undertaken to produce the item format for the VBC. Some gaps in skill objective sequences were filled by creating new items. The authors report that new skill objectives were derived from their work with vocational rehabilitation clients in sheltered facilities, or from field-based rehabilitation programs.

Test/retest reliability of two observers viewing videotapes of five clients at work settings averaged 0.98 (100–96%). Interrater reliability ranged from 0.84–1.00 for each of seven categories of skill objectives and averaged 0.95.

Because the VBC items were developed through careful comparison with other behavior checklists, the authors reported content validity to be "high." In four separate studies, correlations between employers' reports of necessary vocational skills and the skills contained in VBC objectives averaged 0.97.

Halpern et al. (1982) believed that the VBC has many apparent strengths. The item format (specification of setting, behavior, instruction, and standard) emphasizes the relationship between assessment and instruction. The item pool, which was developed from checklists requested from a broad array of rehabilitation services, represents the collective judgment of a broad variety of rehabilitation professionals. Finally, because the VBC is criterion-referenced, users can adapt or modify the checklist for their own specific purposes.

Two problems exist with the VBC. First, because of the great breadth of content that is covered, comprehensive assessment across domains requires much time and energy of both examiners and examinees. Second, several of the items are ambiguous, which leads to occasional difficulty in interpreting the outcomes of assessment. These concerns notwithstanding, the VBC seems to be an effective approach to program-related assessment.

### Adaptive Behavior Scale (ABS)

The ABS[2] was designed to provide an objective description of retarded persons' abilities to meet the normal demands of the general environment. The ABS may be used as a measure or description of retarded individuals' personal independence in daily living, preferably in conjunction with other available infor-

---

[2]The ABS is available from the American Association on Mental Deficiency, 5101 Wisconsin Ave., N.W., Washington, D.C. 20016. 800-538-9547. The scale consists of a test booklet and manual, each priced at $1.50. Discounts are offered, depending on the quantity ordered. Specimen sets cost $10.00.

mation. The ABS is intended for use with mentally retarded, emotionally maladjusted, and developmentally disabled individuals.

The ABS consists of two parts. Part I includes 66 items across 10 general behavior or skill areas important for achieving independent living status: physical development, independent functioning, language, numbers and time, economic activity, domestic skills, vocational activity, socialization, self-direction, and responsibility. Part II domains contain 44 items that cover maladaptive social or personal characteristics: violent and destructive behavior, antisocial behavior, rebellious behavior, untrustworthy behavior, withdrawal, stereotyped behavior and odd mannerisms, inappropriate interpersonal manners, unacceptable vocal habits, unacceptable or eccentric habits, self-abusive behavior, hyperactive tendencies, sexually abberrant behavior, psychological disturbances, and use of medications.

Users may select one of three methods for completing the ABS: 1) where possible, collect information by direct personal observation of all relevant behaviors (this is the recommended method); 2) interview individuals who are "knowledgeable" about the person(s) being assessed; and 3) have "knowledgeable" persons fill out the ABS forms on the basis of direct observation or general knowledge of the person being assessed.

The percentile ranks for the ABS were developed using approximately 4,000 mildly to profoundly mentally retarded persons in 68 residential facilities throughout the United States before 1968.

Interrater reliabilities for the 1974 version of the ABS were derived from independent observations of ward attendants from both morning and evening shifts. The rater-agreement reliability estimates for Part 1 domains ranged from 0.71 (self-direction) to 0.93 (physical development), with a mean score of 0.86. Only one scale from Part 2 had a reliability rating above 0.70 (use of medication); others ranged down to 0.37 (unacceptable vocal habits). Mean interrater reliability for Part 2 domains was 0.57.

Concurrent validity studies demonstrate that the ABS Part 1 correlates significantly with IQ scores but lower or not at all with achievement tests. Part 2 domains are independent of both IQ and achievement.

Halpern et al. (1982) explained that the American Association on Mental Deficiency (AAMD) Adaptive Behavior Scale provides only a broad estimate of general adaptive behavior functioning because of 1) the limited number of items in many domains, especially those that measure adult-oriented skills (vocational, domestic, economic); and 2) the lack of specificity in items. Attempts to use the scale to measure specific behavior changes in individual domains have proved generally ineffective. The number of items at the lower developmental levels of the scales, however, make it an especially appropriate broad-based evaluation tool for use with more severely retarded persons.

The ABS can be used with institutionalized and noninstitutionalized retarded persons, so long as the evaluator recognizes that the normative data were derived before 1968, were based on institutionalized persons, and that there is no evidence of reliability or validity for noninstitutionalized individuals.

## San Francisco Vocational Competency Scale (SFVCS)

The SFVCS[3] was developed to assess the "vocational competence" of mentally retarded persons 18 years of age or older participating in sheltered workshops and vocational training programs. Its suggested uses include: 1) selection for training; 2) ongoing assessment; and 3) program evaluation in job training or employment setting.

The SFVCS consists of 30 items relating to four areas of vocational competence. These four areas include motor skills, cognition, responsibility, and social-emotional behavior. Each of the items is presented as a general behavioral statement, followed by four to five statements that describe various degrees of competency regarding that item. The items are not organized, scored, or interpreted according to the four major areas of competence described above. Rather, they are said to be arranged in the sequence in which the behavior would occur during "general work performance" by the individual.

To administer the SFVCS, an examiner obtains information from an interview with someone who knows the examinee, or from personal observation or general knowledge of the examinee's performance in vocational settings. Administration time is estimated to be about 15 minutes.

The evaluator is directed to assign a rating of the degree of competency demonstrated for each item. The evaluator simply circles the number of the statement that best represents the examinee's behavior on each item. Because the total score is the sum of scores for each item, the rater is asked to rate all items. Vocational competency scores range from a minimum of 30 to a maximum of 138.

Percentile norms are available for interpreting the examinee's total score relative to the norm group, which is described below.

The norm group was made up of 562 mentally retarded male and female workshop clients, representing 45 workshops from all regions of the country.

Internal consistency reliability coefficient values are reported as 0.95 for both male and female subjects. A test/retest stability coefficient value of 0.85 resulted from two administrations of the instrument separated by a 1-month interval.

No validity studies are presented in the manual.

---

[3]The SFVCS is available from The Psychological Corporation, 757 Third Ave., New York 10017. The scale consists of a scale booklet and manual. A specimen set may be purchased for $1.65 and the cost for a package of 25 forms is $5.25. 212-888-3500.

Halpern et al. (1982) stated that no guidelines beyond a description of the norm group are provided for interpreting the scores, and no validity studies that would offer a basis for interpreting scores are available at this time. Also, no evidence of interrater reliability is presented. Because the SFVCS is essentially a rating scale, a description of interrater reliability would offer a sense of how accurate raters' perceptions are.

It seems that the greatest utilities of the SFVCS are: 1) general screening of individuals for placement into sheltered work settings; and, perhaps, 2) program evaluation in vocational settings; or 3) description of retarded individuals' characteristic behavior at work for purposes of instructional planning. Users should regard the SFVCS as useful primarily as a supplementary tool to other, more program-related instruments.

## Camelot Behavioral Checklist (CBC)[4]

The CBC is intended to aid in the evaluation of behavioral competencies important to the vocational/personal adaptation of moderately and severely retarded individuals. The author reports that the information provided by the CBC is relevant for both administrative and programming needs because the items are arranged in relative order of difficulty. As a result, the evaluator can identify both specific training needs and obtain a summary or classification score directly based on training objectives.

The CBC is a behavioral checklist that consists of 399 items that are behavioral descriptions of competencies necessary for personal and vocational adjustment. The items are arranged into 40 subdomains across 10 domains. The 10 major domains are: self-help, physical development, home duties, vocational behavior, economic behavior, independent travel, numerical skills, communication skills, social behaviors, and responsibility. The sub-domains (toilet use, grooming, and eating behaviors, for example) are included in the domain, Self-Help. Items in each domain are arranged in order of sophistication or complexity. For example, the first item under Eating Behaviors is "drinks from glass;" the eighth is "uses napkin;" the nineteenth is "selects meal in cafeteria."

The checklist is completed by memory, through interview with a knowledgeable person or by direct observation and testing. Direct observation is the most appropriate after training objectives are tentatively selected. Scoring is easily accomplished by marking items with a plus to indicate that the behavior

---

[4]The CBC is available from Ray Foster, Camelot Behavioral Systems, P.O. Box 3447, Lawrence, KS 66044. 913-842-4898. It is 45¢ per copy. Also available are a manual ($3.50) and a Skill Acquisition Program Bibliography ($6.00), which compiles 1,700 curriculum programs that address the skills in the Camelot. All of these programs are commercially available and referenced in the Bibliography.

can be performed, or a minus to indicate that the competency is not currently performed. A score total is obtained for each of the 10 domains and for the entire test by summing the plusses.

The CBC offers two levels of interpretation. First, items can be considered on face value as training objectives. The sequencing of items by levels of difficulty facilitates the development and planning of short-term goals.

Second, normative values are available for each domain, subdomain, and for a total score. The behaviors in each scale are placed to show order of difficulty and are spaced to show degree of difficulty. Percentile profiles flank each side of the score sheet for norm group comparisons. As a result, visual inspection and interpretation of the score profile is greatly enhanced. The percentages referenced are specific to the norming sample and may fluctuate with the average functioning of the group tested. In most cases,normative interpretation of the CBC offers only general or supplementary information for decision-making in planning.

The content of CBC was generated primarily from a review of other similar instruments. Items were rejected if they did not constitute adequate training objectives, if they were not amenable to further task analysis, or if they failed to discriminate among examinees of different levels of functioning. The items cover a range of competencies that might be expected to be observed among moderately and severely retarded individuals.

After initial item selection, the CBC was revised based on data from a single sample of 624 institutionalized retarded persons. The manual does not state the characteristics (age, sex, IQ, or placement) of the norming sample.

Interrater reliabilities were calculated by comparing ratings of two ''teams'' of specialists for each subdomain area. Interrater reliabilities ranged from 0.79 (Independent Travel) to 0.98 (Communication Skills). Total score interrater reliability was 0.93.

Construct validity was examined through intercorrelation studies of several psychometric instruments with the CBC. Correlations ranged from 0.33 (Leiter) to 0.86 (Stanford-Binet). Other correlations reported were $r$ values of 0.50 (WISC), 0.78 (WAIS), and 0.63 (PPVT).

Halpern (1982) noted the arrangement of items by difficulty level, which may help evaluators make comparisons of individual examinee skills with a reference group. However, users should avoid judging individual examinee potential from comparison with a norm group. The score is only a statement of current functioning.

One scoring problem exists in that the instructions call for a plus to be marked if an individual is physically unable to perform a behavior. The author intends that the plus should indicate ''no need for training.'' Because plus usually means ''can do,'' this particular scoring is especially open to misinterpretation.

## PERSONALITY ASSESSMENT

One of the important goals in rehabilitation is to assist the disabled client in achieving satisfaction in a job or similar productive outlet. This goal implies more than skill proficiency. Individual needs, motivation, ability to get along with others, and a capacity to cope with employment-related demands, are all aspects of personal functioning that are of major importance for the clients' suitable job adjustment and success. Moreover, many clients beginning the rehabilitation process bring with them continued problems of anxiety, difficulties in continuing with a job or training program, and behavioral patterns, such as overdependency and aggressiveness, that are antithetical for an appropriate placement in a job setting. All of these considerations emphasize the need for an evaluation of personality functioning in rehabilitation.

In the early days of the rehabilitation movement, when services emphasized physical restoration, the assessment of personality was considered to be irrelevant for most clients. When vocational rehabilitation was asked to undertake work with the mentally retarded, the severely disabled, the mentally ill, the alcoholic, and later the socially disadvantaged, many counselors resisted these populations, claiming that the client problems were "too severe." But when these persons were accepted for rehabilitation services, some counselors were determined to apply the same evaluation procedures that had succeeded with their previous clients. These approaches largely ignored the personality functioning of the disabled person. When the proportion of failures grew, and, out of necessity, the impact of personality functioning on job adjustment was explored, the practice of evaluating a client's personality characteristics gradually became more common in vocational rehabilitation. In fact, counselors learned that some personality traits may predispose the client to function well in some occupational areas and badly in others.

The purpose of personality assessment in rehabilitation is to identify those personality strengths or deficits that impact on job demands, where and how the client can function effectively, and what training might be needed to enhance those behaviors demanded for suitable job adjustment (Maki et al., 1979). In rehabilitation, the term "personality" refers to that client information related to typical behaviors as distinct from the intellectual attributes of the individual. Consequently, "personality" is defined as:

> . . . the system whereby the individual characteristically organizes and processes biophysical and environmental inputs to produce behavior in interactions with the larger surrounding systems (Sundberg, 1977, p. 12).

In contrast to the traditional meaning that personality "connotes the superficial impression created by an individual's behavior" (Shertzer and Linden, 1979, p. 314), the term now further conveys the dynamic exchange between physiologic status and/or environmental experience. Within the work environment, personality is directly related "to the degree to which it reflects work behaviors" (Maki et al., 1979, p. 120). Neff (1971) believed that the work personality refers to the concrete set of interrelated motives, coping style, and defensive maneuvers with which an individual confronts the demands of work. For the rehabilitation worker, then, personality is a constellation of interests, needs, values, and behaviors that allows an individual to meet appropriate work rules in a particular job setting.

In vocational evaluation, personality assessment should focus on behaviors necessary for employment or productive output. To provide some direction to this evaluation, the following questions could be explored by the rehabilitation professional:

1. Have clients shown emotional reactions toward the disability that may be obstacles to adequate vocational adjustment?
2. How is the client likely to respond in a high production/high stress type of job?
3. Will the client respond appropriately to supervision on the job?
4. On a job that brings a large amount of close association or collaboration with other workers, can the client adjust to this demand?
5. How does the client understand the daily adjustmental implications of his or her disability?

In vocational rehabilitation, the traditional way to obtain an evaluation of personality functioning is to authorize a referral for a "psychological workup" from a psychologist or a psychiatrist. The report by the psychiatrist usually consists of a brief description of the client, a sociopsychologic history, and a clinical summary of the present condition. The result is a diagnosis. The psychologist's report emphasizes the findings of testing and a summary of client behaviors. Unfortunately, these reports often contain information which is not vocationally relevant, or they do not provide an assessment of the client's residual emotional strengths that can be used in vocational training or employment. When reading these reports, the rehabilitation professional frequently has to translate the meaning of the described behaviors into vocationally relevant terms.

What is needed in vocational rehabilitation for an appropriate personality evaluation is the description of a client's behavior in observable, quantifiable, understandable, and functional terms (Field, 1979). Because a rehabilitation counselor is primarily responsible for planning and developing the client's rehabilitation process, which also implies collecting relevant and essential information needed for client planning, the counselor should be concerned about obtaining information on the client's personality or behavior functioning that is vocationally oriented. As client planning assumes that the counselor understands the particular behaviors that are needed to perform certain jobs adequately, so the assessment should focus on those behaviors that the client typically shows that are relevant to job situations.

Table 8.1 identifies personalilty traits that should be explored during the interview. The relationship of these characteristics to vocational functioning is also indicated. This figure actually expands the model presented in Chapter 1 and explained in Table 1.1. It also includes personality factors that are found in the guidelines of client functioning discussed in Chapter 4.

In personality assessment, a definite personality pattern or cluster of behavior problems is not associated with a particular disability. Problems associated with motivation or interpersonal relationships can be found with clients having orthopedic problems, visual impairments, or emotional difficulties. Yet, certain behavioral deficits, like high distractability or continued lack of sustained concentration, are very often identified among those persons with neurologic illnesses or severe emotional problems. Also, medications that are used with certain conditions, particularly mental disorders, may cause passivity or related effects. All of these factors should be attended to by the rehabilitation professional, for they may influence the client's response to rehabilitation demands.

## COLLECTING INFORMATION
## ON PERSONALITY FUNCTIONING

As explained earlier in this chapter, much information about a client's behavior can be gained by utilizing well the interview situation. The same is true with personality assessment. Along with the opportunities offered by the intake interview, there are other methods of obtaining information on the client's personality traits. There are paper-and-pencil surveys, such as projective performance tests, and personality inventories. Some examples of projective performance measures are free-association tests, the Rohrshach, and the Thematic Apperception Test. These methods require a great deal of education and training to administer and interpret correctly, and such training is usually not in the professional preparation of the rehabilitation worker. Rather, psychologists are more specifically trained to administer these evaluation tools.

Many personality inventories used in the 1980s require some training in their administration and interpretation, but do not have such intensive training demands as the projective measures. In the following pages, five personality measures are recommended for use in rehabilitation, some of which could be interpreted by the rehabilitation worker. When using these tests it must be remembered that their administration, scoring, interpretation, and reporting should be under the supervision of a person who meets the qualifications as defined by state law and the American Psychological Association standards (Sax, 1981). Although these tests were not developed primarily for use in

Table 8.1.    Identification of personality traits

| Personality traits | Personality measure | Vocational functioning problem areas |
|---|---|---|
| Mood/temperament (general appearance and behavior) | MMPI 16PF | Relationship to supervisors and other workers Frustration tolerance Adjustment to strains and pressures of work environment |
| Attitude Toward self Toward others (Orientation toward other people) | PSI Tennessee Self-Concept | Sense of responsibility Successful job performance Cooperativeness On-the-job social skills Self-confidence in the work situation Follow instructions/work safety Self-presentation (dress, appearance, grooming, posture, method of talking to others) |
| Motivation Energy level Goal-directedness | EPPS 16 PF | Seeks rehabilitation goals Energy on job Meet work demands, such as punctuality or continuing at task Work habits Response to pleasant or unpleasant tasks Acceptance of work role |
| Adjustment to disability Coping resources Capacity to face one's problems Strengths of client | PSI MMPI 16 PF | Reality orientation— accepts limitations Dependent or independent role in work situation Coping mechanisms for dealing with stress in the job |
| Needs: Security Variety recognition Status responsibility Creativity Achievement independence | EPPS 16 PF | Change orientation Adaptability Ability to take risks with self |

predicting behavior in work situations, the information they give, combined with an interpretation perspective that is job-focused, can be quite useful in rehabilitation.

Personality development, however, is not like the development in a school environment of such cognitive areas as verbal and numerical skills. A client can respond in very different ways in different contexts. Thus, as Anastasi (1982) stated that the:

> . . . same response to a given question on a personality inventory may have a different significance from one person to another (p. 527).

In rehabilitation, the professional wants to know how an individual will respond within an independent living, training, or employment situation. Because of this need and the uncertain predictive validity of the personality measure for an individual, the personality test itself provides an estimate of the client's *current* emotional functioning. From interview information exploring both the client's past behavior and current emotional functioning in other areas than vocational, i.e., family and social, the rehabilitation professional will be able to have some ideas of personality-related problems in a training or work situation. For example, a 35-year-old disabled man who was injured on the job now, after physical rehabilitation treatment, wants to return to work. A personality may suggest withdrawn or alienated behaviors, but work experience might have been highly productive. For accurate rehabilitation planning, other factors must be considered in order to develop appropriate goals. The client's current reaction to the disability, perception of work expectations, environmental influences, and opportunities for work adjustment should all be identified before predictions are made of the client's behavior in an employment setting.

## PERSONALITY INVENTORIES

### The Minnesota Multiphasic Personality Inventory (MMPI)

The MMPI[5] is the most widely used personality inventory. Consisting of 550 affirmative statements, the test is designed for adults from about age 16 upward. The inventory items range widely in content, and the measure provides scores on ten "clinical scales," described as the following:

1.  *Hypochondriasis (Hs)*   Thirty-three items derived from patients showing abnormal concern with bodily function

---

[5]The MMPI is available from The Psychological Corporation, 757 Third Ave., New York 10017. 212-888-3500.

2.  *Depression (D)*   Sixty items derived from patients showing extreme pessimism, feelings of hopelessness, and slowing of thought and action
3.  *Conversion Hysteria (Hy)*   Sixty items from neurotic patients using physical or mental symptoms as a way of unconsciously avoiding difficult conflicts and responsibilities
4.  *Psychopathic Deviate (Pd)*   Fifty items from patients who show a repeated and flagrant disregard for social customs, an emotional shallowness, and an inability to learn from punishing experiences
5.  *Masculinity-Feminity (MF)*   Sixty items from patients showing homoeroticism and items differentiating between men and women
6.  *Paranoia (Pa)*   Forty items from patients showing abnormal suspiciousness and delusions of grandeur or persecution
7.  *Psychoasthenia (Pt)*   Forty-eight items based on neurotic patients showing obsessions, compulsion, abnormal fears and guilt, and indecisiveness
8.  *Schizophrenia (Sc)*   Seventy-eight items from patients showing bizarre or unusual thoughts or behavior who are often withdrawn and experiencing delusions and hallucinations
9.  *Hypomania (Ma)*   Forty-six items from patients characterized by emotional excitement, overactivity, and flight of ideas
10. *Social Introversion (O or Si)*   Seventy items from persons showing shyness, little interest in people, and insecurity

Many volumes have been written about the inventory, and hundreds of additional scales have been developed beyond the basic scales described above. These scales also stimulated much research with varied types of clients. Moreover, the manual reports retest reliabilities on normal and abnormal adult samples from the 0.50s to the low 0.90s. Anastasi (1982) explained that certain scales, e.g., depression, assess behavior that is so variable over time as to render retest reliability inappropriate.

Anastasi (1982) stated that, in general, the greater the number and magnitude of deviant scores on the MMPI, the more likely it is that the individual is severely disturbed. Anastasi (1982) further believed that the principal applications of the MMPI are to be found in differential diagnosis. This inventory is essentially a clinical instrument and its proper interpretation calls for considerable psychologic sophistication. Although several computerized systems for completely automated profile interpretations have been developed, training is still necessary in order to interpret the results to clients. Many of these automated interpretations are largely descriptive summaries, while others provide highly interpretive statements.

***Vocational Implications***   Caution must be used in the choice of this instrument for certain clients. As a screening device, other measures described in this chapter might be more appropriate. For many of the emotionally disturbed, for example, this inventory might simply be too long. Administration in two or three sessions might have to be considered. Also, for many clients who have no history of emotional disturbance and currently show good adjustmental patterns to their disability, differential diagnosis might not be necessary. But when a client is suspected to have a strong emotional overlay to adaptive problems, the MMPI could provide some useful information. For example, with the client who reports continued back pain, the MMPI can suggest emotional factors that should be considered when developing rehabilitation plans. Many of the clients described in Chapter 2 might be using their pain as a source of secondary gain or a reason for their ambivalence. Furthermore, this measure can suggest a level of a disabled person's depression, thus identifying the professional adjustment problems for different types of occupational situations. However, unless a rehabilitation professional has special training, another qualified person should interpret the results for the MMPI.

### Edwards Personnel Preference Schedule (EPPS)

The EPPS[6] was designed to be an instrument for research and counseling and to provide a quick and convenient measure of a number of relatively independent *normal* personality variables. Percentile scores are given for 15 personality variables: 1) achievement; 2) deference; 3) order; 4) exhibition; 5) autonomy; 6) affiliation; 7) intraception; 8) succorance; 9) dominance; 10) abasement; 11) nurturance; 12) change; 13) endurance; 14) heterosexuality; and 15) aggression.

The EPPS consists of 225 items, each having two short statements. Clients choose the statement that best describes them. Items have been carefully selected to minimize the influence of social desirability. A separate answer sheet is used. This untimed group or individually administered test takes between 40 and 55 minutes to complete.

In considering the EPPS for the handicapped, no reading level is given in the manual. However, because the test is designed for college students and adults, the reading level is fairly high. In its present form, this test is not usable for the visually impaired; nor is it usable for the deaf and mentally retarded, unless the person has a high level of reading comprehension.

To be noted with the EPPS is that ipsative scores are used, namely, the frame of reference is the individual rather than a normative sample. In other words, the strength of each need is seen in relation to the strength of the client's other needs.

---

[6]The EPPS is available from The Psychological Corporation, 757 Third Ave., New York 10017. 212-888-3500.

Retest reliabilities of the 15 scales reported in the manual range from 0.74 to 0.88 (Anastasi, 1982). Published validation studies have yielded conflicting and inconclusive results, and Anastasi (1982) believed that the measure is in need of revision to eliminate certain technical weaknesses, particularly with regard to item form and score interpretation. However, the inventory is still rather widely used in rehabilitation facilities, and when the rehabilitation worker understands the meaning of the different needs explained in the manual, he or she can then interpret the profile, which is developed from the client's responses.

*Vocational Implications*    Many of the EPPS scales can provide insights on the client's unique personal attitudes and needs. Both are as much a part of a disabled person's vocational and training choices as they are of his or her friendships and love affairs. The "change," "endurance," and "order" scales can suggest adaptability patterns in a work situation as well as the client's work flexibility and change orientation.

## Sixteen Personality Factor Questionnaire (16 PF), Form E

Form E is the new "low literate" form of the 16 PF[7] and like other forms of the 16 PF, the manual states that it is designed to "make avail-able . . . information about an individual's standing on the majority of primary personality factors." Final scores are given on 16 bipolar primary factors: 1) reserved/outgoing; 2) less/more intelligent; 3) affected by feelings/emotionally stable; 4) humble/assertive; 5) sober/happy-go-lucky; 6) expedient/conscientious; 7) shy/venturesome; 8) tough/tender-minded; 9) trusting/suspicious; 10) practical/imaginative; 11) forthright/shrewd; 12) self-assured/apprehensive; 13) conservative/experimentary; 14) group-dependent/self-sufficient; 15) undisciplined/self-conflict-controlled; and 16) relaxed/tense. Scores are reported in standard ten scores (stanine).

Form E uses forced choice items such as: "Would you rather play baseball *or* go fishing?" The person selects the activity, feeling, preference, etc. that he would rather do or be. A few questions, however, require a reasoned, factual answer: "After 2,3,4,5, does 6 come next *or* does 7 come next?" The 16 PF manual contains no information on the average time needed to complete Form E. The 128-item test is not timed.

When considering this test for the handicapped, the publisher estimates that Form E requires between a third- and sixth-grade reading level. Answers are always recorded on a separate answer sheet, which can be either hand- or machine-scored. Although no information is specifically given, Form E is

---

[7]The 16 PF, Form E is available from The Institute for Personality and Ability Testing, 1602 Coronado Dr., Champaign, IL 61820. 217-352-4739.

designed for "personality evaluation for vocational and general guidance of culturally disadvantaged and intellectually limited persons." It is not applicable to the blind in its present form. Because of its low reading level, Form E should be usable with the deaf who read fairly well. Also, a rehabilitation professional who understands basic personality concepts can, after reading the manual carefully, interpret the 16 PF profile to the client. Sufficient information on the profile is provided to do this appropriately.

*Vocational Implications*    Many of the 16 personality factors can be applied to the client's rehabilitation planning. Factors C (Emotionally Stable), E (Assertive or Conforming), F (Enthusiastic), Q2 (Self-Sufficient or Group Dependent) are particularly relevant to adjustment issues in a training or occupational situation. Furthermore, they can indicate a pattern of adjustment to disability, itself, which is a critical variable in successful rehabilitation. Factor H (Venturesome or Shy) suggests a client's change orientation or work flexibility. Also, a disabled person who scores low on Factor C (Affected by Feelings or Emotionally Stable) tends to be low in frustration tolerance for unsatisfactory work conditions, easily annoyed, and perhaps evading necessary job demands. Moreover, many of the factors in this measure can alert the rehabilitation professional to such client characteristics as Low Energy for Work Demands (Factor G); Overly Pessimistic about Possibilities for Job Adjustment (Factor F); or Continued Difficulty in Getting Along with Others, Working with People, and Accepting Supervision (Factor L).

### The Psychological Screening Inventory (PSI)

This measure[8] was developed to meet the need for a brief mental health screening device in situations where time and professional manpower may be at a premium. It is intended only as a screening device, to be used in identifying persons who might profit by receiving more intensive attention. There are five scales of the PSI: 1) Alienation (AL); 2) Social Nonconformity (SN); 3) Discomfort (DI); 4) Expression (EX); and 5) Defensiveness (DE), which is designed to assess the degree of defensiveness characterizing the test-taker's responses.

The PSI consists of 130 personal statements or items to be answered true or false. It is printed on the front and back of a single 8½- by 11-inch sheet. Items are at a fifth- sixth-grade level, and the test can normally be completed in 15 minutes. It can be administered either in group or individual settings, both with a minimum of instructions. In its present form, the test is not usable for the

---

[8]The PSI is available from the Research Psychologists Press, Inc., P.O. Box 984, Port Huron, MI 48060. 800-538-9547.

visually impaired. However, if the deaf have at least a fifth-grade reading comprehension level, it can be applicable.

*Vocational Implications*   The PSI can be particularly useful in re-habilitation, for it can provide a beginning awareness of how a client is coping with a disability. The scales of alienation, discomfort, and expression are especially valuable for this purpose. For example, the Discomfort Scale was designed to assess the personality dimension of anxiety or perceived mal-adjustment. Persons who score highly on this dimension tend to complain of varied somatic symptoms and admit to many psychologic discomforts and difficulties. When a rehabilitation professional wants to understand how the client's handling of pain is associated with a disability, this scale provides some suggestions that could be further explored in counseling. An accompanying high score on the Alienation Scale may indicate that because of disability, the client is withdrawing from family and social involvements. Consequently, high Discomfort and Alienation scores for a disabled client could suggest difficulties in adjustment to the strains and pressures of a work environment or many of the demands of competitive work, e.g., getting along with co-workers or main-taining an adequate production rate.

## Tennessee Self-Concept Scale

This test[9] is designed to be used with both healthy and maladjusted people. Atkins et al. (1982) explained that self-concept involves the dynamic inter-action of the client's beliefs, needs, body image, sexual identity, values, and expectations. Many of these factors can be explored when interviewing dis-abled persons, but understanding their self-concept is a critical element for understanding the psychologic make-up of an individual. The Tennessee Self-Concept Scale explores many dimensions of self-concept, such as family self, physical self, moral self, and identity.

The scale consists of 90 items, equally divided for positive and negative responses. It is self-administering and requires no instruction beyond those on the inside cover of the test booklet. The answer sheet is arranged so that the subjects respond to every other item and then repeat the procedure to complete the sheet. The "Counseling Form" answer sheet is easy to interpret because the score sheet can be presented directly to the client for interpretation and discussion. However, the manual should be read before any interpretation is given to the client. A trained rehabilitation professional should be able to understand the concepts explained in the manual.

---

[9]The Tennessee Self-Concept Scale is available from the Counselor Recordings and Tests, Acklen Station, Nashville, TN.

This scale has particular use for rehabilitation professionals because it can provide information and suggestions on the sources of the client's self-esteem and pattern of adjustment to disability. No reading level is indicated in the test manual. A review of the items indicates that at least a sixth-grade reading level is necessary. In its present form, the test is not usable for the visually impaired and is applicable to the deaf only if their reading comprehension is at this sixth-grade level.

It is important to understand, however, that the normative group for the development of the varied scales did not include the disabled population. This should be explained to the client.

***Vocational Implications*** Self-concept is an important concept in rehabilitation planning, for it influences the client's motivation and is linked to self-confidence in work situations. Also, the Physical Self, Personal Self, and Social Self Scales can indicate clients' attitudes toward their own disability. A high score on "Family Self" may suggest a coping resource for the client. When the scales, apart from Physical Self, reveal high scores, it might indicate to the rehabilitation professional that the client has many perceived strengths for adjusting to work situations. These can be explored in counseling with the client.

## SELECTED ISSUES IN PERSONALITY ASSESSMENT

### Cautions

Responses to a personality inventory comprise clients' attempts to describe for themselves and specific others, such as the rehabilitation professional, how they see themselves in terms of the behaviors described in each inventory item. Such inventories provide a picture of the extent to which clients are able to face themselves or are willing to have others see them as they think they are. Personality inventories probe into feelings and attitudes that many people normally conceal and regard as private. It is the rehabilitation professional's responsibility, consequently, to create conditions which assist the client in generating information useful in self-understanding or self-acceptance.

There are many ways in which clients avoid this self-revelation. They may fake information during evaluation in order to avoid threatening feedback. When responding to personality inventories, they may offer a positive response regardless of what questions are asked. Or, they may simply attempt to manipulate or convince the rehabilitation professional that they must enter a certain occupation. An additional difficulty is the forced choice technique used in constructing the varied items. Clients are asked to pick one or two items most descriptive of themselves. Yet, not all possible combinations of stimuli are presented, and a given item may consist of two alternatives of equal social desirability. A situation is created in which the person may have no logical basis for making a choice (Shertzer and Linden, 1979).

Although all of these difficulties cannot be eliminated, they may be reduced by the professional's careful structuring of the assessment situation, or by thoroughly preparing the client for taking the different paper-and-pencil tests given in rehabilitation assessment. To help the client feel more comfortable when performing a personality inventory, the rehabilitation professional can explain the purpose of the particular test, respond to the client's possible anxiety, stress the importance of obtaining an accurate picture of the client for effective rehabilitation planning, and emphasize the necessity of confidence in the assessment results.

### Uses for What Groups?

When personality assessment is performed with a client, certain tests described in this chapter may be more useful than others. The main purpose of these measures is to screen the client or gain more supportive information for the professional's perceptions acquired during the interview. With these goals in mind, the following approaches are recommended:

*Screening or Supportive Information*
*Step 1*    PSI
*Step 2*    Tennessee Self-Concept Scale
An understanding of the client's self-concept is helpful when evaluating attitudes toward self and motivation for rehabilitation. Also, the results of the PSI suggest how the client is reacting, behaviorally, to the disability. For example, is the client showing much discomfort and feeling greatly alienated from others?

*Client's Understanding of Needs and Personality Factors*
*Step 1*    EPPS
*Step 2*    16 PF, Form E
To be useful for rehabilitation planning, the results of these inventories must be interpreted in the perspective of rehabilitation needs and goals. For example, if a client shows high achievement, affiliation, and endurance scores on the EPPS, then this information can suggest some client motivational factors which, in turn, can be considered when developing rehabilitation plans. If with the above traits, further information obtained from the 16 PF indicates high scores on assertiveness, conscientiousness, practical, and controlled, personality factors, then this personality style of the client in a work or independent

living situation might be suggested. In other words, the results of the two measures can be interpreted together, and such interpretation will enable the client to gain added self-insight into rehabilitation strengths and weaknesses.

### Differential Diagnosis
*Step 1*   MMPI, when appropriate
*Step 2*   Tennessee Self-Concept Scale

***Other Approaches***   Information about behavior functioning, for example, can also be obtained by placing the client into a real or simulated, but controlled setting for the purpose of a behavioral observation of the work personality. This is called situational evaluation. Behavior rating scales, such as those described in the first section of this chapter, can be used to collect this information. Also, Field (1979) developed a formal, structured assessment system, called the Vocational Diagnosis and Assessment of Residual Employability (VDARE). This process, predicated on the *Dictionary of Occupational Titles* (1977) employs the principle of transferability of skills, enabling the rehabilitation professional to translate client information into meaningful terms.

## CONCLUSION

Personality assessment is one of the most important areas of client self-knowledge. The measures described in this chapter have all been utilized by the author. Other inventories could be suggested, but these measures have proven particularly helpful and are, therefore, recommended. Although tests cannot always accurately describe a client's basic underlying motivations, they do provide a sample of behavior. Such indications can facilitate personal insight (Biggs and Keller, 1982). For many clients, the evaluation process in rehabilitation is not really an end in itself, but can be the first step back to self-awareness. Rehabilitation plans that evolve from vocational assessment build upon this self-understanding. Clients who are aware of their own strengths and weaknesses and realize that some deficits may have to be modified before training or job placement often become more involved in the formulation of rehabilitation plans.

In rehabilitation, effective personality assessment begins with the rehabilitation professional's own awareness of the close relationship between behavioral traits and job- or other productivity-related adjustment. This awareness enables the rehabilitation professional to make referrals to psychologic consultants for personality information on the client that will be more specific and relevant to rehabilitation needs. Also, in understanding both the relationship between work and personality and the fundamental ingredients of personality assessment, the rehabilitation professional can generate referral questions or utilize appropriate evaluation measures that will provide more useful information for rehabilitation planning.


## CASE STUDY


The following case shows the importance of perceiving the relationship between behavioral traits, even those which are temporary, and adjustment to a training or employment.

*Helen, age 43, presents herself for vocational evaluation after being referred to you by her state vocational rehabilitation counselor. Two years ago, she suffered a stroke, which left her with partial paralysis of the left side. She has little use of her left hand and walks with a noticeable limp. Otherwise, all other physical functions are intact. During the intake interview, Helen explains that she has been married for 23 years, has two children, both of whom have left home and are married. She claims that she has derived most of the meaning in life through her children and roles as a wife and mother. Although before her stroke she was an active member for ten years both of a bridge group and Garden Club, her social and avocational outlets were few. Her husband has been a plant supervisor with an industrial firm since their marriage, and apart from bowling once a week, prefers to stay at home with his family and to work in the garden on weekends. Helen reports that her husband has been a good supporter and father.*

*Helen states that just after her marriage she went to a community college part-time and completed the academic requirements for a two year AA degree in Home Economics. She claims that she liked school. She further explains, however, that since her stroke she becomes easily irritated and is very resentful of her physical limitations. Helen claims that she gets angry at the least provocation, and this behavior is beginning to affect her relationship with her husband and married children.*

With this information, please answer the following questions:

1. What client emotional characteristics or behavioral traits should be modified in order for this client to make a suitable vocational adjustment?
2. What personality measures would you use in exploring Helen's personality characteristics that would have an effect on her vocational rehabilitation?

# REFERENCES

Akridge, R., and Means, B. 1982. Psychosocial adjustment skills training. In: B. Bolton, Vocational Adjustment of Disabled Persons. University Park Press, Baltimore.

Anastasi, A. 1982. Psychological Testing, Macmillan Publishing Co., Inc., New York.

Atkins, B., Lynch, R., and Pullo, R. 1982. A definition of psychosocial aspects of disability. A synthesis of the literature. Vocational Evaluation and Work Adj.Bull., 15:55–61.

Biggs, D., and Keller, K. 1982. A cognitive approach in using tests in counseling. Pers. Guid. J. 60:528–532.

Field, T. 1979. The psychological assessment of vocational functioning. J. Appl. Rehab. Couns. 10:124–129.

Halpern, A., Lehmann, J., Irvin, L., and Heiry, T. 1982. Contemporary Assessment for Mentally Retarded Adolescents and Adults. University Park Press, Baltimore.

Maki, D., Pape, D., and Prout, H. 1979. Personality evaluations: A tool of the rehabilitation counselor. J. Appl. Rehab. Couns. 10:119–123.

Marr, J. 1982. Behavioral analysis of work problems. In: B. Bolton, Vocational Adjustment of Disabled Persons. University Park Press, Baltimore.

Matkin, R., and Rice, J. 1979. Integrating diagnostic and behavioral assessment techniques. Voc. Eval. Work Adj. Bull. Winter 11:18–23.

Neff, W. S. 1971. Work and Human Behavior, Atherton Press, Inc., Chicago.

Sax, A. 1981. New VEWAA/Carf standards for work evaluation and adjustment, Voc. Eval. Work Adj. J., 14:141–142.

Shertzer, B., and Linden, J. 1979. Fundamentals of Individual Appraisal. Houghton Mifflin Co., Boston.

Sundberg, N. D. 1977. Assessment of Persons. Prentice-Hall, Inc., Englewood Cliffs, NJ.

chapter 9
# INTEREST ASSESSMENT
# IN REHABILITATION

In rehabilitation assessment, the exploration of a client's interests frequently becomes the beginning focus for both vocational evaluation and planning. An awareness of the client's interests is helpful in identifying and documenting a vocational goal and intermediate objectives to arrive at that goal. If understanding the client's interests is achieved during the initial interview, the rehabilitation professional can begin to delineate: 1) the objectives of assessment; 2) the identification of needed services; and 3) what would be appropriate outcomes for the client.

Interest exploration can also stimulate counseling by suggesting occupations which had not been previously considered by the client or rehabilitation professional (Phillips, 1982). In order to assist the professional in utilizing interest assessment effectively, this chapter describes the types of client interests, particular issues in interest exploration, and the measurement of interests, including a specialized approach to interest assessment and unique concerns in interpreting interest measures.

## WHAT ARE INTERESTS?

The term, "interest," has been used to mean degree of interest, strength of motivation and drive, or need (Shertzer and Linden, 1979). Super (1949) identified three different types of interests:

1.  *Expressed interest*   the verbal statement of liking for any stimulus such as an object, an activity, a task, or an occupation
2.  *Manifest interest*   the evidence of participation in an activity, occupation or task that can be observed by others
3.  *Tested interest*   interests measured by such objective approaches as free-association measures.

Holland (1959) expanded the notion of interests when he stated that people project their views of themselves and the world of work onto occupational titles. He believed that interests reflect personality and that a career choice depends upon a person's orientation to the environment. Holland identified six occupational environments: realistic, investigative, social, conventional, enterprising, and artistic. Each orientation expresses a somewhat distinctive life-style, which is characterized by an individual's preference for certain values, interests, interpersonal skills, and ways to deal with daily problems. A person's major life-style determines his or her main direction of occupational choice.

## PARTICULAR ISSUES IN INTEREST ASSESSMENT

### Abilities versus Interests

One of the most important generalizations in several decades of research is that interest assessment measures the direction rather than the strength of a person's interests. However, many persons show large discrepancies between interest and achievement. Interests and abilities are not highly correlated (Sundberg, 1977). A client may have a high degree of ability to do something but not be interested in it. Interests identify a domain of preference, and abilities point to the potential level of skill or attainment. Yet, abilities and interests interact. A person's interest in a certain occupational area can often motivate him or her to develop skills in order to become proficient in that line of work.

### Vocational Aspiration versus Realism

Frequently, the interests that are identified by paper-and-pencil inventories conflict with a client's verbalized interests, or clients may express an interest in an area for which they have no measured aptitude or ability. It is not unusual for a client to "fix" on one vocational objective. This "locking in" might indicate parental, family, or other environmental influences. Various approaches can be utilized to resolve this discrepancy, including the identification and analysis of different levels of jobs in the client's interest area. In service-related occupations, for instance, there are differences both in the education and time of training between the jobs of physician and policeman. Both occupations serve people and require a client's commitment and interest to other persons. A description of the duties involved in the performance and training required in each employment area may assist clients in realigning their own career or job expectations.

## THE MEASUREMENT OF INTERESTS

Various approaches for measuring interest include self-estimation, interviews, checklists, questionnaires, and tests, known as inventories. Interest inventories were initially developed in the mid 1920s as "a facilitative response to an established premise which linked occupational interest with job satisfaction" (Phillips, 1978, p. 10). They were developed to assess individual areas of interest and compare subsequent subjective interest scores with the measured interest of successful professionals in a wide variety of occupations. For the past years, inventories have been utilized principally in vocational and educational guidance (Shertzer and Linden, 1979). The inventory is the result of its interaction with the individual and cannot be considered separately in any way. These measures attempt to quantify interests or provide a score to describe a client's feelings of like or dislike. They elaborate acceptance-rejection propositions. Individuals are asked to answer "most liked" and "least liked" to the content of items, which forces them to make a choice. Their choices are self-estimates of their feelings, emotions, and attitudes toward those items, and their responses yield scores of general interest from which, directly or by comparison, interest in particular occupations or fields of activity can be estimated. Shertzer and Linden (1979) believed that this approach assumes that each group of people "under investigation have a pattern of interests in common that is different from that of some other group" (p. 178).

The "choice of interest" inventories should be based on the kind of information provided and not simply on availability, low cost, or time required for administration. If interest measures are used properly, they can be a helpful gauge for evaluating future job satisfaction. But they should be used to complement other methods of assessment, and the test items should be carefully checked for age- and disability-related appropriateness. Interest evaluations may not be appropriate for every client (Phillips, 1978). A person who has incurred a disabling on-the-job injury may be quite satisfied with previous employment but seeks another occupation in a similar interest area. This individual may not feel a need for occupational interest assessment.

When exploring a client's interest areas, the rehabilitation professional should associate this information with results from aptitude tests, review of previous work experience, knowledge gained from the assessment interview, and medical reports. Harmony must be achieved between the disabled person's interests and his or her capabilities. For example, if a client shows a dominant interest and willingness to work in "data"-related occupations, rather than "people"- or "ideas"-related careers, then information is needed about the person's clerical, perceptual speed and accuracy, numerical computation, and, in many instances, spatial relations and eye, hand, finger coordination abilities. In contrast, if interest evaluation results indicate a very strong preference for "ideas"-related occupations, then information should be obtained about the disabled individual's abilities in reading comprehension, language usage, math reasoning, and artistic and creative endeavors.

To facilitate interest exploration, the rehabilitation professional should be strongly aware of the advantages of computer scoring. Interest measures, such as the Strong Campbell and the Career Assessment Inventory, have forms that can be completed, mailed to the nearest computer scoring service, and returned within 10 days. The computer processing provides client "profiles" that can be easily read and interpreted. They may include narrative-style interpretations, which individualize the interest scores and explain in detail the meaning, significance, and limitations of interest measurement (Phillips, 1978).

The following are some recommended interest measures that can be used to generate useful information in rehabilitation assessment. They are grouped into two categories: 1) inventories appropriate for clients with low reading skills; and 2) measures for persons with a higher reading capability.

### Tests Appropriate for Those with Low Reading Skills

*Picture Interest Inventory*    The Picture Interest Inventory,[1] sometimes called the California Picture Interest Inventory, is a nonverbal interest survey. Nine scores are reported: Interpersonal Service, Natural, Mechanical, Business, Esthetic, Scientific, Verbal, Computational, and Time Perspective. The first six are interest scores; the latter three are supplemental scales. The inventory can be administered individually or in a group and can be hand-scored. The test is used in rehabilitation for nonreaders and the mentally retarded. However, the clients must thoroughly understand the directions before taking the inventory.

*Wide Range Interest-Opinion Test (WRIOT)*    According to the test manual, the WRIOT[2] was designed to measure "as many areas and levels of human activity as possible." The interest inventory contains items that represent jobs ranging from unskilled through the highest professional level. It was also developed to measure interests that appeal to a wide variety of groups, from children to disadvantaged and mentally retarded adults. The inventory contains 18 separate cluster descriptions of occupational areas (e.g., Art, Drama, Office Work, Personal Service, Physical Science, and Machine Operation) and seven work attitudes (e.g., Risk Ambition, Agreement, and Interest Spread).

---

[1]The Picture Interest Inventory is available from the California Test Bureau, Del Monte Research Park, Monterey, CA 93940. Phone: 408-649-8400.

[2]The WRIOT is available from Jastak Associates, Inc., Wilmington, DE. Phone: 800-538-9547.

The WRIOT contains 150 three-choice items, containing three clear black-and-white-line illustrations of men and women of various racial groups engaged in different job activities. The drawings are contained in a spiral-bound 5½- by 8½-inch booklets. There is one item per page. Respondents use a separate answer sheet to select the job they would most like to do and the job they would least like to do.

There is no time limit; the average administration time is from 50 to 60 minutes in groups of 30 to 40 and 40 minutes if administered individually. No reading is required for the test items. However, the client must be able to read "least" and "most" on the answer sheet and to identify the letters "A," "B," and "C" as well as the item numbers on the answer sheet and in the test booklet. Duplicate instructions are presented on a separate answer sheet, which is well-designed and easy to use. If the test is administered individually, the professional records the response.

The manual contains special instructions for individual administration to "severely mentally or physically disabled persons." The client first identifies the "best liked" illustration by pointing to or naming it and then picks out the "least liked" illustration in the same way. The professional records each response on the answer sheet. No norms or special interpretation information are available for the handicapped.

In its present form, this test is not recommended for the blind. The deaf should be able to take the WRIOT with little or no change in test materials, although the method of giving instructions would have to be changed.

***Geist Picture Interest Inventory (Revised)—Male and Female***     This measure[3] quantitatively assesses 11 male and 12 female general interest areas: Persuasive, Clerical, Mechanical, Musical, Scientific, Outdoor, Literary, Computational, Artistic, Social Service, Dramatic, and Personnel service. The Geist can facilitate interest exploration with verbally handicapped individuals. The test booklet contains 44 triads of drawings, representing major vocations and avocations, with 130 drawings in all. Only occupations "basic" or recognizable in most parts of the United States are included.

With most clients, the Geist is self-administering. It can be used with individuals or groups and has no time limit. Where there is a severe reading disability, directions and questions under the pictures are read aloud to the client, who circles the drawings of his or her choice. The test can be scored by the examiner, and the manual contains easily understood directions. The Geist also contains a motivation questionnaire for both males and females. This booklet includes the motivational analysis of occupational choices, which in turn, suggests reasons or motivations behind each choice of drawings.

---

[3]The Geist Picture Interest Inventory is available from the Western Psychological Services, 12031 Wilshire Blvd., Los Angeles, CA 90025. Phone: 213-478-2061.

***Vocational Interest and Sophistication Assessment Survey
(VISA)*** VISA[4] is a pictorial interest survey designed especially for the
mentally retarded. The test is administered individually and hand-scored.
There are separate forms for males and females. The male form provides
interest and knowledge scores in seven areas: Garage; Laundry; Food Service;
Maintenance; Farms and Grounds; Materials Handling; and Industry. The
female form provides interest and knowledge in four areas: Business and
Clerical; Housekeeping; Food Services and Laundry; and Sewing.

Although the VISA is a relatively new instrument, it is being used in
rehabilitation facility evaluation programs that primarily serve the mentally
retarded. One of the advantages of using the VISA instead of other nonverbal
picture interest inventories, i.e., The Geist and California Picture Interest
Inventory, is that the VISA focuses on job situations that are more in accord
with job potentials of the mentally retarded. However, this statement relates to
more than the intellectual limitations of the retarded, for it has been demonstrated that the retarded can function in fairly sophisticated situations. Even
when the intellectual limitations are compounded by moderate social and
emotional immaturity, the VISA can serve as an instrument for vocational
exploration and counseling.

***CHOICE*** Based upon the pioneering work of Dr. John Holland, this
inventory[5] is intended for use by individuals who are, themselves, mildly or
moderately mentally retarded. The inventory provides a self-directed, self-
paced opportunity for a client to examine personal interests, aspirations,
preferences, and estimations of self-competencies. To facilitate this self-
direction, information is presented to the client in a variety of ways: color slides
on an audioviewer, a simplified drawing of the slide in the answer book, a
simple caption and the Holland code letter beneath the drawing in the answer
book, and a brief narrative description on audiocassette of the slide and
drawing. Instructions for use of the inventory are also provided on the cassette.
There are four parts of the inventory:

1. Occupational Daydreams—takes the form of a brief, highly structured
   interview of the client by the examiner
2. Activity Scale—activities are organized and presented within the Holland
   categories and the client is asked to mark in the box underneath the
   stimulus drawing in the answer book if the activity is seen as enjoyable
3. Job Scales—the client is required to respond to a series of real jobs which
   are organized and presented within Holland categories

---

[4]VISA is available from J. Parnicky, H. Kahn, and A. Burdett, Ohio State University,
Columbus. Phone: 614-422-9922.

[5]CHOICE is available from the Center of Rehabilitation and Manpower Services, Jull
Hall, University of Maryland, College Park, MD 20742. Phone: 301-454-3026.

4.  Abilities Scale—the client is asked to mark in the box beneath the stimulus picture in the answer book if he or she feels that the competency is one that is already possessed or could be acquired.

In each of the sections, the client is asked to make decisions involving jobs and abilities that may, at first, seem to be unreasonable; however, these seemingly unreasonable choices tap stereotypes, which allows mentally retarded clients to respond within Holland categories as verified by other "more reasonable" items in the inventory. The standardization sample was composed of persons in either rehabilitation facilities or vocational evaluation units in Maryland, Pennsylvania, and the District of Columbia, and scale reliabilities of the Holland code ranged from 0.67 to 0.82. A preliminary study of concurrent validity used Occupational Daydreams as a criterion. The resulting coefficient was 0.58.

## Tests More Appropriate for Those with Higher Reading Ability

*Minnesota Vocational Interest Inventory (MVII)*    According to the manual, the MVII[6] is "designed primarily for use with those persons who contemplate entering occupations that do not require a college degree; thus, it is an inventory of non-professional interests." There are 21 Occupational Scales and 9 Homogeneous Scales. The MVII includes 474 work activities. A forced choice method is utilized, and the clients must pick both the activity they like best and the activity they would least like to do, leaving the third item blank. A total of 316 responses, half "like" and half "dislike," are made. The work activities were chosen from various sources, including skilled tradesmen.

The inventory can be administered in about 45 minutes and is not timed. It was designed for use with students in the ninth grade or above, but the reading level is estimated to be about the sixth grade. The MVII is available in booklet form, and responses are indicated in the booklet itself. Separate answer sheets are also available.

For the severely visually impaired, this test is not useful in its present form. However, this measure is appropriate for use when deaf clients have they necessary reading comprehension skills and directions are given through the use of signing or lipreading.

*Gordon Occupational Checklist*    This interest inventory[7] was designed for use with individuals who are not college-bound but who are ready to discuss vocational plans. As such, it is primarily a vocational counseling tool rather

---

[6]MVII is available from Vocational Psychology Research, Elliot Hall, University of Minnesota, Minneapolis. 55455.

[7]The Gordon Occupational Checklist is available from The Psychological Corporation, 757 Third Ave., New York 10017. Phone: 212-888-3500.

than a true interest survey. Scores are reported in Business, Outdoor, Arts, Technology, and Services, and the results are based on the frequency that individuals underline and circle activities they would like to do full-time and jobs they would especially like, respectively. This test enables the rehabilitation professional to obtain an overview of the client's areas of expressed interest as well as specific occupational preferences. The inventory consists of 240 activities that are performed in many different kinds of jobs.

The Gordon is administered in group or individual sessions and is hand-scored. It requires a sixth-grade reading level. The test is typically finished in 20 to 25 minutes. Although not suitable for the blind, it can be taken by the deaf who have the requisite reading skills.

***Strong Vocational Interest Blank for Men and Women (SCII)***   The SCII[8] is one of the oldest and most scientifically developed interest surveys. The inventory is easy to administer, requires at least a sixth-grade reading level, and it is necessary to use a computer for scoring. Because the test authors have integrated Holland's (1959) theory of career development with the empirical approach traditionally used in scoring and interpreting the SCII, clients receive scores displayed on scales based on the Holland typology. The Holland theme scale contributes a conceptual framework within which to organize and interpret the data reported on the total SCII profile for both men and women.

There are 23 basic Occupational Scales in the SCII. This test is mainly applicable for use only with those persons who are oriented toward professional, semi-professional, or managerial occupations that attract college graduates. For others, the relevance of the instrument is questionable. Also, the interpretations of the SCII should be made only by persons who have had supervised experience in evaluating clients' objective interests.

***Kuder Occupational Interest Survey (Form DD)***   In a forced choice, triad format, this inventory[9] includes such occupational areas as: Outdoors, Mechanical, Computational, Scientific, Persuasive, Artistic, Literary, Musical, Social Service, and Clerical. Seven personal-oriented areas are also included: Group Activity, Stable Situations, Working with Ideas, Avoiding Conflict, Directing Others, Working Independently, and Acting Spontaneously. This measure employs a forced choice, three-item response format. Clients select the item they prefer or would like most, and the one they least prefer. For clients who want to explore their pattern of interests honestly, this inventory is a useful instrument.

---

[8]The SCII is available from the National Computer Systems, Inc., 4401 West 76th St., Minneapolis, MN 55435. Phone: 612-830-7600 or 800-538-9547.

[9]The Kuder Occupational Interest Survey (Form DD) is available from Science Research Associates, Inc., 259 East Erie St., Chicago, IL 60611. Phone: 312-984-7000.

The test is administered easily; its directions are explicit and may be understood readily. No time limit is specified, and most clients can complete the form in approximately 30 minutes. Scores are given on a profile covering 10 occupational areas. At least a sixth-grade reading level is required, and the inventory can be applicable for persons who are college-bound or seek shorter training. The inventory can be used with deaf clients if their reading level is adequate. Because the test is not timed, it can be orally administered to the blind.

*The Self-Directed Search (SDS)*    The result of more than 20 years of research by Holland (1959), the SDS[10] is a self-administered, self-scored, and self-interpreted vocational counseling tool. This measure has two main purposes: 1) to provide a vocational counseling experience for people who do not have access to professional counselors or who cannot afford their services; and 2) to multiply the number of people a counselor can serve. Cutts (1977) explained that persons who have vocational questions such as: "What career shall I follow? Is my tentative choice reasonable?" or "What alternatives do I have in career choice?" and adults who are wondering about their current job status should be aided by this inventory.

The SDS is considered self-interpreting, but the manual states that the counselor is expected to aid in the interpretation. Assistance may be needed in explaining the five profiles in the assessment booklet. Each contains the estimate, on each of the five scales, of a person's resemblance to each of the six personality types (Realistic, Investigative, Artistic, Social, Enterprising, or Conventional). Cutts (1977) stated that because the order of the six types is always the same, the five profiles should have the same general shape. The professional should be aware that the implications of a well-defined, highly differentiated profile (showing high scores in some areas and low in others) versus a flat profile, which is undifferentiated, reflects confusion and presents a variety of problems and questions in counseling.

The SDS scales have a moderate degree of internal consistency. Samples of 2,000 to 6,000 college freshmen show a range from 0.67 to 0.94. Retest reliabilities show that the SDS summary codes have the highest degree of reliability as compared to the subscales that reflect a lower degree of reliability. Also, the item content and format reflect clear content validity. Items are stated in direct ways that require minimal interpretation and are related to the scale. Content is consistent with well-established vocational knowledge.

The SDS includes two booklets—an assessment booklet and an occupational classification booklet. To use this inventory, a client fills out the assessment booklet and obtains a three-letter occupational code. The code is

---

[10]The SDS is available from the Consulting Psychologists Press, Inc., 577 College Ave., Palo Alto, CA 94306. Phone: 800-538-9547.

then used to locate suitable occupations in the occupational classification booklet, *The Occupational Finder*. Through a series of questions related to occupational daydreams, competencies, and preferences for activities and occupations, the assessment booklet provides an estimate of the client's interests in a number of occupational areas.

There is also a Form E of the SDS that was published in 1970 and is designed for students as young as the fourth-grade as well as for adults with limited reading skills. The directions use words that are known by 80% of fourth-graders in the United States. The regular form of the test requires at least a sixth-grade reading level, and clients who have both college and noncollege training in mind will find the SDS most useful. Clients can usually complete the SDS booklet in approximately 40 minutes.

The SDS can serve as a beginning measure for interest exploration, but it can be used periodically throughout a person's entire career. The SDS offers many alternative occupations.

*Career Assessment Inventory (CAI)*    Developed to cover the vocational area of occupations requiring less than a 4-year college degree, this inventory[11] overlaps to some extent with the more ''nonprofessional'' occupations covered by the Kuder and Strong Tests (Johansson, 1976). The majority of items developed for the CAI were based upon an understanding of job descriptions of various occupations and related activities detailed in the *Dictionary of Occupational Titles* and the *Occupational Outlook Handbook*. A determined effort was made to avoid items that would imply a career or interest that would be applicable more to one sex than another. The professional reviews of the test items and the field-testing with sixth- and eighth-graders provided the necessary data for the final wording of the CAI. The first 151 items are activity-type items, the next 43 relate to school subjects, and the remaining 101 include occupational titles.

The measure is written at a sixth-grade reading level and requires between 20 and 40 minutes to complete. The interpretive profile measures theh client's interest on three separate scales:

*Scale 1*    Gives a graphic representation of how the client's individual orientation to work relates to six basic occupational themes: Realistic, Artistic, Conventional, Enterprising, Social, and Investigative

*Scale 2*    Reveals the strength or weakness of the client's interest in approximately 23 academic areas such as mathematics, social science, and teaching

*Scale 3*    Compares the client's interest with people already employed in 75 occupations on the CAI

---

[11]CAI is available from National Computer Systems, Inc., Minneapolis, MI 55435. Phone: 612-830-7600.

Reliability studies indicated that test and retest scores for the various samples showed very stable patterns for the groups. Also, the concurrent validity data presented for both the student samples and adult samples were of the same magnitude as data evidenced by similar scales on the Strong-Campbell Interest Inventory and the Strong Vocational Interest Blanks (Johansson, 1976).

This inventory is computer-scored, and the information obtained from the measure can be very useful to both the client and the professional for rehabilitation planning purposes. The CAI covers a wide range of occupations, and offers many suggestions for associations between the client's interest and particular occupations.

*Interest Check List*    Developed by the U.S. Department of Labor, this inventory's[12] primary purpose is to serve as an interviewing aid when the rehabilitation professional feels that further information on a client's interest is desired. There are 115 activities on the check list, and they are divided into 23 job clusters. This inventory requires at least a sixth-grade reading level and 20 to 30 minutes to complete. The items and job categories were taken from the *Dictionary of Occupational Titles*, and are related more to occupations requiring limited post-secondary education. It can be hand-scored by the examiner, and the inventory is especially valuable in facilitating interest exploration with the client during the initial phase of the rehabilitation process.

*Minnesota Importance Questionnaire (MIQ)*    This measure[13] is a 210-item pair comparison instrument designed to measure 20 vocationally relevant need dimensions that refer to specific reinforcing conditions found to be important to job satisfaction (Roessler and Rubin, 1982). Bolton (1982) explained that the needs, which are learned through previous reinforcing experiences, are defined as classes of preference for reinforcers. Twenty dimensions of vocational need were formulated:

| | |
|---|---|
| Ability utilization | Moral values |
| Achievement | Recognition |
| Activity | Responsibility |
| Advancement | Security |
| Authority | Social service |
| Company policies | Social status |
| Compensation | Supervision—human relations |

---

[12]The Interest Check List is available from the U.S. Department of Labor, Manpower Administration, Bureau of Employment Security, Washington, DC 20210. (U.S. Government Printing Office).

[13]The MIQ is available from the Vocational Psychology Research, Elliot Hall, University of Minnesota, Minneapolis. 55455. Phone: 800-538-9547.

Co-workers              Supervision—technical
Creativity              Variety
Independence            Working conditions

The MIQ is a self-report instrument, and its completion requires at least a fifth-grade reading ability. The time necessary to administer this measure averages about 35 minutes. Hand-scoring is possible, but the complexity of the scoring process makes it impractical. Computer-scoring is available.

Harrison et al. (1981) reported that concerning reliability, MIQ profiles are relatively stable over periods approaching 1 year. Validity was examined by looking at how different groups perform. Because this questionnaire was developed in the context of the Theory of Work Adjustment, a number of studies support the validity of correspondence between MIQ need profiles and occupational reinforcer patterns as a predictor of job satisfaction (Harrison et al., 1981). The Theory of Work Adjustment states that job satisfaction is predicted by the correspondence between an individual's needs and the re-inforcers in the work environment.

The MIQ can be used not only to assess the impact of disability, but also to help the client identify an appropriate broader set of occupations in terms of need-reinforcer correspondence and ability-ability requirement correspon-dence. This inventory identifies reinforcers most salient for the satisfaction of the client, and knowledge of these can help to focus acquisitions of occu-pational information upon the most relevant occupational characteristics for the individual. The MIQ, consequently, can structure the client's information-seeking process. Yet, this is a sophisticated instrument, and while the MIQ norms permit comparisons with 148 occupations selected to represent the major levels and fields in the world of work, it should be interpreted by a professional who has a thorough grasp of the technical nature of the instrument. The professional should also first understand the Theory of Work Adjustment (Davis et al., 1968). Computer-scoring is of great assistance when interpreting the MIQ, and is available from the same location as the questionnaire, itself.

## COUNSELING HELPS IN INTEREST EXPLORATION

Table 9.1 relates the usefulness of the different inventories that measure interest to varied levels of formal preparation required by occupations. Because interest exploration can facilitate vocational or life planning when it is begun early in the rehabilitation process, the professional will find it helpful to structure this area of evaluation. The following guidelines are suggested when developing this assessment:

*Interest Exploration with Clients Who Have at least a Fifth-Grade Reading Ability*
    *Step 1*    MIQ or Interest Check List

Table 9.1.   Usefulness of inventories for occupational preparation

| Inventory | Formal preparation required by occupation | | | |
|---|---|---|---|---|
| | No high school degree | High school degree | 2 years preparation beyond high school | 3 or more years preparation beyond high school |
| Kuder DD | U[a] | U | U | U |
| CAI | U | U | U | NU |
| Picture Interest Inventory | U | U | U | NU |
| WRIOT | U | U | LU | NU |
| CHOICE | U | LU | NU | NU |
| Geist | U | U | LU | NU |
| VISA | U | U | LU | NU |
| MVII | U | U | U | NU |
| Gordon Occupational Checklist | U | U | U | NU |
| SCII | U | U | U | U |
| SDS | U | U | U | U |
| Interest Check List | U | U | U | NU |

[a]U, useful; LU, limited usefulness; NU, not useful.

*Step 2*   To particularize interest areas for occupations requiring preparation at least 3 years beyond high school:
   SCII (computer-scored) or
   SDS (hand-scored)

*Or*   To particularize interest areas for occupations requiring preparation either not beyond high school or two years maximum training after high school:
   CAI (computer-scored)
   MVII (computer-scored)

**Interest Exploration with Clients Who Have below a Fifth-Grade Reading Ability**

*Step 1*   Interest Check List, but many of the items may have to be read aloud

*Step 2*   Gordon Occupational Checklist (hand-scored) or
   CHOICE (hand-scored) or
   WRIOT (hand-scored) or
   GEIST (hand-scored) or
   VISA (hand-scored) or
   Picture Interest Inventory (hand-scored)

*Step 3*   For all reading groups, identification of clients' interests are in:
   Business sales and management (Enterprising), or
   Business operations (Conventional), or
   Technologies and trades (Realistic), or

Natural, social, and medical sciences (Investigative), or
Creative and applied arts (Artistic), or
Social, health, and personal services (Social)

With a beginning knowledge of the client's interests in these job clusters (which relate to Holland's, 1959, typology), the rehabilitation professional can then consult resources that provide detailed descriptions of a wide variety of occupations. One volume that is particularly valuable is a *Guide for Occupational Information*, produced by the U.S. Department of Labor. The data in this publication is organized into 12 interest areas, 66 work groups, and 348 subgroups. Each subgroup has its 6-digit unique code and title, taken from the *Dictionary of Occupational Titles*. Within each subgroup, related occupations are identified. For the 66 work groups, descriptive information gives the kinds of job activities performed, the requirements made on the worker, clues for relating individuals to the type of work, preparation for entry into jobs, and other pertinent items. One of the appendices has information on how to organize career and occupational information resources. It contains techniques and procedures for cataloging and filing occupational information according to the structure in the *Guide for Occupational Information*.

When using the guide and when assessment suggests interests in different work groups, then each work group can be explored to determine if the client still wants to consider that area and whether the training requirements are in harmony with the individual's capabilities. Subgroups that identify many occupations should be examined to assess whether one or more of them seems to suit the client's interests and qualifications better than the others.

When the exploration of all the relevant groups has been completed, with identification of possible occupations of particular interest, then the collected information is organized. This information can then be used, with other data and facts, for rehabilitation planning. The *Guide for Occupational Information* provides a convenient crossover from information about the disabled person to potentially suitable fields of work or other areas of productivity.

## A Specialized Approach to Interest Assessment

Within the last 15 years, more interest measures have been devised for nonprofessional occupations and for persons planning to enter the work force after high school. However, there is still much work to be done for designing more effective assessment instruments for the physically and mentally disabled. Other methods for interest exploration must also be used for those clients who have a very low reading ability or a very limited knowledge about jobs and activities. During the interview with a client, direct questions could be utilized in order to gain information about existing interest areas. This information may still be unreliable, superficial, and unrealistic. Such questions can elicit responses that are susceptible to a client's tendency to respond by giving socially approved answers. But even apart from the difficulties in using direct questions, the interview can still be employed effectively to solicit information about a client's interests. Friel and Carkhuff (1974) devised a model to assist someone in identifying interests as well as expanding interest options. It involves understanding the client's total functioning in physical, emotional, and intellectual areas. This approach can be modified for use in an interview situation. It implies that the rehabilitation professional must become very active when assisting someone in exploring interest areas. The six steps to this approach are modified by the author for application to the interview.

*Step 1*   Assist the client to explore interests by asking such questions as:

From the jobs that you have had, what did you particularly like or dislike?
    For example, did you like working on your own, or because your supervisor was friendly to you?
In those jobs, what did you feel you could do especially well?
When you were in school, what subjects did you particularly like and dislike? Why?
From the people that you know in your life, what jobs do they have that are of particular interest to you?
When you watch television and see people doing various jobs, are there any that are of special interest to you?
What do you enjoy doing in your spare time?

It is important for the rehabilitation professional to understand the reasons behind an identified interest. For example, is it because of some external pressure, e.g., what parents or friends told the client that he or she would like? An added resource that can at least facilitate the client's exploration of interests are newspaper want ads, especially those in the Sunday edition. The professional can read these ads to the client and then encourage a response, or the client can carefully read them, check any openings that have an interest for him or her, and then discuss them with the rehabilitation professional.

*Step 2*   Assist the client in exploring his or her values by asking such questions as:

When you were working, what do you feel was important to you?
What is the reason that it was important to you? For example, was it important to work with your hands, or not to have close supervision, or you liked the particular job, or you knew it was something you could do well?

The goal in these questions is to develop an understanding of what a client means by a particular value.

*Step 3*   Categorize the information that has been generated about the client's values. Friel and Carkhuff (1974) suggested organizing these values into the physical, emotion/interpersonal, and intellectual areas. For example:

| Area | Value |
|------|-------|
| Physical | Dressing well on the job |
| | Working in a comfortable office atmosphere |
| Emotional/interpersonal | Having job security |
| | Having people close by when working |
| | Interacting frequently with people |
| Intellectual | Liking the opportunity to make decisions |

***Step 4***  Further categorize the information into:

*People occupations*—includes the areas of service (nurse or social worker), education (teacher), business (salesman), providing goods and services, and recreation (coach and artist)

*Things occupations*—includes business (accountant or secretary), technology (providing mechanical services, e.g., mechanic or electronic technician), outdoors (forest ranger or landscaper), and science (developing research and methods, e.g., biologist)

***Step 5***  Now, help clients to identify which of the interest categories best fits their values. For example, if the client mentions that the most important work value to him is job security, then an interest area appropriate to that dominant value should be chosen. It could be helpful to the client to display his or her values in the physical, intellectual, and interest areas in one column and then match these values to the occupational information gathered under data and things. The specific occupations identified by the professional must be in harmony with the client's stated values; the more occupations that are suggested, the more extensive will be the client's own exploration.

***Step 6***  Finally, identify the educational and occupational requirements demanded of particular employment areas that are congruent with the client's values. Some jobs require less than a high school diploma; others may require a high school diploma or its equivalent, namely, apprenticeship training after high school, 2 years of junior or community college, or 4 or more years of college. Clients should also decide how much education they want. The professional should find out the educational capability of the client from school records or previous paper-and-pencil testing. Of particular value during this interest exploration is the *Dictionary of Occupational Titles*, published by the United States Department of Labor. If the professional knows how to use this valuable resource, the number of occupational alternatives can be greatly expanded. Once a main interest area is identified and clients are aware that it is in harmony with their dominant values, then this book provides a large amount of information about the particular occupations relevant to this interest area.

Taking these six steps sequentially is often a lengthy exploration process, but it is a very legitimate use of the rehabilitation professional's time because it

encourages the client's involvement in both interest exploration and rehabilitation programming. Most of the steps are designed to elicit the client's
thoughts and feelings about past, present, and future career activities.


## CONCLUSION

Although the assessment of human behavior is an integral part of vocational
evaluation, how much can be said about a person from a test score? Interest
inventories may suggest what alternative courses of action are really feasible or
satisfying for a client and the effective use of the interview can further help to
identify different paths to rehabilitation goals. But the question remains:
"Which one of these possible alternatives does the client really wish to or
should take?" This issue is discussed in the next chapter: Interpreting Assessment Information.


## CASE STUDY

In the following case, the difficulties of interest exploration become evident.
The client has had one career field for many years and is now considering a
change.

*Oscar, age 37, has been referred to you by a family counselor for*
*vocational exploration. It was clear to the counselor that he has a major*
*drinking problem, which apparently is a manifestation of more deeply*
*rooted personality problems. Six months ago, he joined Alcoholics Anony-*
*mous (AA), which he now continues in by his choice. In AA, he learned*
*that his drinking controls him and that he is an alcoholic.*

*Oscar has been married twice; each marriage ended by his wife leav-*
*ing him. Reportedly, he got fired from job after job, was physically and*
*verbally abusive to his wives and states that he has a great deal of anger*
*toward a former boss who fired him from his position as regional sales*
*manager. Of further interest is that Oscar's mother died when he was 8,*
*and he was sent to live with his father's sister in another state. He at-*
*tended public school, graduated from high school, and then entered a*
*community college for 2 years, majoring in business management. He then*
*joined the army for 3 years, and upon completion of his military service,*
*obtained a job with an auto parts firm. He also completed his college de-*
*gree in business by attending night classes for 5 years.*

*Oscar reports that he started drinking very heavily after completing*
*his education and beginning his career in business. He believes the pres-*
*sures to succeed were almost overwhelming, and he thought that drinking*

*would help him to cope. He also states that he has hostile feelings toward his father because he believes the father abandoned him. He claims he is bitter toward women—"They all left me." At the same time Oscar believes he is very dependent on women. Moreover, he has grown increasingly hopeless about loving or being loved by a woman. He believes that although he has a college degree in business, he must attempt to look at other fields because: "I no longer have my interest in business since it contributed to my drinking problem."*

Please answer the following questions:

1. Does the proceeding information provide any suggestions for the client's occupational interests other than business?
2. What approach would you primarily use to explore Oscar's interests—the interview or paper-and-pencil measures?
3. Using the approach described in the last pages of this chapter, how would you help Oscar to identify his main interests?

## REFERENCES

Bolton, B. (ed.) 1982. Vocational Adjustment of Disabled Persons. University Park Press, Baltimore.

Cutts, C. 1977. Test Review—the Self-Directed Search. Meas. Eval. Guid. 10:117–120.

Davis, R., Lofquist, L., and Weiss, D. 1968. A Theory of Work Adjustment, Revised Ed. Minnesota Studies In Vocational Rehabilitation, XXIII. Industrial Relations Center, University of Minnesota, Minneapolis.

Friel, T., and Carkhuff, R. 1974. The Art of Developing a Career. Human Services Development Press, Amherst, MA.

Harrison, D., Garnett, J., and Watson, A. 1981. Client Assessment Measures in Rehabilitation. Rehabilitation Research Institute, University of Michigan, Ann Arbor.

Holland, J. 1959. A theory of vocational choice. J. Couns. Psychol. 6:35–45.

Johansson, C. 1976. Career Assessment Inventory. National Computer Systems, Inc., Minneapolis, MN.

Phillips, J. 1982. Occupational interest inventories: An often untapped resource. J. Appl. Rehab. Couns. 9:10–16.

Roessler, B., and Rubin, S. 1982. Case Management and Rehabilitation Counseling. University Park Press, Baltimore.

Shertzer, B., and Linden, J. 1979. Fundamentals of Individual Appraisal. Houghton Mifflin Co., Boston.

Sundberg, N. 1977. Assessment of Persons. Prentice-Hall, Inc., Englewood Cliffs, NJ.

Super, D. 1949. Appraising Vocational Fitness, 1st Ed. Harper and Row Publishers, New York.

chapter 10

# INTERPRETING
# ASSESSMENT
# INFORMATION

One of the most important aspects of vocational assessment is how the rehabilitation professional communicates to the client the information gained from the evaluation. This communication involves interpreting test data in an understandable way, helping clients to make decisions about their future plans, and perhaps alleviating some difficulties that might be obstacles to effective rehabilitation planning, such as unrealistic vocational aspirations or poor motivations for training. Especially for the disabled client, reporting assessment data may be crucial to making a decision regarding which course will lead to possible employment. For the professional, this interpretation session demands skills in integrating assessment data about the abilities, education, and motivation of individuals with what is known about the nature of various occupations (Shertzer and Linden, 1979).

Because rehabilitation assessment should be part of the continued counseling process with the client reaching productive goals, the time of reporting evaluation information requires particular counseling skills. Also, the rehabilitation professional often has to interpret test information gained from nonvocational sources (such as a psychiatrist or psychologist) into vocational terms. This vocational translation necessitates a knowledge of customary instruments used by such sources and even special training in order to make the test results meaningful to the client. Some of the principles underlying this training are explained in this chapter. This chapter also identifies the general principles involved in interpreting and communicating assessment information to the client, explains the types of interpretation, discusses the actual situation of communicating evaluative information to clients, indicates the special problems often presented in the interpretative session, and offers some responses to these questions. The role of the rehabilitation professional in developing resources for occupational information is also discussed. Selected occupational literature is identified along with ways to generate knowledge about the local world of work.

## TYPES OF INTERPRETATION

Goldman (1971) identified four kinds of interpretation—descriptive, genetic, predictive, and evaluative, all of which fit within the structure of rehabilitation assessment.

### Descriptive

This interpretation asks such question as: "What kind of a person is this client?" "What are his (or her) hobbies, vocational interests, particular capabilities, and personal strengths?" "What does the evaluation reveal about this client, especially when the person is compared to other people on specific test scores like aptitude functioning?" "Furthermore, does the client do better in one area than another?"

### Genetic

In this aspect of interpretation, various reasons are explored as to why or how the client is functioning in a certain manner. For example, if the client has a work history in outdoor activities, but interest-testing reveals that he or she actually has little interest in this area, then the reasons for this discrepancy could be explored. Low aptitude scores could also be discussed. Particular obstacles, either from the client's environment (i.e., family) or from within the client (i.e., attitude or emotional disposition) could be identified. Such obstacles might represent reasons why the client is against a particular vocational direction, especially when evaluation strongly suggests an exploration of the latter area.

### Predictive

There are many factors that constitute the client's vocational or training success. Prediction should be done cautiously during the reporting of evaluation data because of such realities as motivation, the client's own adjustment to disability, and environmental forces impacting on the client as he or she "moves" from medical treatment or inactivity to more active involvement in the rehabilitation process. If interpreted properly, most evaluation information suggests reasons why a certain vocational direction is feasible for the client. Soliciting clients' feedback during interpretation can also facilitate their awareness of what is needed for an effective adjustment to training or to employment.

### Evaluative

In this area of interpretation, the emphasis is more on such objective considerations as what are specific behavioral and ability-related job demands, what does the *Dictionary of Occupational Titles* say about job qualifications, and what occupations are particularly in demand in the client's geographical area. The results from the assessment are then compared or matched to this objective information. From this comparison, the professional can begin to determine what occupation or level of training would be more feasible to enter and how long a course of vocational training should be pursued. This area of interpretation, however, necessitates value judgments by the rehabilitation professional, which in turn generates recommendations for the client.

In reporting evaluation information, all of these varied kinds of interpretation are utilized. When considering the interpretation of assessment results, the validities of evaluation measures must be carefully identified. If an instrument has a low predictive ability and has been used in evaluation, then this should be discussed when communicating the results to the client. As explained in Chapter 5, the validity issue is a continuing problem when using traditional assessment tools with those who are disabled. The disabled population was probably not included in the norm group, and although the measure may be strong in content validity, which has reasonably good descriptive use during the interpretation session, it should not be utilized for prediction.

## GENERAL PRINCIPLES OF INTERPRETATION

Many guidelines make the interpretation session an effective experience for both the rehabilitation worker and the client.

### Principle 1

*The rehabilitation worker should communicate evaluation information at the level of the client's understanding* Hopefully, at this time in the evaluation process, the professional has some knowledge of the client's mental abilities as well as the deficits that may limit the client's capability of understanding important assessment facts. Someone who has chronic anxiety or who has been showing continued resistance to exploring new alternatives for life planning will have a difficult time endorsing assessment feedback. In these instances, the client's own point of view, attitudes, or goals can be used as a point of reference or departure. In preparing for the interpretive session, the professional can then identify information that may be favorable or unfavorable to the client's point of reference. This information can be balanced or the "for and against" evidence summarized, at which point an explanation can be offered as to why the client should shift goals or consider a certain direction for rehabilitation planning.

## Principle 2

*The recommendations that are offered in this reporting of information session should be made in terms of alternatives so that the client can then make a choice*    It is the client who basically interprets the test information (Biggs and Keller, 1982). But the professional must understand the different options that are available to the client. Knowing how to use the *Dictionary of Occupational Titles*, published by the United States Department of Labor, is an invaluable asset in assessment. This resource identifies the many occupational choices available in the labor market and gives the requirements for each job. The discussion of alternatives or the exploration of different job options feasible for the client reflects the professional's experience in handling job-related information and knowing the different opportunities that may exist within the client's community.

## Principle 3

*The client should participate as much as possible in this interpretive session*    Promoting client involvement ensures that the client will appropriately evaluate the test results (Biggs and Keller, 1982). Although it might be easier for the rehabilitation professional simply to present the test results or other related information to the client without soliciting any feedback and then make recommendations without much time allowed to deal with the client's response, this approach will usually not be facilitative for realistic rehabilitation planning. If clients participate in gaining an understanding of assessment results, they will then be likely to introduce new information about themselves from other sources and to produce new insights regarding the significance of all the information (Goldman, 1971). In fact, the more clients contribute to the results provided by the assessment measures and the more the rehabilitation professional is "client-centered"-oriented and puts stress on the client's feelings about the assessment data, the more accepting clients will be of those conclusions and their implications regarding future activities. Importantly, a client who is involved in reporting evaluation information stands a better chance of remembering accurately what is communicated.

## Principle 4

*It is not the test information itself but the rehabilitation professional's and client's perceptions of these results that is important*    Because one of the emphases in reporting evaluation results should be on the attitudes and readiness of clients to use the particular kind of information being given in this session, the professional should also be aware of clients' views toward themselves as clients and toward the rehabilitation process, their expectations about the assessment process itself, and the feasibility of future job-related productivity. Some clients, for example, may see no need to learn more about themselves or to explore options that are even marginally different from their present life-style. The client also may still be attempting to adjust emotionally to the disability. Consequently, the client who perceives there is little hope for a satisfying life may have a quite low self-concept. How clients perceive test scores are often associated with their self-views. Clients will have great difficulty accepting information that conflicts with their self-concepts. It is the professional's responsibility to facilitate the kind of interaction that will lead the client to a more accurate perception of the assessment data.

## Principle 5

*During this information imparting session, the professional should avoid persuasive methods that might convey brusqueness or aggressiveness*     The evaluation data should speak for itself and be the motivational tool for rehabilitation planning—not the professional's personality alone. Of course, the professional provides suggestions, options, attractive choices, and reasonable alternatives. However, it is the client's final decision whether to act on such recommendations. One of the goals of this session is not to force the professional's interpretation of assessment data upon clients, but rather to allow clients to relate this new information to their previous experiences and rehabilitation expectations. It is helpful if the evaluation information is presented to the client as objectively as possible. A statement like: "Eight out of ten clients with scores like yours have a good chance of succeeding in this electronics program" is preferable to one which begins: "You should . . . ," "I believe . . . ," or "If these were my scores, I would . . . "

## Principle 6

*The professional should be as familiar as possible with the different tests, measures, or approaches used during the client's evaluation*     Such questions as "How well and what does this instrument measure?" and "What do the scores mean?" should be answered before the interpretation session with the client. This information can be obtained from the test manual or, when testing was done by another source, such as a psychologist, from that person. Moreover, rehabilitation professionals can learn a great deal about a particular paper-and-pencil test by taking the same tests that are used with their clients in vocational assessment. Associated with this principle is the belief that clients should understand which test is being interpreted and what it measures.

## Principle 7

*The client should not be confronted with unsuspected, negative information*     Negative scores or results from the evaluation can be balanced with positive information. For example, the professional may say: "On the one hand, your scores in the mechanical aptitude suggest that you would have a difficult time succeeding in training in that area. But on the other hand, your clerical aptitude is very high and merits serious attention for future planning."

All in all, these principles emphasize that the interpretation session is both a teaching and counseling opportunity for the rehabilitation professional; for the client, it is primarily a learning situation. During the session, clients have the chance to explore alternatives, to discuss their own views about the meaning of the evaluation results, and to gain added self-understanding that might be needed for subsequent life planning decisions. Importantly, however, the professional also has the opportunity to learn more about the client. The extent of this learning depends upon how the evaluation information has been communicated, how the goals of the evaluation process have been formulated earlier with the client, and how clients themselves respond to the learning of this newly discovered information.

## THE ACTUAL INTERPRETATION SESSION

The interpretation meeting with the client should be structured so that the rehabilitation professional has a clear idea of what is to be accomplished. For example, if the goal is to formulate rehabilitation plans for the client, this aim becomes a perspective for the organization of evaluation results. When structuring this session, attention should be given to: 1) emphasizing capabilities that can be utilized in vocational planning; 2) the order in which assessment data will be discussed; 3) how the professional will deal with negative information generated by the evaluation; and 4) what particular data will be used for vocational planning. Also, information should not be forced upon the client, but related to his or her previous experiences. Assessment results should be presented in such a way that clients are encouraged to follow an appropriate rehabilitation direction. All of this demands preparation; when this planning is done, the reporting of evaluation becomes much more effective.

The interpretation session can be "structured" into four phases.

### First Phase (Introduction)

At the beginning of the session, the professional should help the client feel at ease and receptive toward assessment information. Reviewing the goals of evaluation and soliciting responses from the client on how he or she felt about the evaluation could help to reduce feelings of anxiety. Clients are usually anxious because of the evaluative and judgmental aspects of assessment. For example, they may fear that tests will be bearers of bad news. Clients may also perceive that the results may change their expectations about a definite area of training. Providing them with the opportunity to talk about these concerns may give the professional some ideas about how to present the evaluation results. When the professional provides the chance for clients to express their thoughts and uses an active listening style to show that he or she is genuinely interested in what is being said, then the clients' cooperation in acting upon assessment information is frequently promoted. Clients may have many concerns about the evaluation information. Asking them about how they felt during the time that the tests were administered will achieve an understanding of attitudinal factors that may have influenced them during the assessment procedures (Miller, 1982).

## Second Phase

When the professional believes that the client is receptive to listening to the evaluation results, the original purposes of the rehabilitation assessment and what tests or measures were used should then be discussed. Interest tests should be identified first, for their information is usually less threatening to the client and can establish a direction for the feedback of the other evaluation data in the personality, aptitude, and intelligence areas. Why these particular assessment tools in all the evaluation areas were selected and what they measure could also be reviewed. Furthermore, concepts such as norms, percentiles, percentile ranks, and stanines may need to be thoroughly explained (Miller, 1982).

## Third Phase

After reviewing all the measures used for a particular client's evaluation, the professional can explain the results of each assessment area, beginning with interest inventories. The client is usually shown the interest profile, told about the information it presents, and then particular results are identified. In this phase of test reporting, statistical data or test-score numbers must be translated for the client. Percentiles probably are the safest and most informative numbers to use, provided their two essential characteristics are made clear: 1) that they refer not to the percentage of questions answered correctly but to the percentage of people whose performances the client has equalled or surpassed; and 2) specifically, who are the people with whom the client is being compared. The second point, a definite description of the comparison or "norm" group, is particularly important in making the meaning of test results clear. The reporting of numbers should be minimized when communicating test results and if used, should only be done incidentally. One suggestion for a response is: "Your results are similar to those people who . . . "

After imparting the interest information, the client should be asked about his or her own relevant feelings or reflections. "Do you feel these results present an accurate picture of you?" and "Is this information a surprise to you?'' are two questions that will solicit client responses. The client should be able to understand the assessment results and talk about what they mean to him or her.

When the interest results are given, then achievement and ability or work results can be reported. Frequently, the interest results are encouraging to the client and set the stage for a very productive reporting session. Any negative data should be communicated carefully. In reporting these results, the professional should emphasize the information that identifies the client's vocational strengths and the patterns of strengths and weaknesses interpreted in terms of the client's educational and work history. It is important to present this information objectively, using norm comparisons when they are available. Attention should also be given to the consistency of the results with the client's past and present level of functioning. Also, two questions need to be answered in light of the achievement/ability results: 1) Do the results suggest that the client could handle the work or training required at other, higher levels?; and 2) What does this information mean in terms of an occupational choice?

Because assessment reporting has already identified general areas of interest, it is most helpful now if the professional suggests particular interest areas, respective occupations, and the physical, emotional, and intellectual qualifications for each area. In this regard, the *Dictionary of Occupational Titles* (1978 Ed.) is a valuable resource. Before the interpretation session, the professional can examine the client's assessment results and use the *Dictionary of Occupational Titles* to consider different occupations and their qualifications that are appropriate to these results. (This resource is further described in the last section of this chapter.)

After these results have been explained and the information has been related to the client's past experience, statements about vocational goals, and prior interest exploration, then feedback should again be solicited from the client. It is necessary that the client understand the results as they relate to future rehabilitation planning, and encouraging the exploration of feelings and perceptions about this data will further facilitate this comprehension.

Following this interaction, the intelligence test results can be communicated if these measures have been utilized in assessment. The rehabilitation professional should be cautious about giving the client a definite IQ score. Out of all the evaluation results, often clients remember just their particular IQ score, which distorts its meaning for rehabilitation planning. Also, the score may vary to a small degree, depending on both testing conditions and the client's current level of functioning. Rather than report the IQ number, a range (such as ''Average,'' ''Bright Normal,'' or ''Superior'') can be given.

Personality assessment then follows and frequently, this part of the interpretation session is very threatening to clients. To alleviate some of the client's anxiety, the purpose of each test and what it measures can be explained. Furthermore, the professional should avoid terminology that has unfavorable emotional connotations, such as "neurosis," or "emotional stability." The particular test results can also be related to occupational goals or job requirements. Often, these personality measures reveal negative information about the client that may have as its source the client's troubled past. The professional should decide whether this data has any relevant bearing on current rehabilitation planning. For example, test results or evaluation may reveal that the client has certain phobias or experiences severe anxiety, both of which may affect work adjustment. Therefore, the professional may recommend therapy before any training is pursued. In this area of interpretation, it is particularly important for the professional to identify personality strengths that relate strongly to work functioning. Limitations that might affect employment must also be presented, but these are more readily acknowledged when viewed through the perception of some strong personality assets.

**Fourth Phase (Conclusion)**

When terminating the reporting of assessment information, the rehabilitation professional should keep in mind those results that are important for rehabilitation planning. This information should again be identified in summary fashion, and then rehabililtation directions for training or employment can be suggested. Clients should be asked to provide some feedback on what they have learned from the evaluation and what results they consider the most important. They should leave the interpretation session with an understanding of themselves that raises hope and strong expectations for their future. This often demands that rehabilitation professionals frequently repeat in the interpretation session those results that show capabilities for employment; however, it is time well-spent. The results often become motivational factors for later rehabilitation involvement. The professional should remember that the interpretation of test results usually leads to the development of rehabilitation plans. Any planning should involve the client, and options need to be explored with the client. Table 10.1 shows a summary of an actual interpretation session.

**SPECIAL CONCERNS IN INTERPRETATION**

Different problems often arise during the interpretation session. Problems that are not handled promptly can eliminate the effectiveness of this important part of assessment. Three concerns frequently occur when the professional provides feedback on evaluation results.

**Contradictory Test Scores**

Occasionally, two evaluation measures may give two different scores on the same factor or individual trait. How can those differences be reconciled? For

Table 10.1.    Summary of actual interpretation session

| Phase | Tasks |
|---|---|
| First phase (Introduction) | 1. Know about measures to be interpreted to the client.<br>2. Establish a relationship.<br>3. Review goals of evaluation for the client. |
| Second phase | 1. Give the client an opportunity to talk about the assessment experience.<br>2. Summarize in a general manner the overall results of evaluation, emphasizing positive test results.<br>3. Solicit feedback from the client. |
| Third phase | 1. Interpret carefully each evaluation measure—Interest, Aptitude/Ability, Intelligence, and Personality. Use such guidelines as norms, percentiles, etc.<br>2. Solicit feedback about the client's feelings concerning the results.<br>3. Deal with such problems as contradictory test scores, reluctance, and unrealistic vocational aspirations.<br>4. Suggest particular interest areas, the respective occupations, and the qualifications for each in the physical, emotional, and intellectual areas. |
| Fourth phase (Conclusion) | 1. Summarize results for the client and discuss how this information can relate to rehabilitation planning.<br>2. Ask the client for further feedback, especially about what has been learned from the evaluation experience.<br>3. Develop rehabilitation plans. |

example, can the discrepancy between the results of two interest inventories be resolved when one of them shows a high score in business-related activities, and the other a low score? In responding to these differences, three basic viewpoints can be considered, as identified by Goldman (1971).

*Differences between the Tests Themselves*    There may be differences in the types of items found on paper-and-pencil tests, e.g., free choice versus forced choice. The latter might be more irritating because of the necessity of making choices, even when the client feels no preference for use of the alternative choices. Or, the norm groups used in developing normative data for the test might be quite different both in age and intelligence levels. The characteristics that the test measures might also be quite different. The Quick

Test, for example, measures school ability and then provides an IQ score; the Shipley-Hartford Test, however, includes both Verbal and Abstract reasoning and then gives an IQ score. The same client taking both tests may score lower on the Shipley-Hartford Test because of less developed abstract reasoning ability.

*Differences within the Individual*   On two occasions during rehabilitation assessment, a client may function physically and psychologically in different ways. Fatigue; the presence of mental distractions; situational anxiety; acute, temporary stress; and motivation could all be sources for the difference in scores on two measures evaluating the same area. When the professional notes this difference, he or she should explore with the client reasons for the discrepancy.

*Differences in Test Administration and Scoring*   Occasionally, the conditions in the testing room or environment (e.g., overheated or too cold) represent inhibiting factors to test performance. Or, the test administrator may increase anxiety among the clients. Many professionals induce tension because of the way they present themselves while others try to relax clients before a testing experience. These realities may contribute to a difference in the way a client handles test items. Consequently, on two occasions, scores on the same measure may differ. Again, the professional should ask the client for reasons why the scores are different, especially when there may be no difference between the tests, themselves.

## Reluctance To Believe Test Scores or Follow the Professional's Recommendations

During the interpretation session, the client may seem unwilling to believe the assessment results or reluctant to act eventually on this information. This problem needs attention because one of the goals of this session is to use assessment data to help clients become motivated enough to pursue appropriate rehabilitation goals. The first step in alleviating this concern is to identify the source of the reluctance. The client's responses could be influenced by hostility toward the professional as an authority figure, hearing assessment information that apparently goes against the client's perceived self-concept, or the client's predetermined resolve to follow a course of action, regardless of the evaluation results. Also, because of past failure experiences the client may lack the flexibility to take risks or attempt new ventures suggested by evaluation results and rehabilitation planning. Change is viewed as very threatening, and there is a marked hesitancy to try new directions. Whatever the reason, the source of the client's reluctance should be explored and identified.

During this exploration, empathy with the client should be established. When the client is aware that the rehabilitation professional is an active listener and also expresses warmth, sincerity, and genuine interest, usually there will be more willingness to reveal obstacles that could deter rehabilitation. Empathy can convey client acceptance and facilitate professional trust.

Once the source of the reluctance is identified, the professional can begin to deal with the problem. The training and occupational alternatives suggested by evaluation information often have to be made attractive to the client. Any suggested course of action must be perceived by the client as personally rewarding. Also, providing emotional support for those clients who hesitate to take a risk while at the same time emphasizing the assets revealed by the evaluation may generate movement toward rehabilitation goals. Frequently, when clients enhance their attitudes toward self and have confidence in the professional, they are motivated to overcome apparent obstacles to vocational planning. For example, often the family represents the client's source of reluctance because he or she is afraid to act counter to the expectations of family members. It takes a considerable amount of courage for the client to tell the family that he or she is going to follow a certain direction in rehabilitation, even when the family does not endorse the choice. When the client believes that a certain course of action is the most appropriate, trusts the rehabilitation professional, and feels that this training or the next step in the rehabilitation process will eventually bring personal satisfaction, then the client may follow this direction over the family's wishes.

## Unrealistic Vocational Aspirations

Although this difficulty is briefly discussed in a previous chapter, it often arises again during the interpretation session. Because of the client's limited awareness of his or her abilities, little exposure to the working world, and a fear of certain training areas that lead to employment, the client's own perception of the best rehabilitation goals may be very different from what the evaluation information suggests. When this problem inhibits appropriate rehabilitation planning, the professional must carefully explore with the clients their educational and work history, level of skill proficiency suggested by the evaluation results, and feasible training or employment possibilities. After the identification of the client's work-related qualifications, various employment alternatives can be presented, based on emotional, physical, and intellectual qualifications. The *Dictionary of Occupational Titles* provides information on job requirements and working conditions. The professional should also know about salary and promotional possibilities. If this information is given in relationship to the client's training and job capabilities, with emphasizing as many employment alternatives as possible, the client will at least have a considerable amount of useful information to make a choice.

It is the client's responsibility to make the decision about what vocational direction should be pursued. When the rehabilitation professional is patient, identifies the sources of the client's unrealistic vocational goals, and attempts to make rehabilitation alternatives as appealing as possible, there is a greater possibility that the client will carefully consider the professional's recommendations. Many times, it is also helpful for clients to talk to someone in a field toward which they may be unrealistically aspiring. This "reality exposure" helps clients to confront personal options and obtain some concrete information on their feasibility. Often, these encounters help to break down clients' resistance and allow them to acknowledge the impracticality of an initial vocational choice. Moreover, workers can also recommend that the client meet people in those occupations or training opportunities that are more in harmony with his or her evaluation results.

## Professional's Role in Developing Occupational Information

A knowledge of occupational resources and local opportunities for employment considerably enhances the credibility of the interpretation of test results to clients. Goldman (1972) suggested that if counselors, for example, continue to use tests, they must collect information about local experiences. This would make interpretive statements more meaningful and bring a perspective for understanding assessment results. Using varied occupational information resources can provide a more realistic picture of evaluation results, which will add more credibility for rehabilitation planning. During the interpretive session, it is also important to increase the client's options for training or employment. A knowledge of occupational resources facilitates the exploration of alternatives.

To develop an awareness or increase an understanding of occupational information, selected occupational literature is described and approaches are identified for generating information on the local world of work.

### Occupational Literature

*Dictionary of Occupational Titles (DOT)*   First published in 1939, the 4th Edition of the DOT contains valuable information relating to approximately 20,000 jobs. It is a single volume of 1,400 pages. There are three basic arrangements of occupational titles: 1) The "Occupational Group Arrangement" is appropriate if the professional has sufficient information about the job tasks, wants to know about other closely related occupations, and/or wants to be sure he or she has chosen the most appropriate classifications using the other arrangements; 2) "Occupational Titles," arranged by industry designation, is appropriate if the professional only knows the industry in which the job is located and wants to know about other jobs in an industry or work in a specific industry; and 3) The "Alphabetical Index of Occupational Titles," which is appropriate if only the occupational title is known, and the professional cannot obtain better information (Herr and Cramer, 1979).

All the jobs are designated by a nine-digit number. The first of the nine digits refers to an occupational category. There are nine such categories:

1. Professional, technical, and managerial occupations
2. Clerical and sales occupations
3. Service occupations
4. Agricultural, fishery, forestry, and related occupations
5. Processing occupations
6. Machine trades occupations
7. Benchwork occupations
8. Structural work occupations
9. Miscellaneous occupations

These categories are divided into 82 two-digit occupational divisions, which are then subdivided into 549 three-digit occupational groups. Figure 10.1 further explains the DOT code, and Figure 10.2 illustrates a DOT definition.

*Occupational Outlook Handbook*   This book, written for adults and for high school and college students, is published every 2 years by the United States Bureau of Labor Statistics and printed by the United States Government Printing Office. It contains occupational projections and the latest information on more than 850 occupations in 30 industries. These 850 occupations are organized into 300 occupational briefs and grouped into 13 clusters of related jobs. The DOT numbers are used to identify an occupation, and each of the

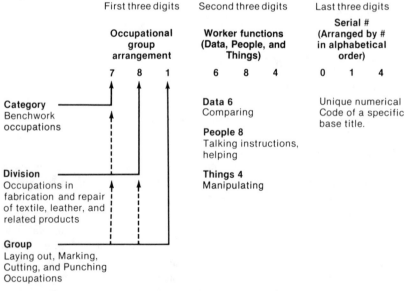

*Figure 10.1.  Parts of the DOT code.*

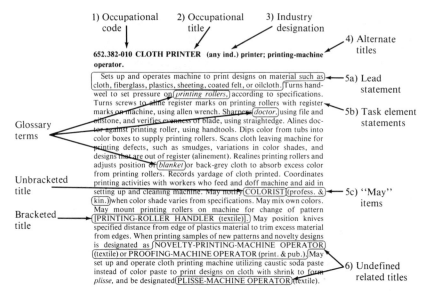

1) Occupational   2) Occupational   3) Industry
   code              title            designation
                                                          4) Alternate
                                                             titles
**652.382-010 CLOTH PRINTER** (any ind.) printer; printing-machine
operator.

Sets up and operates machine to print designs on material such as   ◄— 5a) Lead
cloth, fiberglass, plastics, sheeting, coated felt, or oilcloth. Turns hand-        statement
weel to set pressure on *printing rollers,* according to specifications.
Turns screws to aline register marks on printing rollers with register
marks on machine, using allen wrench. Sharpens *doctor,* using file and   ◄— 5b) Task element
oilstone, and verifies evenness of blade, using straightedge. Alines doc-       statements
tor against printing roller, using handtools. Dips color from tubs into
color boxes to supply printing rollers. Scans cloth leaving machine for
printing defects, such as smudges, variations in color shades, and
designs that are out of register (alinement). Realines printing rollers and
adjusts position of *blanket* or back-grey cloth to absorb excess color
from printing rollers. Records yardage of cloth printed. Coordinates
printing activities with workers who feed and doff machine and aid in
setting up and cleaning machine. May notify COLORIST (profess. &   ◄— 5c) "May"
kin.) when color shade varies from specifications. May mix own colors.       items
May mount printing rollers on machine for change of pattern
PRINTING-ROLLER HANDLER (textile)]. May position knives
specified distance from edge of plastics material to trim excess material
from edges. When printing samples of new patterns and novelty designs
is designated as NOVELTY-PRINTING-MACHINE OPERATOR
(textile) or PROOFING-MACHINE OPERATOR (print. & pub.). May
set up and operate cloth printing machine utilizing caustic soda paste   ◄ 6) Undefined
instead of color paste to print designs on cloth with shrink to form       related titles
plisse, and be designated PLISSE-MACHINE OPERATOR (textile).

Glossary terms

Unbracketed title

Bracketed title

*Figure 10.2. Parts of a DOT definition.*

occupation descriptions includes the nature of the work, places of employment, training, other qualifications, advancement, employment, outlook, earnings and working conditions, and where to write for additional information. It is revised every 2 years and is a valuable reference book (Fredrickson, 1982).

***Approaches for Generating Information on Local Working Opportunities*** The rehabilitation professional should be familiar with the varied resources that provide information on job opportunities. Some resources are:

1.  Private and independent schools
2.  Apprenticeships (the best source of information—the regional representative for apprenticeships in the client's area)
3.  Professional and trade associations and labor unions
4.  State and private employment agencies
5.  Local newspapers
6.  The Chamber of Commerce

When seeking information about possible employment opportunities, certain guidelines will provide the most useful facts. In 1980, The National Vocational Guidance Association published guidelines (Fredrickson, 1982); those relevant to rehabilitation assessment are as follows:

1.  Duties and Nature of Work
2.  Work Setting and Conditions
3.  Personal Qualifications

4.  Social and Psychological Factors
5.  Preparation Required
6.  Special Requirements
7.  Methods of Entering
8.  Earnings and Other Benefits
9.  Usual Advancement Possibilities

## CONCLUSION

A central aim of rehabilitation assessment is to identify the client's vocational assets and capabilities. Then, some tentative recommendations are provided from which rehabilitation plans are developed. The communication of the evaluation results is a necessary step, both to identify those assets and to formulate appropriate plans. How the rehabilitation professional handles the interpretive session often determines whether the client will achieve rehabilitation goals.

## CASE STUDY

The following case illustrates the difficulties in the reporting of the assessment results to the client.

*Robert, age 29, had been a truck driver with the same firm for 8 years before this on-the-job injury. While transferring materials to a loading dock, he fell and injured his back to such an extent that the doctors have indicated that he must change jobs if he is to be gainfully employed in the future. Concerning his personal history, Robert dropped out of school in the tenth grade, had various unskilled jobs for 3 years while living at home, and then at age 17, obtained a position in the housing construction industry. When that field hit an all-time low for buyers of homes, he was laid off but found a job as a truck driver. He states that he liked the job very much, but now realizes that because of his back condition, he will be unable to continue in that field. Robert claims he has been very upset about this loss, especially because his employer told him that there were no other jobs available in the company. He has also been married for 6 years and has two children. His wife works as a waitress. Robert reports that his marriage has been a happy one, although family life has been tense since his unemployment.*

*Just before vocational evaluation, Robert indicated that he really has had no hobbies outside of fishing and coaching a neighborhood softball team. His family told him that he should think about becoming a computer repairman because "There is good money in that field."*

Robert is accepted for rehabilitation and spends 8 days at a vocational assessment center. As a rehabilitation professional and Robert's rehabilitation counselor, the results of the following tests are sent to you:

1. QT
   96 IQ score
2. Bennett Mechanical Aptitude:
   55 percentile as compared with adults entering training
3. WRAT
   Reading: eighth-grade level
   Spelling: sixth-grade level
   Arithmetic: ninth-grade level
4. PSI
   Highest score on discomfort, with a somewhat high score on alienation
   All other scores within Average range
5. Kuder Interest Inventory:
   Highest scores in Outdoors and Clerical
   All other scores in the Middle range

The evaluator reports that Robert was cooperative and friendly during evaluation and particularly liked the clerical- and mechanical-related work samples; For proficiency, he scored in the Below Average range in the former, and the Above Average range in the latter. He also mentions that he talked frequently with the other clients about his injury and often stated that with workmen's Compensation payments and with his wife working, they were getting by financially.

With this brief information, please answer the following questions:

1. What do you foresee as problems in communicating the assessment results to this client?
2. What are the discrepancies between Robert's expressed interest and the test results?
3. How would you proceed in communicating the assessment results to Robert? Also, how would you help this client to develop with you realistic rehabilitation plans?

## REFERENCES

Biggs, D., and Keller, K. 1982. A Cognitive Approach to Using Tests in Counseling, Pers. Guid. J. 60:528–532.
Fredrickson, R. 1982. Career Information. Prentice-Hall, Inc., Englewood Cliffs, NJ.
Goldman, L. 1971. Using Tests in Counseling (2nd Ed.) Goodyear Publishing, Co. Santa Monica, CA.

Goldman, L. 1972. Tests and Counseling: The Marriage that Failed. Meas. Eval. Guid. 4:213–220.

Herr, E., and Cramer, S. 1979. Career Guidance Through the Life Span. Little, Brown and Co., Boston.

Miller, G. M. 1982. Deriving Meaning from Standardized Tests: Interpreting Test Results to Clients. Meas. Eval. Guid. 15:87–93.

Shertzer, B., and Linden, J. 1979. Fundamentals of Individual Appraisal. Houghton Mifflin Co., Boston.

chapter 11
# ASSESSMENT FOR INDEPENDENT LIVING

For over 50 years, the main purpose of any rehabilitation assessment was to determine employability. Exploration of job potential was seen as the primary goal of vocational evaluation. Although job-related factors are still vitally important, other assessment goals have been introduced since the beginning of independent living legislation in 1978. This legislation facilitated the growth of independent living services. The movement itself has reshaped the thinking of disability professionals and researchers, generating new service delivery models and encouraging new research directions (DeJong, 1978).

Independent living is a general term describing a situation in which a disabled individual is able to live as independently as possible. The application of the concept of independent living has provoked different interpretations. Some speak of it in terms of services that might not have an immediate employment objective and are over and above those traditionally provided. Others explain it from a more philosophical and political perspective in terms of a person exercising control over his or her life based on options that minimize dependence upon agencies, institutions, family, and, to some degree, the very services that the professionals are eager to provide (Galvin, 1980; Wright, 1981). However, the essence of independent living is a person controlling his or her life, based on the choice of acceptable options that minimize reliance on others when making decisions and performing everyday activities. It refers to the ability of the severely disabled person to participate actively in society—to work, own a home, raise a family, and participate to the fullest extent possible in normal activities.

Although the concept of independent living is very broad, it focuses upon the individual. This focus necessarily includes many levels of functional independence. But independent living is not dependent upon particular programs that foster functional independence. Rather, it is based upon the individual's ability to choose and achieve a desired life-style and to function freely in society. Independent living, consequently, can be achieved by a wide variety of actions and/or services. DeJong (1978) identified six services that have become closely associated with the movement for independent living: advocacy services, peer counseling, attendant care services, the removal of architectural barriers, adapted housing, and adapted transportation.

The 1978 Rehabilitation Amendments, particularly Titles VI and VII, identify both special employment opportunities for the handicapped and comprehensive services, the latter including services for severely disabled individuals, centers for independent living, independent living services for the older blind, and protection and advocacy for the rights of severely handicapped individuals. The special employment opportunities emphasize community services employment pilot programs for handicapped individuals and projects with industry. In other words, these amendments state that vocational services may be offered to those for whom competitive employment may not be a reality in the proximate or perhaps distant future. The legislation further suggests that before employment can be considered, a severely disabled's quality of life must be enhanced. With this restoration into ''independent living,'' vocational goals might become feasible.

When a disabled individual comes for rehabilitation-related services and wants to make the transition from dependent to independent living, an assessment should be conducted to determine what are the client's residual capabilities and what services are needed to bridge the ''dependent'' to ''independent'' gap. Wright (1981) believed that the determination of functional limitations and capacities is the basic evaluation. The main focus of the assessment is actually how the disability limits independence (Boland and Alonso, 1982). Wright (1981) also explained that evaluation information

> . . . should be closely related to assessment goals: the interpretation of living skills as they relate to present task performance ability; the determination of required client services (e.g., adjustment training, recreation therapy, assistive devices); and the provision of environmental modification or equipment redesign (p. 738).

In other words, evaluation can also identify what skills the client needs in order to function successfully in the community. Social skills, personal care skills, and community survival skills, for example, are not only critical to job placement but are essential for effective daily living.

The rehabilitation professional is confronted with the necessity of utilizing a rather broad assessment approach. This approach should not only identify the needed services for independent living but also the client's functional capacities which, through development and some environmental modification, could be used in some kind of employment. The model of client functioning (see Chapter 1) pinpoints the many functional capacities that are relevant to both independent living and eventual employment. The beginning of any relevant approach, however, is to determine the special goals or the particular focus of the evaluation. This chapter outlines various areas that should be explored in independent living and then discusses some approaches to evaluate these areas.

## FOCUS OF INDEPENDENT LIVING ASSESSMENT

Individuals participating in an evaluation for independent living rehabilitation/ habilitation usually represent many different levels of disabilities and have needs which are also quite different. Some individuals who have little developed capability seem to have considerable potential that can be developed through a training process. Others may have only a few problems in living independently, and the evaluation should be comprehensive enough so as to identify client areas that offer the greatest possibility for training and eventual work adjustment. The assessment should also be more client-centered, with the opportunity for the client to make choices and decisions throughout the evaluation process.

One goal of the evaluation should be to explore independent living tasks that can lead to greater life satisfaction from achievement in the areas of socialization, personal care, and vocational skills. Assessment then focuses upon movement capability, manual dexterity, personal grooming, home-making activities, transportation capabilities, and personal management concerns. Practitioners (Halpern, 1982; Wright, 1981) in the independent living field suggested that many possible skill areas be explored when considering the eventual feasibility of a vocational direction. Five areas, in particular, should receive assessment attention:

1. *Transportation and Mobility*   Can the client walk to a training facility or job? If public transportation is available, is the client able to take the bus? Is a bus or van available that can be used? Are friends or family free and willing to take the client to training or a job? Is the client able to learn to drive?

2. *Communication*   Are clients able to express their needs in an acceptable manner? Are they able to understand what the employer and co-workers are saying or gesturing for them to do? If the client uses sign language, what system is utilized, e.g., American Sign Language, Total Communication, Finger Spelling or miming?

3. *Self-Care and Appearance*   These areas should include toileting, independence, eating, neatness, independence in selected dressing skills, and oral hygiene skills.

4. *Socialization*   Does the client show behaviors that are antisocial or seriously maladaptive? In the positive direction, does the client display social behaviors that elicit favorable or accepting response from others? These include smiling, appropriate greeting, initiating verbal communications, and responding appropriately to friendly questions.

5. *Functional Reading and Computation*   These skills may only have to be evaluated when employability is being explored, and then only after a job analysis has been performed and the target skills necessary for the completion of the job have been identified.

In other words, the rehabilitation professional should evaluate the degree of independence that has been reached, what help (training, equipment, or attendant care) is required, and what the person's overall performance in selfcare is at home and traveling (Wright, 1981). Added to these concerns are activities relevant to the work setting. Furthermore, a necessary goal of independent living evaluation is an assessment of the client's psychosocial environment. In assisting the move toward independence, parental influence that might, for example, facilitate or deter this transition should be assessed. Do family members perceive the person as living independently? If so, will they continue their support throughout the process of achieving independence? Parents may show overprotective behaviors and encourage their son or daughter to give up their independent living center. An understanding of these behaviors may prevent difficulties from turning into overwhelming obstacles to the client's independence.

With family considerations, an independent living assessment should include the client's ability to handle money, prepare food, perform general household tasks, make sound judgments concerning personal safety, and undertake personal relationships. To obtain information about these areas, the rehabilitation professional can ask: "What type of bills are you responsible for?" "Can you make a bed?" "How do you cope with distress?" "What hobbies or interests do you have and is there anyone with whom you enjoy doing these hobbies?" Also, knowing the client's present and past living arrangements is important, for a transition to a more independent living situation may have to be made in order for the client to reach productive, employment-related goals.

During the entire assessment process, the client should gradually become aware of self-strengths and capacities. A knowledge of these assets will facilitate more appropriate decision-making. According to Schwab (1981), further characteristics of the evaluation process for independent living are:

*Flexibility*   Assessment programs should allow for the wide spectrum of client capability because some individuals have few problems in living independently while others have little developed capacity.

*Realistic standards*   What criteria can be used to measure client capability? The evaluation process must center on the next steps in a client's self-development program because independent living tasks should lead to greater life satisfaction in the areas of socialization, personal care, and vocational skills.

*Usability*   The assessment should be conducive to client decision making and efficient in the use of staff time.

*Ethicality*   The evaluation program should not require information that would invade individual privacy rights.

Using some general guidelines for assessment in independent living, the rehabilitation professional should consider agency and client needs in examining more particular approaches and ascertaining which one is the most appropriate. After careful review of many approaches, several assessment measures are recommended, many of which contain primarily structured lists of activities or tasks performed by the disabled person under the observation of the rehabilitation professional. Further information for the particular evaluation tool may be provided verbally by the client. Generally, these instruments do not reflect vigorous psychometric methods but do resemble some of the situational techniques used in work evaluation (Wright, 1981). Measurement criterion issues, such as validity, reliability, standardization in administration, and norms are not that fully developed in these recommended evaluation activities. Wright (1981) explained that:

> Performance measures of ADL (Activities of Daily Living) can reflect a variety of factors, including: time, speed, quality, endurance, improvement with practice, effect of personal variables (e.g., incentives), effect of environmental variables (e.g., assistive devices) (p. 741).

When completed, these measures represent a valuable source of information for rehabilitation planning purposes. They assist the professional in recognizing those deficits that need remediation for community living. Developmentally disabled persons and others who have been institutionalized or sheltered may not have had the opportunity to participate in ordinary life experiences (Wright, 1981). To become independent, many must learn community living skills, such as budgeting, personal hygiene and attire, shopping, socializing, and relating to other people.

Descriptions of these evaluation tools have been modified from a publication entitled: "Client Assessment Measures in Rehabilitation," a Federal grant-supported research project of the Rehabilitation Research Institute, University of Michigan.


## EVALUATION TOOLS


### Barthel Index—Granger Adaptation

The Barthel Index[1] (originally named the *Maryland Disability Index*) was developed by F. I. Mahoney and D. W. Barthel in 1965 and modified by Carl V. Granger in the mid 1970s. This scale, a measure of functional limitations, assesses the degree to which a person can function independently in performing ADL, including self-care, mobility, and bladder and bowel control. The index

---

[1]Additional information about the Barthel Index can be obtained from Carl V. Granger, M.D., Director, Brown University/The Memorial Hospital, Institute for Rehabilitation and Restorative Care, Family Care Center, 89 Pond St., Pawtucket, RI. 02860, or Maureen McNamara, Coordinator, Medical Rehabilitation Evaluation Center, 89 Pond St., Pawtucket, RI. 02860. Phone: 401-725-0980.

is a behaviorally anchored scale, containing 15 items. The areas investigated include the following: feeding, bathing, grooming, dressing, toilet transfers, chair/bed transfers, ambulation, stair climbing, and bladder and bowel control.

The index is designed for use with physically disabled clients in particular. It was originally developed for hospital/rehabilitation settings but has been widely used in other settings, such as state vocational rehabilitation agencies. The index may provide case managers with a quick reference that can be used to help indicate general patterns in improved client functioning in personal ADL and the general level of assistance a client needs. It may also help determine the functional prognosis before stroke rehabilitation and in studies of cost-effectiveness.

In completing the index, it is necessary to observe or interview the client or professionals working with the client. Minimal professional judgment is needed. The value of each item is based on the patient's independence versus need for assistance in performing an activity. The preferred scoring system consists of four levels of rating on the dependence-independence continuum. (A three-level system can be used when raters are not optimally trained or ratings are completed by telephone or from the records.) The higher the score, the higher the degree of independence. A score of 0 indicates complete dependence. A total score is calculated by summing the ratings of the 15 items, providing an indication of the severity of the disability. The range of possible scores and the corresponding severity classifications are as follows: 0–20, totally dependent; 21–60, severely dependent; 61–80, moderately dependent; 81–99, slightly dependent; and 100, independent. The index can be completed by hand and a severity of disability score obtained in approximately 5 minutes.

Concerning reliability, 307 severely disabled adults, former patients at 10 geographically selected comprehensive medical rehabilitation centers, were subjects in a study in which the Barthel Index was administered. Test/retest reliability was 0.89, and intercoder reliability was above 0.95.

The use of the Barthel Index as a functional assessment instrument measuring personal care need was examined in a study of 89 chronically ill patients who were living at home but receiving basic care services. On an individual basis, the Barthel score was correlated with the total number of tasks that the individual could perform independently. There was a 0.91 correlation, significant at the 0.00001 level.

Used properly, the index measures the client's level of independence in personal ADL. A second advantage is that it can be completed quickly. Some of the limitations of the Barthel Index include the following: 1) it defines the need for personal care assistance only; 2) it must be supplemented with other assessments for determining eligibility or developing rehabilitation plans; and 3) the evaluation does not detail the tasks to be performed in a rehabilitation training program, except by the categories that are assessed.

## California Client Gains Scale

The Research section of the California Department of Rehabilitation began to develop this measure[2] in 1979 as part of its Independent Living Research Study. This scale is intended to measure change in clients served at independent living centers and consists of 93 items covering demographic and disability information as well as different aspects of a client's life: financial skills, use of leisure and productive time, activities of daily living skills, health skills, and use of medical services, social and psychologic well-being, and housing. (The housing items were not used in the final analysis because of their poor quality). A variety of response types are used: multi-point scales, agree/disagree, yes/no, and a few short answer fill-ins.

The measure is designed for use with independent living center clients. A shortened version of this scale has also been developed. This *California Independent Living Survey* is useful as a client outcome measure in various applications with independent living centers. Except for a new housing scale, all of the items were taken from the original form. An item/total correlation analysis was used to reduce the scale from the original form to a more practical 30-item scale, which can be completed in approximately 15 minutes.

This is a self-administered scale to be completed at intake and at two or more points after the client has been receiving services from a center—at about 6-month intervals for perhaps 18 months. Coding values are assigned to each or as a composite of all of the skill areas. Difference scores for groups of clients can be summed and averaged. A *t*-test can then be used to determine if a significant change has occurred.

A reliability test was conducted from pilot test data gathered in two independent living centers in southern California. After item analysis was performed to remove ineffective scale items, a Hoyt reliability coefficient of 0.87 was obtained. Two validity studies were conducted. The first compared the gain scores for clients having achieved independence with those of a sample of independent living center intake clients. The developers reported that the results indicated that the scale does measure independence as the word is used in independent living centers. The second study compared the scores of independent living center clients living in institutions with those of clients living on their own. Again, the developers reported significant results in the expected direction.

The developers felt that the Gains Scale may be an alternative to the functional assessment approach, which they feel is not suited for measuring

---

[2]Additional information about the California Client Gains Scale and the shortened version, the California Independent Living Survey can be obtained from: Gene Hiehle, Research Section, California Dept. of Recreation, 830 K St. Mall, Sacramento 95814. Phone: 916-322-8500.

client change in the independent living setting. The scale's length makes it too cumbersome to be useful in ongoing outcome evaluations.

## Functional Assessment Profile (FAP)

The FAP[3] was developed by an intra-agency task force within the Massachusetts Rehabilitation Commission in 1976. The FAP identifies a client's functional assets and liabilities in the rehabilitation process.

Ten functional areas related to the performance of work and activities of daily living are assessed through the following means: open-ended behavior description; degree of limitation (i.e., asset, no limitation, minor limitation, or major limitation); compensation (i.e., fully compensated, partial compensation, no compensation now, or no possible compensation), and open-ended comments. The ten functional areas include problem solving, interpersonal relationships, communication, self-care, object manipulation, mobility, time management, energy reserved, self-direction, and work.

This measure is appropriate for all vocational rehabilitation clients. However, because of the time involved in completing the FAP, its use may be limited to particularly difficult cases, cases in Status 24, or transfer cases. Also, it is not necessary to administer the entire FAP to all clients; the most relevant of the ten functional areas may be addressed to a given individual.

The FAP is primarily used by counselors in order to facilitate the rehabilitation process: conducting preliminary diagnostic studies, determining eligibility/severity, evaluating the adequacy of the diagnostic study, developing the Individualized Written Rehabilitation Program (IWRP), and providing guidance and counseling. It is useful to supervisors for case evaluation and team consultation and to vocational evaluators in facilities. It is appropriate as a framework for clinical problem solving and not recommended as a rating tool for program evaluation.

The FAP is completed by the counselor on the FAP Grid, although the client and others involved in the client's rehabilitation can play a part as well. A *User's Guide* is provided that includes instructions, relevant definitions, possible questions for obtaining necessary information, and several short case studies as examples. The counselor should be trained in behavioral observations and familiar with the definitions and directions in the *User's Guide*. It is recommended that the counselor review an actual case with a person already trained in the profile's use for greatest ease in utilizing the FAP.

Assessment can be made through the rehabilitation process in order to monitor progress toward the client's goal. Administration time can vary from a

---

[3]The FAP, including *User's Guide* and *Trainer's Guide*, can be obtained from the Staff Development Unit, Massachusetts Rehabilitation Commission, 20 Providence St., Boston, MA. 02116. Phone: 617-727-2183.

few minutes to 3 hours, depending on the application of the profile. A quick screening of a case for information requirements or the assessment of one functional area can take about 10 to 20 minutes. However, sorting out all of the information acquired through a thorough diagnostic study into functional capacities and limitations and planning for the IWRP can take up to 3 hours.

Because the profile is not a rating scale or a test, there is no scoring procedure. There is no evidence of reliability or validity. Plans for such studies were discarded when the developers ascertained that it was best utilized as a framework for clinical problem solving rather than a rating instrument.

This system of functional assessment is flexible. It allows the counselor to analyze and use the information gathered on a client as it makes sense to him or her. Also, a connection between the assessment of the client and planning for treatment is established through the compensation section.

Regarding limitations, the assessment itself cannot be any better than the clinical skills of the counselor doing the assessment. Second, use of the profile demands comfort in expressing medical concepts in behavioral terms. Third, the profile is only useful as a clinical tool and not for program evaluation or statistical comparison.

## Functional Life Scale (FLS)

The FLS[4] was developed by John E. Sarno, Martha T. Sarno, and Eric Levita at the Institute of Rehabilitation Medicine of the New York University Medical Center in 1973. The FLS is designed to quantitatively measure an individual's ability to participate in basic activities common to most people. It focuses on functions actually performed rather than on the capacity to perform or the elements which constitute performance. It can be used to assess disability and functional limitations and to measure client change as a result of participation in rehabilitation programs.

The FLS contains 44 items designed to assess five categories: Cognition, Activities of Daily Living (ADL), Activities in the Home, Outside Activities, and Social Interaction, which includes Vocational Status. The four qualities of Self-Initiation, Frequency, Speed, and Overall Efficiency are rated for each item, where appropriate. Each item is rated for these qualities along a five-point scale, designed as follows: 0—Does Not Perform Activity At All; 1—Very Poorly; 2—Deficient; 3—Approaches Normal; and 4—Normal.

The FLS is designed for use with all disabled clients who are in their homes and the community. The ultimate concern is how the client functions in the real world. The FLS is useful to both case managers and program managers.

---

[4]The FLS can be obtained from: John E. Sarno, M.D., Institute of Rehabilitation Medicine, 400 East 34th St., New York 10016. Phone: 212-340-7300.

For case managers, it provides an indication of the client's functioning and may be useful in identifying problem areas and needed services. For program managers, the FLS provides an indication of the severity of the disabilities of the client population, which is useful in program planning. Change scores alert program managers and case managers of the success or failure of their programs. Because inappropriate items can be omitted, the flexibility of the FLS is increased.

The FLS requires a combination of self-report and professional judgment. It can be administered before, during, and/or following the rehabilitation process. Raters must be trained to make accurate judgments, but it is not necessary that the raters be physicians because medical judgment is not required.

Total scores for each item are calculated by summing the quality ratings for that item. It is this total score that is important because it defines what the client actually does. Because the same score can be achieved for various reasons, total scores for the various qualities can be used to determine the contribution of such factors as motivation and speed. Scores for a given category (e.g., Cognition) are taken as a proportion of the possible maximum score after adjustment for items that are not applicable.

Concerning reliability, test/retest reliability was assessed through the Pearson product moment coefficient of correlation. The $r$ values for each of the raters for self-initiation scores, 0.90; frequency scores, 0.90; speed scores, 0.90; overall efficiency scores, 0.88; and overall scores, 0.91, were all significant beyond the 0.001 level, establishing the stability of the ratings over time.

Concurrent validity of the FLS was estimated by comparing its ratings with the external and independent "clinical judgment" of the physiatrist. The physiatrist ranked 31 patients on a nine-point scale after completing clinical examinations. Comparisons between clinical evaluation and FLS ratings, using the Spearman rank order correlation, yielded a value of 0.69, $p < 0.001$ of the basis of a two-tailed test. The results show a relatively high degree of congruence between ratings on the FLS and independent clinical estimates by a physiatrist.

A major advantage of the FLS is that it provides a quantitative measure of a very nebulous but important clinical dimension. It focuses on actual functioning rather than on the abilities to function. This approach avoids the discrepancies often found between ability and behavior, which are sometimes influenced by the interactive influence of physical, psychologic, social, economic, and cultural factors. Concerning limitations, the FLS requires further standardization and the derivation of norms on larger populations and different types of disabled persons (i.e., those with multiple sclerosis, Parkinson's disease, or epilepsy).

**Independent Living Behavior Checklist (ILBC)—Experimental Edition**

The ILBC[5] was developed by Richard T. Walls, Thomas Zane, and John E. Thvedt at the West Virginia Rehabilitation Research and Training Center and was copyrighted in 1979. The ILBC provides a measure of objective skills relevant to independent living by defining the degree to which a client or trainee, using whatever adaptive devices required, can function without constant aid and/or supervision.

The ILBC is a list of 343 independent living skill objectives specified in terms of conditions of performance, specific behavior, and standards of performance. The objectives assess skills in the following six categories: Mobility Skills, Self-Care Skills, Home Maintenance And Safety Skills, Food Skills, Social and Communication Skills, and Functional Academic Skills.

The ILBC is useful for any client whose independent living skills need to be identified and/or developed. Specific client groups might include mentally retarded, blind, quadraplegics, clients institutionalized for long periods of time, and the severely disabled. The ILBC can be used in a variety of settings, such as sheltered workshops, rehabilitation facilities, and educational/training programs.

The ILBC is valuable to various professionals associated with the rehabilitation and/or training of independent living clients. Counselors preparing Individualized Written Rehabilitation Plans (IWRPs) will find that the ILBC provides a means for setting goals and evaluating the client's progress. It defines independent living skills clearly, specifies a broad range of skills applicable to a variety of necessary ADL, and sets clear standards for mastery of skills. For program managers and program evaluation specialists, skill objectives are specified in terms of conditions, behavior, and standards, which permits documentation of client or trainee progress as well as a measure of the effectiveness of services and/or training. Additionally, the IBLC provides them a means for setting goals, determining accountability, documenting legislative requirements, and outlining an objectively specified curriculum for independent living skills. The flexibility of this instrument is heightened in that only skill objectives deemed relevant need to be used, and additional skill objectives can be developed as needed.

Using the ILBC requires professional judgment, but paraprofessionals can easily be trained. The ILBC can be administered as often as necessary for maintaining an accurate view of the client's competence. In some instances, a single assessment of skill objectives may be sufficient; in other cases, a periodic assessment of client or trainee skills is desirable. Administration is achieved by

---

[5]Copies of the ILBC and other pertinent information is available from the Publications Department, West Virginia Rehabilitation Research and Training Center, 1 Dunbar Plaza, Suite E, Dunbar, WV. 25064. A complete set of ILBC materials costs $8.00. Phone: 304-348-2375.

observing the client; the time necessary varies, depending on the number of objectives deemed appropriate for the individual client.

For scoring, a Skill Summary Chart and Skill Objective Profile are developed. The Skill Summary Chart is used as an overall record of all the skill objectives achieved by the client in all six categories. The skills mastered by the client in initial assessment and in training, as well as the date the skill was demonstrated or completed, are entered on the Skill Summary Chart. The dates that training was begun and completed (the skill was mastered) are recorded. The Summary column provides a concise view of the skill objectives mastered in either initial assessment or training, and so summarizing the individual client's progress to date in each skill category.

The Skill Objective Profile allows for a quick survey of overall client progress in each of the six skill categories. The profile is constructed by dividing the number of skill objectives mastered in a category by the total number of skill objectives considered applicable to the client in that category, multiplied by 100. The instrument is hand-scorable.

More than 200 behavior checklists were obtained from individuals, rehabilitation facilities, and schools in the United States and other countries. One hundred sixty-six of the checklists contained items relevant to independent living. Of these, the authors found 53 constructed well enough to suggest objective ways to assess independent living behaviors. The items were sorted into the six categories that make up the major divisions of the ILBC. Over-lapping or duplicate items were eliminated, and extensive rewriting and modification of the remaining items was undertaken to produce the item format. Some gaps in skill objective sequences were filled by creating new items. The authors reported that new skill objectives were derived from their work with vocational rehabilitation clients in sheltered workshops, deinstitu-tionalization training, rehabilitation facilities, or field-based rehabilitation programs.

Intra- and interrater reliability is high for the ILBC. What the authors claimed as ''high criterion-related validity'' should be reported as good content validity. No real criterion-related validity studies are reported in the usual sense of the term, namely, the prediction of examinees' performance on related behaviors as measured by some other means (Halpern et al., 1982).

The ILBC includes a manual that contains all test items and directions as well as blank recording forms to use for monitoring individual performance.

Two problems appear to exist with the ILBC. Because of the breadth of content that is covered, comprehensive assessment across domains requires much time and energy of both examiners and examinees. Also, several of the items are ambiguous, which leads to occasional difficulty in interpreting the outcome of assessment. These concerns notwithstanding, the ILBC seems to be an effective program-related approach to assessment (Halpern et al., 1982).

**Independent Living Assessment Instrument**

Developed in 1981 by Nancy Traxler, a rehabilitation counselor, and the Montgomery County Association of Retarded Citizens, this measure assists in the evaluation of a client for living independently, particularly in his or her own apartment. It also helps to identify the supports within the community that can help to attain and maintain this goal of independent living. It is designed to be used in an intake interview, which explores independent living skills. The questions cover the following areas: hygiene; personal cleanliness and clothing; apartment cleanliness and care; kitchen skills; body care; first aid;. emergency and safety; use of public transportation; community resources and leisure time; emotional behavior assessment; and financial responsibility.

The instrument consists of two pages of questions, intended as a guideline to follow during the interview session. The questions should be open-ended in order to elicit the maximum amount of informational conversation from the client. Because there is no time limit, a question may be re-asked or clarified. Some questions may lead to further information. The professional should especially listen for the following:

1.   What does the client want from the agency, service or housing program?
2.   Is the client realistic about independent living goals?
3.   Is this person ready to live independently?
4.   Which services are needed to help this person realize:
     His or her goal of living independently
     The level of independent living he or she will be able to achieve
     His or her ability to learn specific and necessary independent living skills
     The type of independent skills one will not be able to achieve
     Which supports will be needed to bridge this gap in a compensatory manner.

There have been no validity and reliability studies on this instrument, but rehabilitation professionals will find it particularly useful for obtaining relevant independent living information in the interview. Specific situations in which the measures could be used are:

1.   Social workers in a hospital, nursing home, or institution where they must find residential placement for persons, such as those who have lost their level of care and the concomitant reimbursement level under the state's Medicaid program
2.   Rehabilitation counselors in a state agency when a feasible vocational goal cannot be immediately determined
3.   Peer counselors in an Independent Living Service Center
4.   Family therapists working with a family with one handicapped member, and where independent living becomes an issue and a goal for that family's therapy

The Independent Living Assessment Instrument is reprinted in the Chapter Appendix.

## PARTICULAR ASSESSMENT ISSUES IN INDEPENDENT LIVING

The usual process of independent living rehabilitation is client-centered, inductive in nature, and the status of the client is recognized as dependency (Boland and Alonso, 1982). The type of intervention is dictated by the type of problem, i.e., housing, transportation, health, etc. The goal of independent living rehabilitation is need reduction, and perhaps when this is achieved, vocational goals can be developed for the client.

In working with the client for independent living goals, especially when assessment is going to be conducted, the rehabilitation professional should have special information about the additional needs of these most severely handicapped people and the appropriate resources available (Wright, 1981). With this knowledge, the professional should pay particular attention to the role of counseling. Counseling in independent living rehabilitation is critical to client success, and professional preparation is needed. Issues like adjustment to disability, utilization of functional capabilities, and assertiveness can become focuses of counseling. Counseling needs may also be developed from the assessment situation.

Implied in the utilization of the different measures described in this chapter is the variety of settings in which these measures can be used. The following are the recommended applications of these instruments:

1.  Intake interview for state agency to determine independent living needs:
    a.  FLS
    b.  FAP
    c.  Barthel Index—Granger Adaptation
    d.  Independent Living Assessment Instrument
    e.  ILBC
    *(Except for the FLS, the administration times for the above measures are somewhat lengthy. However, they can be utilized as guidelines for the interview. Also, the FAP may be limited to particularly difficult caes, and it is not necessary to administer it in its entirety to all clients.)*
2.  Assessment conducted in a hospital or nursing home, and independent living centers:
    a.  California Client Gains Scale
    b.  Barthel Index—Granger Adaptation
    c.  Independent Living Assessment Instrument
    d.  FLS

There is considerable overlap, however, with all of these measures and their use may depend upon availability, professional training, and the amount of time needed to complete the instrument. Added concerns may be the validity and reliability studies associated with a specific measure, although these studies with each instrument either do not exist or are quite limited.

## CONCLUSION

Although the assessment approaches identified in this chapter are not exhaustive, they still provide an understanding of the many evaluation opportunities available for the severely disabled. With this population, there are multiple rehabilitation outcomes, goals which are consistent with provisions in the Rehabilitation Act of 1973 and its amendments and reflected in the funding support for research and demonstration projects on independent living rehabilitation. Rehabilitation focuses upon the restoration of the individual to the maximal level of functioning possible: medically, physically, mentally, psychologically, vocationally, and economically. The preceding pages provide some guidelines for determining the capabilities of clients to reach these goals. It is a determination vital to effective rehabilitation efforts.

## CASE STUDY

*Jane, age 27, is a quadraplegic residing in a nursing home for 2 years. Eighteen months before this living arrangement, she was seriously injured in an automobile accident, which killed her mother and best girlfriend. Jane's father passed away when she was age 11. After prolonged medical treatment in a rehabilitation hospital, she was transferred to the nursing home because of her need for continued care and the identified absence of any relatives to provide support. The medical staff now feels, however, that Jane should consider a more independent living arrangement. To the staff she seems anxious to explore other alternatives to her present care arrangements. She often talks to the very few younger patients of her need to socialize with more young adult people. She is confined to a motorized wheelchair and needs assistance with toileting, dressing, and related self-care activities. With mechanical devices, she has some use of her hands and arms and can feed herself, although with difficulty.*

*Before her injury, Jane was employed as an executive secretary with a large legal firm. She shared an apartment with her best friend (the one who was killed in the car accident). She was an active member of her church and also enjoyed sewing. Jane mentions that she has been very unhappy in the nursing home and has experienced many periods of depression. As a rehabilitation professional, you have been asked to interview Jane in order to explore the possibility of a transfer to an independent living center.*

1.  How would you evaluate Jane's willingness to live independently?
2.  From the assessment resources described in this chapter, what measure do you believe would be the most appropriate to evaluate Jane's independent living capabilities?
3.  How would you involve Jane in the independent living assessment?


## REFERENCES

Boland, J., and Alonso, G. 1982. A Comparison: Independent living rehabilitation and vocational rehabilitation. J. Rehab. Jan./Feb./March:56–59.
DeJong, G. 1978. The movement for independent living: Origins, ideology, and implications for disability research. A paper presented at the annual meeting of the American Congress of Rehabilitation Medicine, New Orleans, LA, November 17th.
Galvin, D. 1980. Policy issues in independent living rehabilitation. A paper presented at the 1980 World Congress of Rehabilitation International, Winnipeg, Manitoba, Canada, June 22–27.
Halpern, A., Lehmann, J., Irvin, L., and Heiry, T. 1982. Contemporary Assessment for Mentally Retarded Adolescents and Adults. University Park Press, Baltimore.
Schwab, L. 1981. Independent Living Assessment for Persons with Disabilities. Dept. of Human Development and the Family, Lincoln, NE.
Wright, G. 1981. Total Rehabilitation. Little, Brown, and Company, Boston.

# Chapter 11 Appendices

## Appendix A:
## INDEPENDENT LIVING
## ASSESSMENT INSTRUMENT

I.   **Independent Living Assessment** (Verbal)
     Goal:  *To discriminate ability for safe independent living within an*
            *an apartment setting*
     A.  Hygiene/Personal Cleanliness/Clothing
         1.  How did you dress today?
         2.  Did the weather outside influence your choice of clothes?
         3.  Do you like to take a bath or a shower?
         4.  Can you describe your routine for bathing or showering and
             dressing to me?
         5.  How do you shop for clothes? Do you like to go by yourself or
             with a friend?
         6.  When is it important to wash your hands?
         7.  How often do you brush your teeth?
         8.  How often do you wash your hair?
         9.  How do you handle hygiene when you have your period?
     B.  Apartment Cleanliness and Care
         1.  Do you do all of your own housekeeping? If you need help
             with it, who do you ask and how?
         2.  What would you do if your toilet backed up onto the bathroom
             floor?
         3.  Where is the garbage kept?
         4.  What would you do if you saw bugs in your apartment?
         5.  Who would you call if:
             a.  The sink was clogged?
             b.  Something was broken?
             c.  The heat was not working?
         6.  Do you have a special day to do your laundry? Do you do it
             with assistance or independently?

C.  Kitchen Skills
    1.  What are your favorite meals to cook?
    2.  Tell me about the word "nutrition."
    3.  Do you shop for food on your own, or with another person?
    4.  Can you show me where you keep:
        a.  TV dinners?
        b.  Hamburger, other meats?
        c.  Cheese
        d.  Unopened cans of fruit?
        e.  Open cans of food?
        f.  Milk?
        g.  Cereal?
    5.  What happens to food when the refrigerator breaks?
    6.  How can you tell if food is spoiled?
    7.  Can you show me how you:
        a.  Wash dishes?
        b.  Broil a steak?
        c.  Bake chicken
        d.  Boil eggs; water?
        e.  Defrost freezer?
        f.  Clean floor?
        g.  Store paper products?
        h.  Clean refrigerator?

D.  Body Care/First Aid/Emergencies/Safety
    1.  What happens when you are sick?
    2.  What would you do if you cut your finger and it was bleeding?
    3.  When might you need to call the emergency number?
    4.  When do you stay home from work because of not feeling well?
    5.  Do you have a doctor whom you see when you are not feeling well? When have you needed to call him?
    6.  If someone has a seizure, what could you do?
    7.  What would you do if you smelled smoke or suspected a fire?
    8.  If there were a fire in your building, what would you do?
    9.  Are there precautions you can take to avoid having a fire occur in your apartment?
   10.  When someone knocks at your door, do you open it right away?
   11.  If someone were breaking into your apartment, what would you do?
   12.  When someone buzzes your apartment, do you check to see who it is before allowing them to enter the building?

E.   Use of Public Transporation/Community Resources/Leisure Time
1.   How often do you take the metro bus?
2.   How did you learn the routes that you use?
3.   How do you find out about new activities?
4.   Do you travel alone at times? Are there times when you prefer going with a friend?
5.   How do you get to the grocery store? Is there a 7-11 or something similar nearby for quick trips?
6.   How do you spend evenings home alone when nothing special is going on?


II.   **Emotional/Behavior Assessment** (Verbal)
Goal:   *To assess social coping skills and appropriate ways of handling independent living issues*
A.   Do you have any special friends you feel very close to and spend a lot of time with?
B.   How do you handle problems between you and your close friends?
C.   How do you let people know you like them?
D.   How do you handle disagreements between you and your roommate (if applicable)?
E.   Tell me some wrong ways to handle anger.
F.   Do you feel angry at times? How do you handle it?
G.   Have you ever liked being interested in the same man (woman) as a friend of yours? What did you do?
H.   Have you ever had a problem at work because you lost your temper? How did it work out?
I.   What is the difference between borrowing and stealing?


III.   **Financial Responsibility**
A.   Do you have bills to pay?
B.   How do you remember to pay bills?
C.   What happens when you forget to pay a bill?
D.   Do you have a savings account?
E.   Do you have a checking account?
F.   What do you do with your check when you get it?
G.   Can you show me how you budget your money?
H.   Role play a financial transaction:
1.   paying rent
2.   going to store

# Appendix B:

# INTAKE ASSESSMENT RATING SCALE

1 = Very poor judgment; dependent on others
2 = Judgment impaired; some dependency
3 = Judgment fair; shows room for growth; some dependency
4 = Judgment OK; slight dependency
5 = Shows good judgment and independence

**I.    Independent Living Assessment**

| A. | | B. | | C. | | D. | | E. | |
|----|----|----|----|----|----|----|----|----|----|
| 1. | _____ | 1. | _____ | 1. | _____ | 1. | _____ | 1. | _____ |
| 2. | _____ | 2. | _____ | 2. | _____ | 2. | _____ | 2. | _____ |
| 3. | _____ | 3. | _____ | 3. | _____ | 3. | _____ | 3. | _____ |
| 4. | _____ | 4. | _____ | 4. | _____ | 4. | _____ | 4. | _____ |
| 5. | _____ | 5. | _____ | a. | _____ | 5. | _____ | 5. | _____ |
| 6. | _____ | 6. | _____ | b. | _____ | 6. | _____ | 6. | _____ |
| 7. | _____ | | | c. | _____ | 7. | _____ | | |
| 8. | _____ | | | d. | _____ | 8. | _____ | | |
| 9. | _____ | | | e. | _____ | 9. | _____ | | |
| | | | | f. | _____ | 10. | _____ | | |
| | | | | g. | _____ | 11. | _____ | | |
| | | | | 5. | _____ | 12. | _____ | | |
| | | | | 6. | _____ | | | | |
| | | | | 7. | _____ | | | | |
| | | | | a. | _____ | | | | |
| | | | | b. | _____ | | | | |
| | | | | c. | _____ | | | | |
| | | | | d. | _____ | | | | |
| | | | | e. | _____ | | | | |
| | | | | f. | _____ | | | | |
| | | | | g. | _____ | | | | |
| | | | | h. | _____ | | | | |

Subtotal:_____

**II.** **Emotional/Behavioral Assessment**
A. _____
B. _____
C. _____
D. _____
E. _____
F. _____
G. _____
H. _____
I. _____

Subtotal: _____

**III.** **Financial Responsibility**
A. _____
B. _____
C. _____
D. _____
E. _____
F. _____
G. _____
H. _____
    1. _____
    2. _____

Subtotal: _____

# chapter 12

# THE REHABILITATION PROFESSIONAL AS A CONSUMER

The previous chapters in this volume emphasize the rehabilitation professional as the main person to conduct the vocational assessment. Apart from the initial interview, however, evaluation services will many times be performed by another agency or professional. Chapter 6 on Personality Assessment discusses some reasons for utilizing other resources, such as the lack of training in the administration and interpretation of certain psychologic tests or the agency's decision that the evaluation of personality functioning be conducted by an identified "expert" in that field. The agency's policy could be that all clients must receive a comprehensive evaluation at a specific assessment center. Because of the in-depth assessment opportunities available at an evaluation center, including the specialized training of personnel, services for clients with particular problems might have to be purchased at this resource. When an evaluation is conducted by another agency, the referring rehabilitation professional is a "purchaser" of services. This chapter[1] discusses the many issues and questions that arise in these circumstances and suggests guidelines that can assist rehabilitation professionals in making good decisions when purchasing services.

## ISSUES WHEN PURCHASING SERVICES

### Reason and Time To Evaluate

As the first chapter in this book indicates, clients who present themselves for rehabilitation services bring different goals, varied emotional reactions to their

[1]The author wishes to acknowledge Mr. Joe Shulpulski, Vocational Evaluator, Department of Vocational Rehabilitation, Maryland for his many ideas shared in conversation, which have resulted in the development of the material in the first part of this chapter.

disability experience, and assorted personal needs. After a client is determined eligible for receiving services from a particular agency, then the rehabilitation professional judges what kinds of evaluation would develop an appropriate rehabilitation plan. A physical examination, possibly a psychiatric exam for understanding mental health status, and vocational evaluation are usually the necessary components of this overall evaluation.

The professional should substantiate any beginning hunches about the emotional, physical, and intellectual levels of the client's capabilities. He or she should also update any information in the client's record that also indicates levels of functioning. Either need can serve as a rationale for vocational evaluation. From the time of the initial interview, the professional gains an estimate of what the client seeks from rehabilitation services. The goals of an independent living opportunity, immediate job, or the need to receive appropriate training will all influence what kind of vocational assessment should be pursued.

A good reason to use evaluation resources is when realistic information is needed to support a beginning awareness of a client's abilities or the professional believes that a standardized, sophisticated assessment can help to determine a client's complex functioning. Such resources, however, should not be utilized to keep the client busy for a period of time or, worse, to supply all the answers for the professional who has no idea of what the client can or wants to do. Many clients are also referred for evaluation as a matter of routine, even when the evidence of the client's potential is already available and there is no need to further substantiate this data. In these situations clients often feel that their pursuit of their own perceived rehabilitation goals is being unnecessarily delayed. Because of all these concerns, the initial meeting with the client should ascertain just what are the client's goals and how can vocational evaluation fit into the development of rehabilitation plans.

Timing is also important when referring the client for vocational evaluation services. Timing refers to when assessment should be conducted after a disability-inducing trauma, during hospitalization, or after long-term institutionalization. For most clients, the psychologic adjustment to their mental and physical limitations may take weeks, months, or even longer. Some persons never really adapt to disability-related limitations and prefer a life-style that expresses overdependence or a decided reluctance to become work-productive. Whatever the length of time, a period of psychologic adjustment is to be expected. As clients go through this process of emotional adaptation, feelings of anxiety, depression (with its concomitant anger, confusion, and uncertainty about the future), and helplessness may dominate. When the professional perceives that these feelings strongly exist, a formal, planned evaluation should be delayed. The presence of these emotions at the time of assessment can affect the reliability of the evaluation results.

Many rehabilitation professionals argue that assessment should not be delayed because the process itself could reduce these emotional feelings and thus facilitate the client's progress toward rehabilitation goals. They believe that imparting assessment results that emphasize the client's residual strengths could alleviate their perceptions of hopelessness. However, most disabled persons do need some emotional adaptation to the disability before formal assessment begins. Yet, clients who request rehabilitation services for themselves or who show impatience to be employed again suggest a more positive attitude and psychologic readiness that is conducive to involvement in vocational assessment.

## Formulating Specific Questions

After a client receives vocational evaluation services from another agency, the assessment results are reported to the referring source. This report is crucial to the rehabilitation professional, who is responsible for the case management of the client's rehabilitation, because it should contain information that can be directly used for rehabilitation planning. Yet, this report often conveys testing results and recommendations in impractical language or jargon. Therefore, at the time of referral, questions should be directed to the evaluation source that, in turn, will generate responses feasible for the development of rehabilitation goals. It is assumed that vocational evaluation explores the client's level of intelligence, achievement, and personality functioning as well as his or her interest areas. Many tests that are traditionally used for intelligence and personality assessment, such as the WAIS, the Thematic Apperception Test, and the House-Tree-Person, can also provide information about the client's vocational functioning. What is needed when these measures are used is a rehabilitation perspective offered by the referring source. This direction is developed by the rehabilitation professional's questions suggested at the time of initial referral. The following are some questions which, when asked by the referring source, help to explore the client's job readiness:

1. Is the client aware of activities and situations that would tend to aggravate the disability or impair his or her general health?
2. What aspects of the client's emotional functioning could be viewed as obstacles to appropriate job adjustment?
3. What does the particular assessment measure indicate about those client emotional strengths and achievement areas that can facilitate his or her adjustment to a work environment?
4. What is the relationship between the identified client interest areas and the client's capabilities as indicated by the vocational evaluation?

Of course, there are other questions that can also solicit information about the client's more specific interest areas and behaviors. For example, are the client's behaviors appropriate for such usual job demands as punctuality, attention to a task, and following directions? Importantly, the usefulness of the report from an evaluation agency or professional is largely determined by the type of questions asked.

## What Is the Best Type of Evaluation for the Client?

As discussed earlier in this book, there are many disabled clients for whom the traditional measures of vocational assessment would not be appropriate. For many of the severely disabled, for example, standard aptitude tests emphasize verbal directions, providing little information that can be translated into suitable plans for education and training. Rehabilitation professionals, therefore, must look elsewhere for assessment resources for this population. The professional should carefully appraise the available evaluation resources and determine what resources would provide the most usable information for rehabilitation purposes. For example, a rehabilitation counselor whose case load is mainly with the blind should utilize only those assessment resources that have valid and reliable measures for this client population. Types of assessments other than traditional paper-and-pencil tests will often have to be used. Work sample evaluation for certain clients can be a valuable source of diagnostic data, while a situational assessment might have a more far-reaching applicability than standard measures for the severely disabled.

*Work Samples*   One of the resources available for assessment purposes are the many commercial work sample systems. A work sample itself is a simulated task or work activity of an actual industrial operation. *Actual* work samples are taken directly from business or industry and reproduce the processes actually conducted there; *simulated* work samples are developed by evaluators to simulate jobs. The difference between the two is only a matter of emphasis; both identify either by observation or by measurement specific abilities. The results of a series of individual work samples are usually combined to develop a profile of client potential.

There are many advantages to using work samples, including: 1) the approximation to real-life jobs; 2) the opportunity to assess many personal characteristics in a controlled setting; 3) their appropriateness to the evaluation of many disabled groups, like brain-damaged deaf, and blind individuals; and 4) the realization that during the assessment process, clients can perceive themselves as involved in a work task rather than a test. However, there are some disadvantages to using this method. In its current form, work sample evaluation for the severely mentally retarded is still considered an unsatisfactory source of diagnostic data. The verbal nature of the instructions usually requires a higher language capability than severely retarded individuals commonly display. Also, a lack of standardization of work samples often exists; there is still no assurance that performance on the work samples always predicts performance in actual jobs; and commercial work samples are expensive and need periodic revision so they do not become obsolete.

Even with these limitations, work samples can be very valuable in the assessment of many handicapped persons. In order to use them, the rehabilitation professional must identify the resources in the client's community and what kind of work samples are being used in that agency. The rehabilitation professional should also determine whether the evaluations relate the client's performance on the work samples to the real world of work and, as a result of this type of evaluation, whether the client better understands the demands and expectations of a specific job or group of occupations.

Appendix C on p. 261 of this volume describes commercial work sample systems that are frequently used by different rehabilitation agencies. There is no intent to endorse any one commercial system, but this list could be helpful in identifying what particular system might be especially useful for a client.

***Situational Assessment***   When traditional tests for vocational assessment do not provide relevant information for rehabilitation planning with severely disabled clients, the possibilities of a situational assessment should be carefully explored. After the initial interview, the professional should have a beginning idea of what kind of vocational assessment to pursue. Also, when assessment questions are formulated, the approaches to evaluation and where to obtain reliable and valid information can be identified more easily.

Situational assessment is essentially the observation of people in work situations. It involves a practice of observing, evaluating, and reporting over a period of time. During this assessment, a client's behavior and work performance while working in a job situation with other employees is observed. This type of evaluation also helps the client learn the role of a worker, allows the evaluator to assess many more work behaviors than can be explored with either standardized vocational testing or work sample approaches, and minimizes the typical test-situation anxiety.

For situational assessment to be effective, an appropriate site should be utilized, adequate supervision provided, and a means used to gather information that, in turn, can be translated into rehabilitation planning. Because the observational approach is the basis of situational assessment, these observations must be carefully planned and scheduled, and well-designed rating and observation forms should be used. This demands that the rehabilitation professional understands the work evaluation opportunities in respective agencies, the experience and educational background of the staff, and what kind of ratings are utilized to record the situational assessment information.

## Preparing the Client

Once the decision is made to obtain a certain type of vocational evaluation and the facility or agency to conduct this assessment is selected, the client must be carefully prepared. This is the one area often neglected during the entire rehabilitation process. Assumptions are often made that either the assessment resource will perform this task or clients do not need any preparation apart from the name and address of the evaluation facility and the types of tests or assessment procedures that will be used. Yet, the worker can facilitate the reliability of the entire assessment experience by explaining the purpose of evaluation and how the results can aid the client in achieving realistic rehabilitation goals.

Imparting information and responding to the client's own questions and related concerns should be the focus of this preparation. Professionals should discuss with their clients the purpose of assessment, its part in the rehabilitation process, and how evaluation information can help to identify the client's strengths and indicate obstacles to reaching rehabilitation goals. Procedures that will be used in the assessment can also be explained and then advice given to the client about what is the best way to prepare mentally and physically for the evaluation. For example, getting a good night's sleep the night before and eating a good breakfast can contribute to a better performance during the evaluation. Additional knowledge that should be communicated includes the starting time, how long the assessment usually takes, and the transportation directions to the facility. Finally, the professional should mention that he or she will receive a report from the evaluation resource and will discuss it with the client. This can often alleviate client concerns about learning the assessment results. If it is the policy of the particular agency or other evaluation resource to carefully explain test results to the client, then this practice should be mentioned.

It is further suggested that the professional be alert to any signs of client hesitancy or ambiguity about being involved in evaluation. The possible source of this resistance should be identified. For example, many clients know from past experience that they test poorly. The thought of another possible failure experience arouses tremendous anxiety. Information about vocational evaluation opportunities, how the assessment results will be used, and the relationships between assessment and the world of work can all reduce some of this fear. When the client is told that the actual purpose of vocational evaluation is to identify strengths or capabilities that can be used for potentially satisfying, work-related goals, some of the threatening aspects of an upcoming assessment experience are minimized. Much of the anxiety may still remain with many clients, but at least they realize a supportive professional and understand why the evaluation is going to be conducted.

**Evaluating the Report**

Following the vocational evaluation, a report of the results is sent to the referring professional. When the report is received, the following questions should be considered:

1.  Did the report answer specific questions?
2.  Was the evaluation directed to areas that were needed for rehabilitation planning?

3. Are there unresolved discrepancies among the reported test evaluation results?
4. Does the report integrate all the information into a picture of the client that shows vocational capabilities, behaviors, and limitations that are usable for appropriate vocational planning?
5. What are the recommendations for the client? Are they too broad or too specific and are options given? Are the recommendations consistent with the test results? Are they realistic?

Of course, if the professional has serious concerns about the report, the evaluation resource should be contacted. Problems can often be reduced if the professional initially communicates his or her own expectations about the kind of information that should be obtained from the assessment.

All of the above questions represent issues that are to be explored when the professional purchases evaluation services. Acting as a skilled consumer can be just as important as being a well-trained vocational evaluator. After the rehabilitation professional evaluates the report received from the assessment resource, then a further exploration is often conducted with the client in order to determine areas of job feasibility. Or, when the professional has assisted the client to identify work-related interests and capabilities, then an understanding of available jobs and what the jobs demand is necessary. The latter determination can be accomplished through a job analysis.

When used properly, job analysis can generate ideas about whether a client can adapt to training or job demands and can further pinpoint those behavioral demands and work-related capabilities that are necessary to do a job effectively. Through this analysis, job modifications can also be made according to the client's functional limitations. Although job analysis is a skill that can be used frequently during the rehabilitation process, its use is especially important following the collection of assessment information and when counseling or planning is conducted with the client to identify appropriate, occupational objectives.

### Job Analysis Procedure

*Step 1* Identify the particular available jobs in the community. The state employment office, the Chamber of Commerce, and local civic organizations are a few resources for job openings. If available, placement personnel are also a valuable source of information. Whatever the job leads, the range of jobs found in various industries should be known.

*Step 2* Analyze the respective job, taking the job as it is and describing it. This analysis is a logical process to obtain information about the major tasks, setting, and worker qualifications of a specific job. The following outline is one way to do a job analysis. The author has found it very useful in his rehabilitation practice.

1. *The job name or title*    In describing a job, particular attention should be given to what differentiates this job from others. Although several titles may be used for a particular job, distinctive tasks must be emphasized. For example, a clerical job may involve taking dictation, typing, xeroxing, and filing. These functions may be given titles. But what functions does this particular job demand?

2. *What the worker does*    What are the skills involved in doing the job?
   a. What three or four work activities are really necessary to accomplish the purpose of the job?
   b. What is the relationship between each task, and is there a special sequence that the tasks must follow?
   c. Do the tasks necessitate sitting, standing, crawling, walking, climbing, running, stooping, kneeling, lifting, carrying, pushing, pulling, fingering, talking, seeing, listening, feeling, cooperating, muscular discrimination, depth of vision, color perception, oral instructions, written instructions, arithmetical computation, ability for oral expression, intelligence, and ability to handle people? All of these characteristics may be rated as to how important they are to the job. Note that the characteristics required to perform the job and not the characteristics of the present worker on the job are rated.
   d. What are the personality characteristics either required or suggested in order to perform the job successfully?
   e. To do this job, is previous training or experience required? If so, how much and is vocational, technical, or on-the-job training required?
   f. What is the level of required training and mental capabilities for performing the job adequately? For example, how complex is the job, and how much is required in terms of responsibility for the work of others, equipment, materials, and safety? Also, how much initiative, adaptability, mental alertness, and judgment are required?
   g. What specific knowledge is required for this job? This may include knowledge of machines, processes, materials, techniques, and policy and government regulations.

3. *How the worker does the particular task*    What tools, materials, and equipment are used? What are the methods and process used?

4. *The physical setting for the job*    This includes the pay scale, the hours and shifts, and the standards for productive output. What are the physical conditions of the job setting, such as hot, cold, damp, inside, outside, underground, wet, humid, dry, air-conditioned, dirty, greasy, odors, noisy, vibrations, hazards, high places, sudden temperature changes, toxic conditions, and working alone or around others?

Once information needed to perform a job analysis is understood, the worker must collect this information. The professional could utilize the *Dic-*

*tionary of Occupational Titles, 4th Edition*, which contains an abundance of facts about thousands of jobs. But not all work converts to a DOT classification; an available job in the community can be a combination of two or more jobs in the DOT. Also, when the DOT identifies the physical demands of a job, it is assumed that a person possesses the physical capabilities in an amount equal to that job. Without job restructuring or bioengineering, many handicapped people would be eliminated from such jobs.

There are other approaches to the development of a job analysis. A questionnaire can use the format suggested previously. People working in varied occupations who are most familiar with a particular job could then complete the questionnaire. Although a large amount of information can be obtained rapidly, the success of this method depends on the client's ability to provide accurate and easy-to-classify answers. Another method is to utilize an interview format to question employers about the duties and tasks of their jobs. Although this can be quite time-consuming, it gives the rehabilitation professional the opportunity to collect all the desired facts about a particular job. Also, employees could be observed performing their respective jobs at a work station. If this method is used, the information should be carefully recorded on a job observation form. This form could follow the guidelines of a job analysis.

Because the success of a job analysis is affected by the reliability of the information collected, a combination of methods can be used to obtain job information. Whatever the approach, however, job analysis itself is a valuable skill for the rehabilitation professional. It can help to identify the types of jobs that are physically, emotionally, and intellectually appropriate for disabled clients. Such identification can establish a perspective for the client's vocational evaluation.

## CONCLUSION

As a consumer, the rehabilitation professional has the continued opportunity to make choices about the types of services that can be provided for clients. Although the assessment needs of clients differ, the range of available evaluation services should be critically explored in order to plan how these needs will be identified and then met. As a knowledgeable consumer, the professional must identify assessment resources that provide the best chance for generating relevant information for rehabilitation planning. A relevant assessment for the particular client, especially if he or she is severely disabled, has been a rehabilitation problem for a long time. This problem can be minimized as rehabilitation professionals not only assume the role of an enlightened consumer as part of their responsibility but also provide choices for clients that reflect this understanding.

## CASE STUDY

*As a rehabilitation counselor at a state agency, you have interviewed Doris, age 20, who is determined that she is eligible for vocational re-habilitation services. Doris is single, and because of a recent automobile accident, her left hand was severed. Before the accident, she had been working for 3 years at a local factory that makes electrical appliances. She is a high school graduate, lives with her parents, and has been active in various social clubs. Because Doris is now eligible for rehabilitation serv-ices, her counselor believes that a comprehensive vocational evaluation is needed in order to help her be more aware of her employment related ca-pabilities and interests.*

With this information please answer the following questions.

1. What agencies in your community that offer vocational evaluation services would be appropriate for Doris' assessment, and what criteria would you use for this determination?
2. What specific question would you ask this resource in order to obtain suitable information for rehabilitation planning?
3. When talking with Doris before the vocational evaluation, you learn from her that she might be interested in employment as a saleslady or a buyer for a large retail store chain. How would you obtain a job analysis of these particular jobs?
4. How would you prepare Doris for the vocational evaluation experience?

chapter 13

# ASSESSMENT OF THE INDUSTRIALLY INJURED
## Implications for Private Rehabilitation Agencies

A staggering amount of time and money is spent each year attending to the needs of industrially injured workers. Since 1978, insurance companies have spent billions of dollars in employee benefits for disability insurance. Such benefits include medical and surgical expenses incurred because of on-the-job injuries, reimbursement for miles traveled to obtain services, the reception of two-thirds of the injured worker's average gross weekly pay, possibly a stipulated dollar award for loss of function of a body portion, and, if the worker is unable to return to his or her usual employment, the pursuit of a vocational rehabilitation program. These awards and compensation coverage, however, vary widely state to state.

In response to the growing incidence of workers who sustain catastrophic injuries, private rehabilitation firms were developed to assist disabled clients with rehabilitation goals. Working closely with insurance companies who provide compensation coverage, these private resources employ personnel to evaluate the rehabilitation potential of their clients, provide counseling for disability-related, adjustmental concerns, and, when possible, generate job placement opportunities.

Vocational rehabilitation in the private, profit-making sector usually involves three types of clients: 1) the client who returns to his former employer in the same or a modified position; 2) the disabled person who wants to go back to work but isn't sure what he wants to do; or 3) the client who wants to return to work but has no job-seeking skills. The range of disabilities seen in the private sector mainly includes orthopedic problems, with back injuries as the dominant disability. But there are frequently other difficulties associated with the disability. Workman (1983) indicated that the industrially injured worker may have other problems, such as secondary gains, conflicting party involvement, and lack of financial incentives. Many industrially injured persons receive tax-free compensation, for example, and these payments diminish the incentives to participate in a vocational rehabilitation program.

The vocational rehabilitation process pursued in this sector of human services is based upon models developed by the federal-state rehabilitation system. Yet the rehabilitation professional in private practice generates services "from specific referral instructions that may not be necessarily related to the total rehabilitation needs of the injured person." (Workman, 1983, p. 306) Many services could require extensive evaluation and then training in job-seeking skills. Or, assessment may be conducted only as part of a professional's preparation for trial testimony, with no other services provided. But job placement is a central goal for most efforts in the private, profit-making sector. Sanchez (1981), in defining vocational rehabilitation for the California workmen's compensation system, stated that it is "the process of restoring the injured worker to the competitive labor market at a wage level as close as practical to his/her pre-injury level as soon as possible" (p. 131).

Within the vocational rehabilitation process, there is an emphasis on job analysis, labor market surveys, physician visits, attorney contacts, and job placement (Workman, 1983). But the steps that the client may take to reach rehabilitation goals (Workman, 1983) are similar to those traditionally used by state agency programs. They include:

1.  Vocational rehabilitation evaluation
    Initial interview
    Qualified injured worker assessment
    Job analysis
    Information analysis - (medical, personal, social, work history, vocational testing/work evaluation, and labor market analysis)
2.  Development of vocational objectives
3.  Development of rehabilitation plan
4.  Plan implementation
5.  Job placement and follow-up
6.  Case closure

The key ingredient in this entire process is an appropriate, comprehensive evaluation of the injured worker's life situation, behavioral characteristics, and residual physical and intellectual capabilities. Although the ingredients of this assessment do not really differ in type from the evaluations previously discussed in this book, there is a difference of perspective. The injured worker may be receiving benefits or be involved in litigation; or, family influences could represent obstacles to rehabilitation goals and the many years spent in a particular job may be viewed as the culmination of employment efforts. All of these factors are discussed in this chapter, with particular attention given to assessment issues related to the development of different vocational objectives, an interpretation of the medical report, the client's emotional reaction to disability, the family's response to the client's disabling condition, and the professional's preparation for court testimony.

## ASSESSMENT ISSUES RELATED TO THE DEVELOPMENT OF DIFFERENT VOCATIONAL OBJECTIVES

The rehabilitation professional must determine whether the industrially injured worker is prepared to reenter the work situation or is even motivated enough to consider such possibilities and if so, then what training or similar preparation is needed to facilitate this return. A down-to-earth assessment should be made of those factors that affect employability. The interview is the beginning medium through which this evaluation is conducted. It can help to determine the vocational objectives that are feasible for the client. Chapter 2 of this book discusses the utilization of the interview for assessment purposes. It identifies the many areas that need to be explored. With the industrially injured, however, there are further considerations and modifications of the interview structure suggested in that chapter. The following is a recommended format for this interview that can generate information for rehabilitation planning purposes.

*Pre-Interview Period*   Before meeting with the client, all relevant case materials, such as medical reports and work history, should be reviewed. If there is any missing data, topics requiring additional exploration or validation should be identified. During the interview, such topics should be stressed. For example, if the client's records contain very little information about prior work history, this area should be carefully explored.

*Beginning the Interview*   The client's perception of himself or herself as a worker is particularly relevant to employability concerns. To assist clients in evaluating feelings about themselves, it is helpful if they are encouraged to talk about the accident, its emotional impact, and what their needs are if they believe they cannot return to their previous jobs. Early in the interview situation, clients should also discuss their life situations since the accident and their employment expectations for themselves. It is most helpful if the injured worker could also identify any compensatory work-related skills and what has been learned from the previous work experience. Included in this discussion could be such topics as:

1. What was the most satisfying experience in the client's previous job?
2. What is he or she looking for in a job?
3. What are the present limitations to continuing work?

*Conducting the Interview*   With the development of information on the client's current living situation and an awareness of the client's feelings and attitudes about working again, additional factors must be explored for rehabilitation planning. The following outlines these important areas and suggests questions to solicit the respective information:

1. Vocational goal
   a. What kind of a job would the client like to have?
   b. What are the client's preferences for certain types of work activities, such as clerical, outdoor, or service occupations?
   c. What specialized vocational skill training does the client possess, and does he or she have the interest and physical capability to pursue these skills?
   d. What are the areas of physical and mental difficulty that could prevent the client from achieving a vocational goal?
   e. Is there any relationship between the client's education and career possibilities?
2. Client significant factors
   a. What are the current legal involvements, and should vocational training or employment be delayed until these are resolved?
   b. What are the client's transportation needs?
   c. Are there any problems in using community resources?
   d. If necessary, could the client relocate?
   e. What is the attitude of the client's family towards reemployment, and what influences on rehabilitation does the family bring?
   f. Are there unique or particular financial needs that resulted from the accident and the disability?
3. Occupational job significant factors
   a. What credentials (such as education, training, memberships, licenses and certificates) does the client have for further employment?
   b. In previous employment, was the client able to do the job productively, efficiently, and accurately?
   c. What are the client's learning capabilities and speed of learning?
   d. Has the client been a dependable worker, and is he or she capable now of meeting attendance, promptness, and speed of production demands?
   e. In previous employment, was the client able to get along with co-workers and supervisors? Will the client's current emotional reaction to his or her disability be an obstacle to adjusting well to others in a work environment?
4. Getting a job
   a. Will the client be able to get a job, or must he or she be helped?
   b. Is the client able to prepare a personal information package for prospective employers?
   c. Does the client have the initiative to contact employers as well as make telephone inquiries and applications?
   d. Can the client participate appropriately in a job interview?

Such questions may not be generated from the interview, itself. But the interview should be able to provide some initial suggestions for the most feasible vocational objective. With an objective in mind, the rehabilitation professional in the private-for-profit sector can then plan, when necessary, a more detailed or formalized exploration of the injured worker's interests and aptitudes as well as current labor market opportunities. To assist in planning this assessment, the following guidelines are given for the different, possible vocational objectives:

1. Modified job
   a. The onset of a disability represents a discontinuity in what was previously a fairly constant self-concept/environmental interaction (Weinstein, 1983). The client's emotional reaction to the disability event should be evaluated (approaches to this assessment are provided in this chapter.) Often, temperaments must be re-explored to evaluate ongoing applicability to the modified occupational environment. This adjustment includes the abilities to handle job pressure, relationships to fellow workers, and a willingness to meet new job demands.
   b. A job analysis (see Chapter 12) should be conducted and then appropriate modifications made according to the willingness of the employer, the nature of the work environment, and the availability of technology to make the modifications.
2. Other work with same employer
   a. An essential evaluation for this objective is an analysis of transferable skills. Although the client may have a defined physical impairment that prevents return to the same job, many skills and aptitudes remain entirely unaffected. These residual capabilities can be quantified and recombined to meet the requirements of a different job (Weinstein, 1983). Field and Sink (1980), in their development of an evaluation approach, called "Vocational Diagnosis and Assessment of Residual Employability," highlighted five methods of skill identification and skill transference, which enable the professional to quantify the client's residual, occupational related assets:
      Measurement by valid tests
      Measurement by job history
      Measurement by worker's expressed preference
      Measurement by medical report
      A combination of the above
      Assessment by valid tests, job history, and expressed preference (determination of vocational interest) are discussed in other chapters of this book, and the medical report is explained later in this chapter. In addition, specific worker traits associated with past occupations should be identified. Sink and Field (1981) developed a manual method of compiling this data in which the professional collects and

summarizes the job demand characteristics of the individual's work experience, using the trait-factor profiles of the *Dictionary of Occupational Titles*. Once a composite profile is produced, it is altered to reflect the client's current, post-injury, functional capacities (Weinstein, 1983). The profile is stated in the language of jobs and is consistent with traits which were characteristic of the individual prior to the injury.

    b.   After the skill identification a job analysis of opportunities still available with the previous employer should be made.

    c.   Evaluation of the client's emotional adjustment to the disability should also be conducted.

3.   Direct Job Placement

    a.   An assessment of residual/transferable skills.

    b.   An evaluation of the client's emotional adjustment to disability.

    c.   An analysis of jobs currently available in the labor market.

    d.   An analysis of the client's job-getting and job-keeping behaviors, especially how the disabled person might present himself or herself in a job interview situation.

4.   On-the-job training or formal training

The same assessment should be conducted as with direct job placement.

5.   Self-employment

The same assessment as direct job placement can be given, with particular emphasis both on the client's capabilities to meet the distinctive demands of self-employment (e.g., independence, knowledge of business management) and the feasibility of the environment in which the client intends to establish a business.

Earlier chapters in this book provide more detailed information on the varied assessment approaches, each of which can be used for different occupational objectives. The previous employer may also have to be contacted because he or she can give valuable information about the client's work capabilities. Much of this exploration can be done while the client is still involved in litigation or compensation settlements. The injured worker could delay any decision about rehabilitation planning until some decision is reached. But vocational exploration should still be pursued, if for no other reason than to help the client realize that he or she possesses work-related capabilities. This awareness can become a beginning motivating factor for return to employment.

## THE MEDICAL REPORT

The appropriate use of medical information is invaluable to vocational evaluation and planning. When the rehabilitation professional has carefully reviewed the client's medical report, any residual capacities should be identified so that possible transferable skills can be evaluated. The following outlines specific areas in this report:

1. Functional limitations
   a. Work activities possible
   b. Tolerance for work activity
   c. Client concerns about limitations as related to work
   d. Current level of performance in strength, climbing, stooping, reaching, talking, and seeing
   e. What client abilities could be developed, perhaps with the use of devices, to compensate for the disability? Or, has there been substantial deterioration in all possible physical areas that could have been utilized for work?
   f. Does the client have secondary or multiple disabilities with which to cope?
   g. Current level of response to work location, cold, heat, humidity, noise, hazards, and atmospheric conditions
2. Diagnosis
   Readiness for work activities
3. Prognosis
   a. Will condition worsen or improve?
   b. Chronic or temporary condition?
4. Medication
   a. Is the medication taken regularly, and can the client function independently of it?
   b. What are the effects of medication on working? For example, does it cause drowsiness or lethargy?

Understanding the client's medical report can be the first step in formulating realistic rehabilitation plans. Through this awareness, the rehabilitation professional can further comprehend whether: 1) the current disability status precludes employment; 2) the client is unable to work full-time because of a mental or physical condition; or 3) the person can work full-time but must have a sedentary job with low stress and close supervision. This report may also indicate whether the client is limited to occupations requiring light physical activity but is still able to work full-time or there are minimal restrictions to the type of work the client can do.

In many instances, however, rehabilitation professionals may have some specific questions, which may have to be given directly to the physician. Medical report forms are not designed to cover completely every specific situation. It often helps if the examining physician's attention is directed to these things for which specific kinds of information are needed.

## CLIENT'S EMOTIONAL RESPONSE TO DISABILITY

Disabled workers vary in their abilities to deal with occupational and possibly social losses caused by job-related injuries. The time required for medical treatment, the stress of rehabilitation, the lack of mobility, and concern with changing personal appearance may precipitate a number of crises for the injured worker (Versluys, 1980). The client may not be motivated to reach and maintain projected functional levels of performance. Instead, a life of social isolation and dependency on others may be preferred to one in which all the person's energies are utilized in the attempt to reach a maximum level of occupational and family productivity.

Weinstein (1978) identified "disability process," meaning that the work-related disability results from a complex process rather than a discrete accident or illness. The accident is preceded by the development of tension and stress, leading to feelings of inadequacy and depression. He believed that the initiation of the accident process is a matter of personality style that makes the worker unusually sensitive to perceptions of increased expectations and reduced support and approval. Consequently, the worker experiences increased subjective distress and harbors an attitude that makes it difficult to ask for help. When an accident occurs, the worker perceives that his or her distress and possibly resulting impaired performance is caused by an externally generated event, i.e., something that could happen to anyone. Thus, as Weinstein (1978) explained, the accident transforms an "unacceptable disability" into an acceptable one. The disability even becomes a way of life, facilitated by the worker's continued personality characteristics and perhaps reinforced by the social and financial responses to the initial disability.

This reaction to an industrial injury becomes, of course, a deterrant to the achievement of rehabilitation goals and, with varied emotional responses to the accident trauma, needs to be identified. When a person sustains a disability, the usual result is a change in self-concept, which is the result of an altered body image. This body image can profoundly effect the client's readiness for work (Forrest, 1963). The injury may be a devastating experience for the client. Not only may his or her self-concept change but also the person's method of relating to others may be drastically altered (Forrest, 1963). Feelings of inadequacy and self-depreciation may dominate the client's outlook. The area of human activity that usually receives the impact of these feelings is work and productivity.

Following the occurrence of the injury and the accompanying emotional shock that the person's occupational and perhaps family and social life has been severely disrupted is the lingering thought, "Although this has happened, I will soon have a full restoration of my physical capacities. I will be able to do all that I used to do." The worker denies the implications of the injury for employment and physical functioning. At this particular time, the person needs a helping professional who may allow temporary harboring of this denial while at the same time assist him or her in realizing slowly that there may be some permanent limitations.

An understanding of what the injured worker is experiencing emotionally can help considerably when deciding the possibilities of the client's return to work. The emotional reaction of the injured worker usually takes the following sequence:

As the reality of the injury situation becomes more apparent, the client usually becomes angry over the perceived occupational and related economic losses. Depression may begin, dominated by feelings of "What's the use . . . is there going to be any opportunity for me?" Clients may also start to isolate themselves from former friends or accustomed social opportunities. At the same time, however, they become acquainted with possible compensation benefits or family reinforcement that apparent economic deficits can be made up by other family members. Rehabilitation intervention should certainly have begun by this time, offering the disabled person a variety of productive options and attractive alternatives to a possible life of dependency. In other words, appropriate information needs to be communicated.

Clients gradually realize that their disabilities may be permanent and begin to acknowledge their limitations and the necessity to explore other work opportunities. The client's depression may continue but his or her thought processes contain more reality-based information. Support, reassurance that rehabilitation can lead to renewed feelings of productivity, and an identification of residual strengths is particularly needed at this time. Otherwise, the client may feel that dependency and the economic reliance only on compensation benefits may be a more satisfying way of life.

From this stage of acknowledgment, the disabled person begins to adjust to the disability. This adjustment can take the form of positive expressions, including rehabilitation exploration or disengaging from any rehabilitation opportunities. There are many reasons why disabled persons make such a choice—the person's satisfaction with work, the presence or absence of therapeutic intervention, the life (developmental) stage of the person, the individual's reaction to previous crises, the personality makeup of the individual before the disability, and the person's philosophy of life. When the rehabilitation professional observes that an especially negative reaction to the accident is occurring, these factors should be carefully explored. Also, it should be determined whether the client is using symptoms for secondary gain.

If the person is actually getting more reinforcement or benefits from being disabled then nondisabled, it will be very difficult to motivate the client for rehabilitation purposes.

Assessing all of these emotional factors and identifying how the client is coping with the disability can generate invaluable information for the determination of work readiness. Like the different emotional reactions, coping styles can vary. The disability can be minimized through selective inattention, ignoring, denial, or rationalizing the significance of the injury; attempts can be made to "master" or "control" the implications of the disability by identifying other compensating abilities and utilizing the client's energy for productive purposes; or he or she can simply give up and lead a life of inactivity and passivity. An awareness of the injured person's coping style can often influence the direction of rehabilitation intervention.

Atkins et al. (1982) discussed another adjustment process that particularly applies to the injured worker. The basic components of the model are:

1.  Coping

    What is the emotional effect of the disability? Does it include depression, anger, denial, uncertainty, or confusion?

    Has the client had a chance to mourn the loss implied in the disabling condition?

    Has the client begun to enlarge his or her scope of values?

2.  Focus

    Is the client concentrating upon his or her assets and liabilities or only upon disabilities and limitations?

    Does the client extend his or her limitations beyond that which the disability actually dictates?

    Are client limitations underestimated?

3.  Blame

    Where is the responsibility placed for the causation of the disabling condition—on the client, others, or toward the isolated situation, itself? (The last direction of blame is the most conducive to the adjustment process (Wright, 1960).)

4.  Societal influence

    What factors outside the individual influence him or her and affect adjustment?

    What is the disabled individual's perception of the nondisabled environment—family, social relationships, and co-workers?

    Is the individual withdrawing from society or attempting to be accepted by the family and friends?

    Is the disabled person attempting to normalize his or her disability-related limitations and recognize his or her self-worth despite negative attitudes from others?

## THE INJURED WORKER'S FAMILY

Frequently, the critical determinant of whether the disabled person will return to work is the family. Family influence is a decisive factor in rehabilitation. If the family believes, for example, that it is much better for the injured worker to remain permanently at home, and they realize there are other family resources combined with the compensation benefits to provide a stable income, the client may have little motivation for returning to work. Families who are over-protective, highly anxious, and encourage dependent behaviors may prevent total rehabilitation (Versluys, 1980). When the family sees the disabled as being more dependent then he or she is, efforts toward independence are discouraged. The patient is reinforced to behave according to family expectations.

On the other hand, family behaviors that encourage both the injured person to maintain role responsibilities in the home and explore job opportunities can be a deciding factor for employment reentry. Families who communicate attitudes of essential worth to the patient help to stabilize the self-concept, foster a positive attitude toward the future, and facilitate maintenance of rehabilitation gains (Safilios-Rothchild, 1970). During the initial interview with the client, these family dynamics should be explored. Areas such as chronic stress, secondary gain, information, and expectations have particular relevance and questions for generating information.

### Chronic Stress

1. What is the most difficult problem for your family at the present time?
2. How do you think your family has adjusted to your disability?
3. Is there anything different now in your family than from what it used to be, apart from your disability?

### Secondary Gain

1. Has life in your family been better for you since the occurrence of your injury?
2. What kind of financial benefits are you receiving now?
3. What do you believe are the feelings of your family now that you are not working?
4. Does your family expect you to return to work?

### Information

1. How much do you think your family understands about your disability?
2. How much have you learned about the injury and what can and can you not do since the injury happened?

**Expectations**

1. Do you still perform your customary duties around the home? Do you still participate with your family in social activities?
2. Could you please describe what happened in your family life yesterday?
3. What kinds of things does your family expect you to do especially around the house?

Responses to these questions can provide suggestions on how the important people in the client's life view the injury and the possibility of a return to work. Importantly, this information facilitates an understanding of whether those around the client are willing to accept him or her as a worker again. It also identifies the quality of family support for rehabilitation goals.

## PREPARATION FOR COURT TESTIMONY

Since the 1970s, increased demands have been made on rehabilitation professionals to present quantifiable evidence for insurance companies, attorneys, claims agents, physicians, and social security hearings (Godley, 1978). Those in the private-for-profit sector of rehabilitation who serve the industrially injured are more inclined to solicit legal advice than other clients; therefore they may find themselves making court appearances quite frequently. When providing these services for clients, the rehabilitation professional confronts a new variety of responsibilities. These imply that not only is the professional well-prepared to give court testimony about the client, but he or she also possesses a well-developed knowledge of vocational evaluation. In the eyes of the court, the professional is an "expert," and will have to answer in an objective and unbiased manner a wide range of questions concerning the vocational/occupational possibilities of the client.

Sink and King (1978) identified the many questions that could be asked of rehabilitation professionals when testifying on behalf of their clients. The questions, themselves, suggest the type of preparation required in order to make an adequate court presentation. Godley (1978) suggested that such questions could be prepared and reviewed by the professional and attorney before the court appearance. The following outline could be followed by the professional when preparing court testimony, and contains information originally stated by Sink and King (1978):

1. The rehabilitation professional (vocational expert)
   a. Do you have a knowledge of physical and mental disabilities and their relationship to employment potential, and of jobs and their requirements common to the labor market? How did you obtain this information?

b.    Have you had experience in job analysis, and can you give examples of local industries in which you have observed and analyzed jobs?

c.    Have you talked to your client's employer and would they hire the client?

d.    If a job is possible with the employer, what would be the salary level, career ladder sequence, and length of time between steps? What would be the anticipated income in one year? In 5 years?

2.    The client

a.    Describe the details of your client's previous employment, including work performed, tools used, supervision given and received, communication skills required, temperaments, interests, physical demands, and intelligence needed for the job, typical salaries for such jobs, working hours and days, mode of transportation to and from work, and use of arms, hands, fingers, legs, back, etc.

b.    Define for the court the occupational significance of both physical and mental conditions as defined by the physician and the client's daily (social, avocational, recreational) activities, including work around the house, care for or play with children or grandchildren, and does the client drive, attend church, or go shopping?

c.    Describe for the court the occupationally significant characteristics of the jobs the client has held and how the physical (or mental) conditions relate to previous jobs.

d.    Are there any jobs in the labor market that may be done by the client without additional training, or are there jobs in which the client would be employed with additional training or education? If so, what are they and where are they located?

e.    If training or education is needed, is the client qualified for acceptance into training or educational programs? What kind of training/education is required, how long is it, what is the cost, and what are the qualifications for training?

f.    What is the client's perception of going back to work, not working, the physical limitations as stated by the physician, and being trained or educated for another job?

g.    If the client has had a vocational evaluation, describe the types of psychologic tests and/or work samples administered during the assessment process? What are they supposed to evaluate, what are they supposed to measure, and what is their validity? To what kinds of skills or jobs do the work samples relate? If you did not administer the tests or work samples, what are the qualifications of those persons who did so?

Sink and King (1978) explained that the questions should be answered in terms of magnitude, frequency, and duration. To obtain the information requested of many of the questions, the client may be observed or questioned. The *Dictionary of Occupational Titles* should be used for classification for title, worker trait group arrangements, physical demands, working conditions, general educational development, specific vocational preparation, aptitudes, interests, and temperaments. The rehabilitation professional should also have a job market survey that applies to the client's living area.


## CONCLUSION

Among many rehabilitation concerns about the injured worker, the problem of motivation is often dominant. If the worker has been employed for many years and now compensation benefits and family pressures represent strong influences on not returning to a job, rehabilitation will be all the more difficult. This motivation variable is a distinctive focus to evaluation efforts with the industrially injured. If the client possesses all the necessary prerequisites and is ready for immediate placement, well and good. If the disabled person is not, then attention must be given to all those issues that relate to the client working again. Skill development, resolution of emotional feelings, and cooperation from the family should all be attended to if the worker is to achieve rehabilitation goals. The evaluation ''period'' becomes, consequently, not only a time for the identification of job readiness factors, but also an opportunity for the rehabilitation professional to include some counseling with the injured worker to help him or her begin to understand new options for productivity.

For effective evaluation, one of the important presumptions is that the rehabilitation professional knows the local job community and understands the dynamics of job analysis. Many injured workers have well-developed employment skills. From an awareness of the varied job requirements, the rehabilitation professional can suggest appropriate job modifications. Through these changes, the disabled person's compensatory skills can find a new opportunity for usefulness.


## CASE STUDY

*Leonard, age 36, is a construction worker and lives in an apartment in subsidized public housing. He has been married for 11 years and has two children—a daughter, age 10 and a son, age 6. His wife works part-time as a cashier in a local 5 & 10 variety store. In November, 1980, Leonard, while working on the construction of a new office building, fell 11 feet from a scaffold and fractured his left leg, incurred a cervical spine injury, and dislocated his right elbow. He was hospitalized for 5 months and upon discharge, was told by the doctors that he would be limited only to sedentary work.*

*Before entering construction work at age 28, Leonard was a clothing salesman for a large retail chain. He left that job because of poor pay and little job advancement. Leonard also worked as a building supplies sales- man for 3 years but was fired because of continued arguments with his supervisors. Regarding his educational background, Leonard graduated from high school and particularly liked social science-related subjects. He has occasionally attended adult education classes in history.*

*Since his accident, Leonard has been receiving workmen's com- pensation benefits, and with his wife's employment, the money has been sufficient to meet their basic needs. Since his hopsitalization, Leonard attempted for 3 weeks to drive a cab for a friend, but states that his back pains were too persistent and the continued sitting was too uncomfortable for him. Apart from this job, Leonard has been helping his mother with dif- ferent chores around her house. She lives nearby, is 64, has arthritis which limits her mobility, and owns her home. Leonard has one sister, who is married and lives in another state. His father passed away 10 years ago.*

With this information please answer the following questions:

1. What guidelines or structure would you establish for the initial interview with Leonard in order to generate information for vocational planning?
2. What information from Leonard's life history would be particularly useful for rehabilitation purposes?
3. What family factors must be considered that might influence Leonard's vocational rehabilitation?
4. From the information given, what do you perceive are Leonard's vocational strengths?

## REFERENCES

Atkins, B., Lynch, R., and Pullo, R. 1982. A definition of psychosocial aspects of disability: A synthesis of the literature. Voc. Eval. Work Adj. Bull. 15:55–61.
Field, T., and Sink, J. 1980. The Employer's Manual. Udare Service Bureau, Athens, GA.
Forrest, J. 1963. Evaluating job readiness. Paper presented at the Bi-Regional Institute on Placement, March 29th, Oklahoma State University, Oklahoma City.
Godley, S. 1978. Topical review. Voc. Eval. Work Adj. Bull. 11:51–57.
Safilios-Rothschild, C. 1970. The Sociology and Social Psychology of Disability and Rehabilitation. Random House, New York.
Sanchez, I. 1981. The California Worker's Compensation Rehabilitation System. Macmillan, New York.

Sink, J., and Field, T. 1981. Vocational Assessment Planning and Jobs. Udare Service Bureau, Athens, GA.

Versluys, H. 1980. The remediation of role disorders through focused group work. Am. J. Occup. Ther. 34:609–614.

Weinstein, H. 1983. Transferable skills analysis in the rehabilitation process. Rehab. For. 9:25–27.

Weinstein, M. 1978. The concept of the disability process. Psychosomatics. 19:94–97.

Workman, E. 1983. Vocational rehabilitation in the private, profit-making sector. Ann. Rev. Rehab. 3:292–321.

Wright, B. 1960. Physical Disability—A Psychological Approach. Harper and Row, New York.

# chapter 14
# REHABILITATION PLANNING

During the entire assessment process, much information is generated about client functioning. At the beginning of vocational evaluation, the rehabilitation professional usually has either a goal or a perspective for collecting this information. An objective might be to identify client assets needed for employment or training which will lead to a job. Other possible goals are: independent living, the identification of transferable skills for eventual return to a job, or the determination of eligibility for rehabilitation services. When employment or independent goals are being considered, the client should participate in planning immediately following rehabilitation assessment. This planning is an end product of assessment and an essential step for the client to reach appropriate rehabilitation goals.

Many models for the vocational planning process have been developed in the last 10 years. Roessler and Rubin (1982) discussed some different approaches. For example, Dolliver and Nelson (1975) formulated a three-part counseling approach: 1) occupational information; 2) values clarification; and 3) decision making. To reach meaningful vocational alternatives, the client integrates information regarding work with personal values. Then, a feasible goal is selected, and a sequential plan of action is developed.

Carkhuff (1971) built vocational planning around the terms "exploration," "understanding," and "action." The client explores the relationship of vocational objectives to personal capabilities, interests, and situation and then attempts to understand the way in which these different factors influence vocational potential. This personalized understanding then helps the client to develop the steps of the rehabilitation plan (Roessler and Rubin, 1982). MacKay (1975) initiated a two-stage model—identification and integration. In identification, the importance of exploration of self and world is stressed. Hopefully, the client can then identify personal strengths and weaknesses affecting the vocational plan. During the integration phase, the "professional

*221*

assists the client in understanding the personal relevance of the discoveries that have been made during the identification phase" (Roessler and Rubin, 1982, p. 122).

With all of these models, there seems to be a basic process, which has been conceptualized by Roessler and Rubin (1982) as "analysis" and "action." The analysis phase focuses upon occupational information and client feelings. In the action phase, there is the appraisal of client strengths and weaknesses, a statement of goals and problems, a survey of possible resources and services, and a sequence for expected completion of the program (Leung, 1974).

This chapter develops and explains a rehabilitation planning model that has been used in professional practice. As a background to this presentation, components of what is necessary for effective planning are discussed. The case study illustrates the steps in vocational planning.

## WHAT IS NECESSARY FOR EFFECTIVE PLANNING?

During the interpretation of test/assessment results, the ideas and information that are generated (hopefully by both the professional and the client) represent different directions or ways to reach satisfying rehabilitation goals. To perform adequate and meaningful planning necessitates both knowledge and skills on the part of the professional regarding client involvement; the job market, training, and requirements; and the acquisition of specific competencies.

### Involvement of the Client

One of the underlying principles in this book is that input or client participation will be solicited at the very beginning of the assessment process. Earlier chapters identify various ways to accomplish this involvement, including the careful explanation of varied, possible rehabilitation goals, the identification of client assets, and the opportunity to explore different options or alternatives for satisfaction in rehabilitation. All of these ways stimulate client participation in the assessment process. Client involvement is essential during the interpretation session of evaluation results; it can provoke further input into the planning phase of vocational evaluation. Moreover, if there has been client involvement during assessment, such areas as client needs and values will be also identified. An analysis of these areas is crucial for appropriate rehabilitation planning, and most of this information from disabled clients will have to be generated from client discussions rather than psychometric measures.

With this client participation in the vocational planning process, many potential problems relevant to reaching rehabilitation goals may be anticipated. Roessler and Rubin (1982) also identified other important results: such as: 1) being aware of potential vocational objectives; 2) being able to evaluate these objectives for personal relevance, desirability, and practicality; 3) understanding what counseling, restoration, and training steps need to be taken in order to reach the intermediate objectives and vocational goal; and 4) assisting in the development of a concrete, step-by-step rehabilitation plan. All in all, the professional and client must work together (insofar as this is functionally possible for the client) in the development of rehabilitation plans. If this participation is not enthusiastically promoted, there could be a wide gap between client expectations for rehabilitation and what the professional can deliver or what is perceived as possible for the client.

## Knowledge of the Job Market/Training/Requirements

Throughout the rehabilitation assessment process, the professional must consider viable alternatives for employment, training, and independent living. Evaluation is conducted within the context of goals (vocational or independent living). This focus implies that the professional knows occupational information, availability of jobs in the client's geographical area, and the varied opportunities for training. These issues are discussed in the chapter on Test Interpretation.

Rehabilitation planning demands an extensive awareness of occupational resources, such as the *Dictionary of Occupational Titles*, the *Occupational Outlook Handbook*, and assorted publications that identify job requirements and employment conditions and help the professional to place the results of assessment into a reality perspective. Importantly for planning, it enables the rehabilitation professional to generate alternatives or options relevant to training and eventual employment. Roessler (1982) believed, that a:

> " . . . knowledge of work routines, requisites, and rewards has a direct effect on the individual's preferences, values, and self-concept regarding different types of work (p. 172).

## Acquisition of Specific Competencies

For vocational planning, there are certain skills that the rehabilitation professional should possess if this planning is to be effective. Roessler (1982) identified two of them:

1. *An understanding of the problems that impair client efforts to obtain*

*work*    These could be disability-related, concern work experience, or pertain to job availability.
2.  *A knowledge of the world of work*    To select a vocational objective, clients also need to understand job requirements and local employment conditions. To gain this understanding usually implies that the professional possesses this information and is able to communicate it effectively.

Added to these skills or competencies is the ability of the counselor to organize assessment information and formulate and implement a decision-making approach. In the next section of this chapter, a model suggests a structure for organizing evaluation data. Regarding decision-making, many models that have been developed are applicable for the decision-making process in vocational planning (see Clarke et al., 1965; Herr and Cramer, 1979; Pierce et al., 1979). These approaches generally follow the format of: 1) defining the problem; 2) generating alternatives; 3) gathering information; 4) processing information; 5) making plans and selecting goals; and 6) implementing and evaluating plans. What is implied in these systems is a value system which permits decisions to be made among preferences and expectancies for action within a climate of uncertainty (Herr and Cramer, 1979). Of course, for the decision-making approach to be effective also necessitates accurate and complete information about occupational resources, the results of the client's evaluation, and the client's needs and values.

## A PLANNING MODEL

The planning model below provides a structure for organizing assessment information. It incorporates areas of exploration that are discussed both in Chapters 1 and 4. The planning process is conceptualized in stages, and each stage must be completed before moving to the next one.

# A Planning Model

Step 1: **Collecting and Organizing Evaluation Information**

    A.   Sources of Assessment Data
        1.  The interview
        2.  Psychometric or standardized tests
        3.  Work samples
        4.  Situational assessment
        5.  Medical records, psychologists' reports, and so forth

|  | Relevant Results for Vocational or Independent Living Goals |
|---|---|
| B.  Client Areas of Functioning | |
|     1.  Physical characteristics | |
|        a.  General appearance | _____ |
|        b.  Health status | _____ |
|        c.  Motor coordination | _____ |
|        d.  Physical limitations | _____ |
|        e.  Energy level | _____ |
|     2.  Intellectual characteristics | _____ |
|        a.  Educational experience | _____ |
|        b.  Abilities and aptitudes | _____ |
|        c.  Work experience and | _____ |
|           specific skills | _____ |
|           acquired/developed | _____ |
|           work habits | _____ |
|        d.  Disability-related | _____ |
|           knowledge (Under- | _____ |
|           standing assets and | _____ |
|           disability limitations | _____ |
|           in relation to work) | _____ |
|        e.  Cognitive-related | _____ |
|           limitations (Attention | _____ |
|           span, memory) | _____ |
|     3.  Emotional characteristics | |
|        a.  Mood/temperament | _____ |
|        b.  Identified needs | _____ |
|        c.  Motivation | _____ |
|        d.  Adjustment to disability | _____ |

      e.  Coping resources    _____

4.  Interests related to    _____
    employment    _____

5.  Values (Friel and Carkhuff,    _____
    1974)    _____

    a.  Physical (Activity,    _____
       comfort, salary,    _____
       cleanliness, money,    _____
       location, temperature,    _____
       work with hands)    _____

    b.  Intellectual (Specializa-    _____
       tion, learning,    _____
       planning, creativity,    _____
       structure, preparation    _____
       time, chance for    _____
       advancement)    _____

    c.  Emotional/interpersonal    _____
       (Challenging, team-    _____
       work, commitment,    _____
       stability, job security,    _____
       helping people,    _____
       independence,    _____
       unpressured situation,    _____
       structure)    _____

6.  Environmental factors

    a.  Family situation and    _____
       attitude toward    _____
       rehabilitation    _____

    b.  Available financial    _____
       resources    _____

7.  Special considerations

    a.  Medications as they    _____
       would affect job    _____
       performance    _____

    b.  Needed aids (Trans-    _____
       portation, prosthetic    _____
       devices)    _____

    c.  Job modifications    _____
       required    _____

## Step 2:  **Focusing the Evaluation Results**

A.        Client Interest(s)                    Areas of Competence

_____                    _____
_____                    _____
_____                    _____
_____                    _____
_____                    _____

                Values                              Limitations

_____                    _____
_____                    _____
_____                    _____
_____                    _____
_____                    _____

B.        Specify (Prioritize)
                Occupational            Areas of Competence Related
                Interest(s)                    to Interest(s)

_____                    _____

_____                    _____
                                                _____
                                                _____

        Prioritized Values Related to        Limitations Related to
                Interest(s)                        Interest(s)

_____                    _____
_____                    _____
_____                    _____
_____                    _____

C.    Occupational Information Related to Interests
        1.    Available jobs/career opportunities

                _____
                _____
                _____
                _____

        2.    Occupational/entry level requirements

                _____
                _____
                _____
                _____

3.   Training needed and training opportunities

_____

_____

_____

_____

Step 3:   **Selection of Rehabilitation/Occupational/Training/Independent Living Goal**
   A.   Examine again values and competencies in relation to two identified interests. Consider environmental factors and client limitations to achieve rehabilitation goals.
   B.   Examine specifically occupational requirements and job availability in relation to each of the two prioritized interest areas and client competencies and limitations.
   C.   Select Goal: _____

Step 4:   **Formulation of Rehabilitation Plan**

   A.   Major Goal: _____

   B.   Subgoals
        (steps needed to
        achieve major goal)        1.  _____

        Date of
        implementation             _____

        Date of
        completion                 _____

        Resource                   _____

        Monitor                    _____

                                   2.  _____

        Date of
        implementation             _____

        Date of
        completion                 _____

        Monitor                    _____

        Resource                   _____

3. _____

Date of
implementation            _____

Date of
completion                _____

Resource                  _____

Monitor                   _____

4. _____

Date of
implementation            _____

Date of
completion                _____

Resource                  _____

Monitor                   _____

5. _____

Date of
implementation            _____

Date of
completion                _____

Resource                  _____

Monitor                   _____

6. _____

Date of
implementation            _____

Date of
completion                _____

Resource                  _____

Monitor                   _____

## CASE STUDY

*Gary, age 34, is an unemployed airplane mechanic who, 14 months before his first interview with the rehabilitation professional, incurred a serious injury while working. According to accident reports, the client was apparently doing some maintenance work on a 747 when a fellow employee accidentally hit the ladder he was using. Gary lost his balance and fell to the ground, breaking both ankles and severly injuring his back. There were also severe bruises and contusions, and the client was hospitalized for 6 months, particularly to stabilize back problems caused by the accident. The recent doctor's report indicated that Gary is unable to stand for any prolonged period of time and cannot perform the physical demands of climbing, stooping, and bending that were required in his job. In the initial interview, the client explains that he has almost constant back pain, realizes that physical limitations will keep him from returning to his employment, and feels that he is learning to live with his pain. Gary states that he is coming to see you in order to explore employment alternatives. He has contacted his former employer and union officials, and they both have encouraged Gary to pursue rehabilitation opportunities.*

*The client is a high school graduate who maintained a B average in college preparatory subjects. He received particularly good grades in math and science-related subjects. Although accepted at the state university, Gary decided to enlist in the air force because he wanted to marry his high school sweetheart and "For a young person, the service is a better place to be when you are married." He remained in the military for 9 years and achieved the rank of E-6, staff sergeant. His military specialty was airplane maintenance mechanic. During the interview, he explained that his military record was excellent, but that he decided to leave because of relocation demands and the time he had to spend away from his family on the weekends. Upon discharge, he immediately obtained a job with a major airlines company and worked with them for 7 years until the accident.*

*Gary has been married for 16 years and has three childlren—ages 14, 12, and 5. During the interview, he explains that his family life is extremely important to him and states: "My wife and I are very close." The family regularly takes camping trips together, are active members in a local church, and participate in many school functions. He further states that for the past 4 years, his wife has been working as an executive secretary because "We wanted more money for some extras in our life, and she wanted really to get out of the house." Gary also claims that his family is very supportive of rehabilitation efforts because "they want me to do something worthwhile with my life."*

*During this first interview, the client explains that he has had few hobbies, although he likes to read and use his 35mm camera for taking pictures at athletic events. Apart from training associated with his job, he has not taken any formal, post-high school courses. Gary also mentions that he is receiving workmen's compensation payments, which are "quite adequate for us to live on, especially with my wife working." Yet, he explains that he is bored just sitting around the house, and "perhaps there is some training I can take which will put me back in the work force."*

Having gathered this information from the interview, including knowledge about the client's emotional reaction to his disability, and client values as they relate to work, the rehabilitation professional then proceeded with an assessment. The following are the evaluation results.

Step 1:  **Collecting and Organizing Evaluation Information**
     A.   Sources of Assessment Data
          1.   The interview
          2.   Psychometric or standardized tests
               a.   The Quick Test
               b.   Shipley-Hartford
               c.   WRAT
               d.   Differential Aptitude Series
               e.   Kuder Preference
               f.   Pennsylvania Bi-Manual Work Sample
               g.   Strong Campbell Interest Inventory
               h.   PSI
               i.   Edwards Personnel Preference Test
               j.   MMPI
          3.   Medical records

| | Relevant Results for |
|---|---|
| B.  Client Areas of Functioning | Vocational Goals |
|    1.  Physical characteristics (Interview discussion and medical report) | |
|       a.  General appearance | Well-groomed; dresses appropriately and neatly; maintains eye contact; appears assertive of manner. |
|       b.  Health status | Apart from residuals of back injury, good. |

|   |   |   |
|---|---|---|
| c. | Motor coordination (Pennsylvania Bi-manual Work Sample) | Eye/hand coordination above average |
| d. | Physical limitations | Reaching, bending, stooping, climbing |
| e. | Energy level | Client is concerned about pain; has to sit often during the day, but claims he has much energy. |

2. Intellectual characteristics

|   |   |   |
|---|---|---|
| a. | Educational experience | High school graduate, B average; specialized training in airplane mechanics |
| b. | Abilities and aptitudes (WRAT, Quick, Shipley-Hartford, DAT) | Grade 12 functioning in reading and math; 90th percentile in space relations and mechanical ability; IQ functioning in the Bright-Normal range |
| c. | Work experience and specific skills acquired/ developed work habits (Interview discussion) | 15 years airplane mechanic; mechanical comprehension is high; technical knowledge is above average; under-stands and has followed basic work habits—good work record |
| d. | Disability-related knowledge (Interview discussion) | Understands limitations; takes medication regularly; not involved in any activities that would aggravate back condition; attends regularly physical therapy treatments |
| e. | Cognitive-related limitations | Pain experience occasionally affects client's attention while reading and watching TV. Believes that pain will get better. Memory functioning seems good for immediate, recent, and remote recall |

| | |
|---|---|
| 3. Emotional characteristics<br>a. Mood-temperament<br>(Interview discussion) | Friendly, outgoing, but claims frustration tolerance has been lowered since accident. Describes himself as someone who is usually patient with others; claims he is also ambitious, and was interested in reaching seniority/administrative positions within the union; also feels he likes structure and methodical work |
| b. Identified needs<br>(Interview discussion and EPPS) | Job and financial security, recognition; claims does not need that much variety in work; needs good working conditions and advancement opportunities.<br>EPPS: Achievement: 80th percentile, Affiliation: 85th percentile, Change: 20th percentile |
| c. Motivation<br>(Interview discussion) | Claims he is ready to explore rehabilitation/training/ employment related goals |
| d. Adjustment to disability<br>(interview discussion, MMPI, PSI) | Believes that he is very angry because someone was responsible for the accident; but tries to suppress the anger; otherwise, feels that he is coping, but appears to have a "sense of isolation", and privately grieves over not being able to return to his former job; very concerned about allowing his emotions to be visible to others. Profile of MMPI falls within normal limits, although a slight elevation on attention to bodily concerns |

|   |   |
|---|---|
| e.  Coping resources | Family; confidence in mechanical ability; no undue financial worries; has social and church outlets; friends have been supportive |
| 4.  Interests related to employment | Kuder: Scientific: 90th percentile Mechanical: 95th percentile Social Service: 65th percentile Computational: 55th percentile Outdoor: 60th percentile Strong Campbell: General occupational themes Investigative theme: High score S theme: Moderately high Basic interest scales Mechanical activities: Very high Medical service: High Nature: Moderately high Occupational scales Engineer: high Medical tech: high Computer prog: Moderately high |
| 5.  Values (Interview discussion) a.  Physical | Activity, cleanliness, money, location, work with hands |
| b.  Emotional/interpersonal | Stability; challenging; commitment; job security |
| 6.  Environmental factors | Family supportive— eager that client return to work; no serious family problems |
| 7.  Special considerations | Limited standing on job; takes medication for back pain; can drive car; no job modifications required |

Step 2: **Focusing the Evaluation Results**

A.  Client Interest(s)                    Areas of Competence

| | |
|---|---|
| Mechanical | Mechanical ability |
| Scientific | Developed work habits |
| Outdoor | General level of knowledge |
| Computational | good |
| | Numerical abilities |
| | high |
| | Appears well organized in |
| | work habits |

| Values | Limitations |
|---|---|
| Structure | Back condition |
| Location | Limited standing |
| Work with hands | Away from school for many |
| Challenging | years |
| Stability | Pain currently might inhibit |
| Job stability | performance of cognitive |
| | functions |

(The information in Step 2 was developed from interpreting the assessment results to the client and obtaining feedback. Client was asked to rank values and interests and areas of competence were identified from test results.)

B.  Specify (prioritize)              Areas of Competence Related
    Occupational Interest(s)          to Interest(s)

| | |
|---|---|
| 1.  Medical Technician | Computational ability |
| 2.  Computer Programmer | Mechanical conceptual ability |
| 3.  Small engine repairman | Developed work habits |

Prioritized Values                 Limitations Related to
Related to Interest(s)             Interest(s)

| | |
|---|---|
| Structure | Back condition |
| Job security | No specific training in fields |
| Work with hands | |

C.  Occupational Information Related to Interests
    1.  Available jobs/career opportunities
        a.  Jobs appear to be available in health field technology
        b.  Many advertised openings for computer programmers
        c.  Client lives near hospital centers and variety of medical facilities

2.  Occupational/entry level requirements
    a.  Medical Technician: usually four year college degree program
    b.  Computer Programmer: 4 or 2 year college program
    c.  Small Engine Repairman: Vocational Training

Step 3:  **Selection of Rehabiliation/Occupational/Training/
Independent Living Goal**

A.  Attention was focused on values and competencies in relation to occupational areas of medical technology, computer programmer, and small engine repair. Occupational requirements and job availability were also discussed. Client believed that while computer programming would be a satisfying field for him, many health care facilities were located close to his home, and medical technology offered job security, challenging work, advancement, responsibility, and working with his hands. He also stated that he liked the "clean environment" that medical technology offers. Consequently, decisions were made in the perspective of client values and job availability. Also, client believed that he could accomplish a 4-year college program but would have to begin training gradually.

B.  Selected Occupational Goal: medical technologist

Step 4:  **Formulation of Rehabilitation Plan**

A.  Major Goal: To obtain employment as a medical technologist

B.  Subgoals    1.  To visit local 2-year community college and inquire about courses in field related to medical technology

| | |
|---|---|
| Date of implementation | Immediately |
| Date of completion | 2 weeks |
| Resource | College |
| Monitor | Rehabilitation professional |

2. To take two adult education courses offered by community college in liberal arts subjects to develop study skills

| | |
|---|---|
| Date of implementation | Immediately |
| Date of completion | 6 months |
| Resource | Continuing education program |
| Monitor | Rehabilitation professional |

3. To enroll in community college in appropriate program that is transferable to a B.S. degree program in medical technology

| | |
|---|---|
| Date of implementation | 6 months |
| Date of completion | 2 years from date of entry |
| Resource | College |
| Monitor | Rehabilitation professional |

4. To make inquiries in local area about job openings in small engine repair for temporary, part-time work

| | |
|---|---|
| Date of implementation | Immediately |
| Date of completion | 2 years |
| Resource | Local area/employment offices/small shops |
| Monitor | Rehabilitation professional |

5. To maintain physical therapy appointments and inquire about self-help groups to deal with anger about disability

Date of
implementation        Immediately
Date of
completion            6 months–1 year

Resource              Local hospital

Monitor               Rehabilitation professional

6. Upon successful completion of a 2-year college program, to enroll in 4-year B.S. degree program in medical technology

Date of
implementation        Completion of 2-year program
Date of
completion            2–3 years after entry

Resource              College

Monitor               Rehabilitation professional

## CONCLUSION

During rehabilitation planning, the professional utilizes many skills—communication, diagnostic, occupational information, and perhaps placement. An important perspective in the development of many plans, however, is not simply job placement but actually career development (Vandergoot, 1982). During the planning session, the client should learn the many possible options that are available in relationship to competencies and values. As assessment helps a client to identify those strengths and assets that apply to the world of employment or independent living, so planning shows the client how these capabilities relate to different rehabilitation options. Rehabilitation planning is actually similar (although perhaps on a smaller scale) to career preparation, whereby plans are made and implemented to equip the client with specific, marketable job skills (Vandergoot, 1982). Planning should also consider those difficulties that might arise after placement in a job. The client may still have many concerns about the integration of work with other life activities.

What should again be emphasized in rehabilitation planning is the *importance of occupational information*. The professional should have access to reliable information that identifies what job areas are growing or decreasing. Local labor market information must be used sensitively (Vandergoot et al., 1982). When the professional knows about employment and training resources as well as occupational requirements, the planning session will be more valuable for the client.

## REFERENCES

Carkhuff, R. 1971. The Development of Human Resources. Holt, Rinehart and Winston, Inc., New York.
Clarke, R., Gelatt, H., and Levine, L. 1965. A decision-making paradigm for local guidance research. Pers. Guid. J. 44:40–51.
Dolliver, R., and Nelson, R. 1975. Assumptions regarding vocational counseling. Voc. Guid. Q. 24:12–19.
Friel, T., and Carkhuff, R. 1974. The Art of Developing a Career. Human Resource Development Press, Amherst, MA.
Herr, E., and Cramer, S. 1979. Career Guidance Through the Life Span. Little, Brown, and Company, Boston.
Leung, P. 1974. The use of behavior contracts in employability development planning. J. Employ. Couns. 11:150–153.
MacKay, W. 1975. The decision fallacy: Is it if or when? Voc. Guid. Q. 23:227–231.
Pierce, R., Cohen, M., Anthony, W., and Cohen, B. 1979. The Skills of Career Counseling. Carkhuff Institute of Human Technology, Amherst, MA.
Roessler, R. 1982. Vocational planning. In: B. Bolton (ed.), Vocational Adjustment of Disabled Persons. University Park Press, Baltimore.
Roessler, R., and Rubin, S. 1982. Case Management and Rehabilitation Counseling. University Park Press, Baltimore.
Vandergoot, D. 1982. An outline of a career services approach. Rehab. Couns. Bull. 26:79–84.
Vandergoot, D., Swirsky, J., and Rice, K. 1982. Using occupational information in rehabilitation counseling. Rehab. Couns. Bull. 26:94–100.

# Appendices

## Appendix A:
## AN INTERVIEW GUIDE
## FOR DIFFICULT CLIENTS

### INTERESTS

Everyone likes to do certain types of activities more than others. This is true of hobbies, sports, school subjects, and jobs. Knowing your *interests* will help you choose a career and succeed in it.

In almost everything people do, there are different activities—some that we like and others that we don't like. Usually, we are more successful when we enjoy things than when we don't.

Most workers prefer activities in one or more of 10 interest areas. After you understand what activity is, select the one that you think you would like best on a job. Then circle the number next to the activity you have chosen.

1. Activities dealing with things and objects
2. Activities involving business contact with people
3. Activities of a routine, definite, organized nature
4. Activities that involve direct personal contact, to help people or deal with them for other purposes
5. Activities that bring recognition or appreciation by others
6. Activities concerned with people and the communication of ideas
7. Activities of a scientific and technical nature
8. Activities of an unusual, indefinite nature that require creative imagination
9. Activities that are nonsocial and involve the use of machines, processes, or methods
10. Activities that bring personal satisfaction from working on or producing things

Comments:

## GENERAL EDUCATION LEVEL

The things taught in school help us to do better in nearly every part of our lives. Imagine trying to order food in a restaurant if you couldn't read, or trying to make change if you couldn't count, or figuring out how a new toy goes together if you couldn't reason the steps!

Most every job requires that you have some of those same general skills that schools teach. Some jobs require many of these skills while others require fewer of them. We will show you a chart and ask you to rate yourself in each of three areas.

Enter your self-rating below:

Reasoning:     I can _____

Mathematics:   I can _____

Language:      I can _____

Comments:

Besides using general skills learned in school, most people learn specific skills to handle their jobs. They may go to college or trade school, learn on the job, or through an apprentice program—which is a combination of school and work. However they learn, they get skills that take *time*.

How long do you think you are *willing* and *able* to train for a job *after* you leave high school? Circle the number that best answers this question.

1.  Short demonstration only
2.  Anything beyond short demonstration up to and including 30 days
3.  Over 30 days up to and including 3 months
4.  Over 3 months up to and including 6 months
5.  Over 6 months up to and including 1 year
6.  Over 1 year up to and including 2 years
7.  Over 2 years up to and including 4 years

8.  Over 4 years up to and including 10 years
9.  Over 10 years

Comments:

## WORK SITUATIONS

Job satisfaction and success require a great many things. One of these is your *willingness* and *ability* to adjust to situations on the job. These situations are very different on some jobs than others. Knowing the types of situations that you may find in jobs can help you make the best possible choice.

Here are 12 very common situations found in jobs. How many could you adjust to without hating them? Make sure you understand what they are and then circle the number of each situation you think you could handle.

1.  Performing a variety of duties that may often change
2.  Repeating activities or tasks of short duration according to a required procedure or sequence
3.  Doing things only under specific instructions, allowing little or no room for independent action or judgment in working out job problems
4.  Directing, controlling, and planning an entire activity or activities of others
5.  Dealing with people in actual job duties beyond giving and receiving instructions
6.  Working alone and away from other workers, although the work may be related to work other people are doing
7.  Influencing people's opinions, attitudes, or judgments about ideas or things
8.  Working well under pressure when faced with critical or unexpected situations or when taking necessary risks
9.  Rating information by using personal judgment
10. Rating information using standards that can be measured or checked
11. Interpreting feelings, ideas, or facts from a personal point of view
12. Working within precise limits or standards of accuracy

Comments:

## PHYSICAL DEMANDS

Some school and hobby activities make you use your body in different ways. For example, you can run more in basketball, lift more in weightlifting and crouch more in football. Jobs differ in how much they demand you to use your body, too.

Here are six physical demands that jobs have. After you understand what is required in each, think about your abilities, and decide which ones you can do.

1. Lifting. How much?_____ lbs. at most/ _____ lbs. often
2. Climbing and/or balancing: _____
3. Stooping, kneeling, crouching, and/or crawling: _____
4. Reaching, handling, fingering, and/or feeling: _____
5. Talking and/or hearing: _____
6. Seeing: _____

Comments:

## WORKING CONDITIONS

*Where* you do an activity also is important. For example, some sports are inside so that the weather and temperature don't affect you. Other sports are very much affected by weather—like mountain climbing.

Jobs are like that, too. If you don't like being indoors, you probably wouldn't like to be a bookkeeper. Or, if you can't stand hot, humid conditions, you probably wouldn't like to be a ship's mechanic.

What conditions would you want, could you stand, in a job? Here are seven conditions frequently found in jobs. Which ones would suit you?

1. Inside, outside, or both
2. Extremes of cold plus temperature changes
3. Extremes of heat plus temperature changes
4. Wet and humid
5. Noise and vibration
6. Hazards
7. Fumes, odors, toxic conditions, dust and poor ventilation

Comments:

## APTITUDES

Aptitude is a word you have probably heard before. Usually, it goes with the word "test." But aptitude really means the ability to learn something. There are many kinds of aptitude tests because there are many kinds of things to learn.

People who study school subjects and students have found that the ability to learn certain things is important for school. So that is what they put in their "aptitude tests." People who study jobs have found that there are eleven aptitudes that are important for work. Not all aptitudes are needed in any job, and some people succeed on jobs even though they find it difficult to learn some of the things in the job. But the better your aptitude in those areas, the more likely you are to be happy and successful in that job.

Two good ways to find out which areas you have the most aptitude in are by "job aptitude tests" and by looking at what you have already done. Let's start by looking at what you already know about yourself. Here are the 11 aptitude areas. By discussion and looking at yourself, estimate how much of each aptitude you have.

| | | Little | Below average | Average | Above average | A lot |
|---|---|---|---|---|---|---|
| 1. | G, General learning ability | 1 | 1 | 1 | 1 | 1 |
| 2. | V, Verbal | 1 | 1 | 1 | 1 | 1 |
| 3. | N, Numerical | 1 | 1 | 1 | 1 | 1 |
| 4. | S, Spatial | 1 | 1 | 1 | 1 | 1 |
| 5. | P, Form perception | 1 | 1 | 1 | 1 | 1 |
| 6. | Q, Clerical perception | 1 | 1 | 1 | 1 | 1 |
| 7. | K, Motor coordination | 1 | 1 | 1 | 1 | 1 |
| 8. | F, Finger dexterity | 1 | 1 | 1 | 1 | 1 |
| 9. | M, Manual dexterity | 1 | 1 | 1 | 1 | 1 |
| 10. | E, Eye/hand/foot coordination | 1 | 1 | 1 | 1 | 1 |
| 11. | C, Color discrimination | 1 | 1 | 1 | 1 | 1 |

Comments:

## TAKING STOCK OF THE OPINION OF OTHERS

No one lives in isolation from others. You constantly influence and are influenced by others. Certain persons' opinions and expectations are more important to you than are those of others. Sometimes others' opinions are clearly conveyed to you. Often, these opinions may be expressed very indirectly, but they may still be influential.

1. Do you welcome other people's opinions with regard to your vocational planning?
2. Whose opinions do you see as valuable to you in your vocational planning?
3. What two or three persons' opinions are most important to you with regard to your vocational planning (such as mother, father, husband/wife, teacher, friend, etc.)?
   a. _____
   b. _____
   c. _____
4. Do you feel bound to follow their advice?
5. What kind of an occupation do you feel these people you have named expect of you? Be careful here. Don't say anything vague like, "Whatever is best for me." Go beyond this, and consider what kind of job you think they regard as best for you.
6. What alternative kind of occupation might they like to see you enter?
7. In what ways are their expectations similar to or different from *your* expectations?
8. How would they react if you did something else, that is, did not enter this kind of occupation? Again, be thoughtful in your answer.
9. How would you feel about their reactions, especially if they disagreed with your choice?
10. How would you deal with these feelings?
11. What occupation(s) do *you* want for yourself?
    a. _____
    b. _____
    c. _____

## LEISURE TIME ACTIVITIES

The following questions concern leisure time activities. Please answer them as honestly and completely as possible so you can get a clear picture of what you are like.

1. Describe any hobbies you now have.
   What do you like about them?
2. Describe any hobbies you had when growing up.
   What did you like about them?
3. Describe any hobbies you wish you had tried.
   What might you like about them?
   Why haven't you tried them?
4. How many hours per day do you watch TV?
5. What is your favorite spectator sport?
6. What is your favorite participant sport?
7. Do you spend time in your local pub?
8. What social, civic, or political organizations do you belong to?
9. Do you like to read? _____ What?
10. How often do you go to the movies?
11. Do you like to work with your hands? _____ How?
12. Do you own any tools/equipment? _____ What?
13. Have you built anything for your home? _____ What?
14. Have you made any of the decorations in your home? _____ What?
15. Do you have the patience to stick with something slow and time-consuming?
16. Are the results of an activity important to you?
17. How do you react when you are unable to finish a task?
18. Have you had experience with animals, or do you have any pets?
19. What is the best way to relax?
20. What have you done in your leisure time that you most enjoy telling others about?
21. What have you learned about yourself from your leisure time activities that might help you in your future vocational planning?
22. What have you learned from these questions?
23. Do you think these questions are relevant to your future vocational planning? Why?
24. What else would you like to tell me about your leisure time?
25. Do your leisure time interests have job possibilities? ____ yes ____ no
26. If so, list them:
    a. _____
    b. _____
    c. _____

---

This guide was primarily developed by Charles Robinson, M.S. in 1973. It has been used successfully with many low-verbal disabled persons. In fact, information can often be solicited by having the client point to the particular response on the guide.

# Appendix B:
# ACHIEVEMENT TEST
# DEVELOPED BY JOHN O. WILLIS

I. MEASURING
II. COMPUTATION
III. REASONING
IV. FORM COMPLETION
V. COMPLETION OF JOB APPLICATION

## I.   MEASURING

**Please use your ruler to do the following as carefully as you can.**

Draw a line 3 inches long:
Draw a line 2½ inches long:
Draw a line 2¾ inches long:
Draw a line 3⅜ inches long:
Draw a line 2⅞ inches long:
Draw a line 3¹³⁄₁₆ inches long:
Draw a line 2⅛ inches long:

**Please use your ruler to get the answers to these questions.**

How long is this line?_____
How long is this line?_____
How long is this line?_____
How long is this line?_____
How long is this line?_____
How long is this line?_____

**Please draw a box 3¼ Inches long and 2½ inches high in the space below the dotted line**

. . . . . . . . . . . . . . . . . . . . . . . . . . . . . . . . . . . . . . . . . . . . . . . . . . . . . . . .

## II.   COMPUTATION

**Please fill in the blanks.**

A dollar is the same as ____ half dollars, or ____ quarters, or ____ dimes, or ____ nickels, or ____ pennies.

Two dimes and one nickel are the same as _____.

If I have six dimes and something costs 52¢, how much will I have left? _____

There are _____ nickels in a quarter.

There are _____ nickels in a dime.

There are _____ pennies in a nickel.

**Please answer these questions. You may use the back of the page for scratch work if you wish.**

There are 12 people in the room; one-third of them are men.
How many men are there in the room?                    _____

A truck holds 17 boxes. How many boxes can you put in four trucks?                                        _____

I have 15 boxes. There are three shelves to store them on. How many boxes should I put on each shelf?        _____

There are 18 trucks in the garage. If I send seven of them out, how many trucks are left in the garage?      _____

If there are eight cartons on a shelf and 10 cartons in the store-room, how many cartons are there?          _____

If I have worked from 9:30 in the morning until 3:00 in the afternoon, how long have I worked?               _____

If I work from 8:35 in the morning until 11:20 in the morning, how long have I worked?                        _____

**Please do as many as you can. Pay attention to the signs $(+/-/\times/\div/=)$.**

$$
\begin{array}{r} 903524 \\ +645863 \\ \hline \end{array}
\qquad
\begin{array}{r} 1923 \\ -\ 392 \\ 4064 \\ +5805 \\ \hline \end{array}
\qquad
256 + 3259 + 20 =
$$

$$
\begin{array}{r} 364 \\ -203 \\ \hline \end{array}
\quad
\begin{array}{r} 632 \\ -515 \\ \hline \end{array}
\quad
\begin{array}{r} 304 \\ -212 \\ \hline \end{array}
\quad
\begin{array}{r} 206 \\ -189 \\ \hline \end{array}
\quad
\begin{array}{r} 3870598 \\ -2764479 \\ \hline \end{array}
$$

$$
\begin{array}{r} 3 \\ \times 7 \\ \hline \end{array}
\quad
\begin{array}{r} 26 \\ \times\ 4 \\ \hline \end{array}
\quad
\begin{array}{r} 49 \\ \times 13 \\ \hline \end{array}
\quad
\begin{array}{r} 326 \\ \times 203 \\ \hline \end{array}
\quad
\begin{array}{r} 30 \\ \times\ 6 \\ \hline \end{array}
$$

$$
8\overline{)\ 24} \qquad 23\overline{)\ 4625} \qquad 283\overline{)\ 56983} \qquad 28 \div 4 =
$$

$$
9\overline{)\ 0} \qquad 41\overline{)\ 8065} \qquad \dfrac{8}{4=} \qquad 495 \div 12 =
$$

$$
2.63 + 30.2 = \qquad\qquad\qquad \$13.62 - \$2.31 =
$$

$$
\begin{array}{r} 23.2 \\ \times\ 5.1 \\ \hline \end{array}
\qquad
3.2\overline{)\ \ \ 64.3} \qquad
\$2.35 \times 3.5 =
$$

$$
\frac{3}{8} + \frac{2}{8} = \qquad\qquad \frac{3}{5} + \frac{1}{3} = \qquad\qquad \frac{7}{9} - \frac{4}{9} =
$$

$$\frac{3}{5} \times \frac{2}{3} =$$        $$\frac{7}{8} - \frac{3}{4} =$$        $$\frac{7}{9} \div \frac{2}{3} =$$

$3X = 9$        $$\frac{3}{9} = \frac{X}{6}$$        $X + Y = 10$

$X =$            $X =$            $Y = 6$

                              $X =$

| 3 weeks 5 days | 6 feet 4 inches | 2 years 7 months |
|:---:|:---:|:---:|
| +2 weeks 6 days | −3 feet 5 inches | +4 years 8 months |
| weeks   days | feet   inches | years   months |

## What is the area of each of these shapes? (How big are they?)

Area = _____

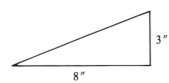

Area = _____

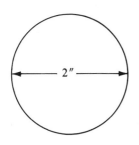

Area = _____

**You are a payroll clerk for a company that employs salesmen. You have to compute their pay. Here are the company policies regarding salesmen.**

1. Salesmen are paid 35% of gross sales as salary.
2. Salesmen are advanced 18% of the previous month's sales income for living expenses.
3. Travel expenses are reimbursable:
   10¢ per mile
   Tolls
   Meals
   Rooms

4.  Withholding for taxes is 20% of sales income, (no withholding on travel expense money or advances), 5.9% of sales income is withheld for Social Security and $60 per month for retirement.

**Salesman "A" turned in the following report for December.**

| | |
|---|---|
| Advance from November sales | $450.30 |
| Travel during December | 754 miles |
| Meals | $240.00 |
| Entertainment | $35.00 |
| Tolls | $7.50 |
| Rooms | $91.75 |
| Gross sales | $2,875.00 |

**Compute his pay slip:**

Commission earnings _____

Refund for travel expense _____

Withholding _____

    Tax _____

    Social security _____

    Retirement _____

Reclaimed November advance _____

January advance _____

Net amount of check _____

Two customers bought the following meals: two hamburgers, one milk shake, one cup of coffee and one hot dog, one egg salad sandwich, one coke, and one cup of tea. Look at the menu below, and write out their bill completely, including the tax and the total if you can.

| Sandwich Menu | |
|---|---|
| Hot dog | .25 |
| BLT | .35 |
| Roast beef | .55 |
| Turkey | .50 |
| Hamburger | .30 |
| Egg salad | .20 |
| Fried egg | .25 |
| **Beverages** | |
| Coffee | .10 |
| Tea | .10 |
| Milk | .15 |
| Milk shake | .30 |
| Coke | .15 |

| Customer Check | | |
|---|---|---|
| | | |
| | | |
| | | |
| | | |
| | | |
| | | |
| | | |
| | | |
| | | |
| Subtotal | | |
| Tax 6% | | |
| Total | | |
| Thank you | | |

Please write the exact time in the space below each clock:

Please draw the exact times on these clocks:

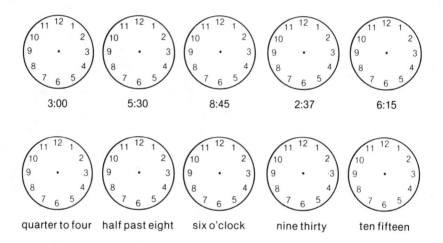

| 3:00 | 5:30 | 8:45 | 2:37 | 6:15 |

| quarter to four | half past eight | six o'clock | nine thirty | ten fifteen |

These are pictures of the odometer of a car. Please answer the questions:

| 1 | 9 | 4 | 6 | 5 | 4 |

| 1 | 9 | 5 | 7 | 0 | 6 |

How far has this car been driven?     How much farther has it gone now?

## III.   REASONING

**Please put these names in alphabetical order:**

Whiting                                    Anderson
Abrams                                     Whitman
Demorest                                   Smith
Whiteman                                   White
Brown

1. _____        6. _____
2. _____        7. _____
3. _____        8. _____
4. _____        9. _____
5. _____

**If the driving time from White Plains, New York to Washington, D.C. is 5 hours and 25 minutes, and I leave at 9:45 a.m., when will I arrive?**_____

**You are a clerk in a store. A customer gives you a $10 bill for $5.52 worth of merchandise. What coins and bills would you give for change?**

    Coins                                    Bills

    _____                _____

    _____

    _____

Total value of coins _____ Total value of the bills _____

## Bus Schedule

| Fresno to Tulare | | | Tulare to Fresno | |
|---|---|---|---|---|
| *Departure* | *Arrival* | | *Departure* | *Arrival* |
| 7:00 AM # | 8:15 AM # | | 8:20 AM # | 9:35 AM # |
| 9:40 AM | 10:55 AM | | 11:00 AM | 12:15 PM |
| 12:20 PM t | 1:35 PM t | | 1:40 PM t | 2:55 PM t |
| 3:00 PM * | 4:15 PM * | | 4:20 PM * | 5:35 PM * |
| 5:40 PM # | 6:55 PM # | | 7:00 PM # | 8:15 PM # |
| 8:20 PM | 9:35 PM | | 9:40 PM | 10:55 PM |

* Sunday only; # Not on weekends; t November to April only

What time does the first bus usually leave Fresno?_____
What time does the first bus usually leave Tulare?_____
At what times can you catch a bus from Tulare to Fresno on a Sunday in July?
_____

Who is the President of the United States? _____
Who is the governor of your state? _____
What town are you in right now? _____
How many inches are there in a yard? _____
What is the capital of your state? _____
Give the name of a newspaper. _____
How old do you have to be to get a driver's license? _____
About how much does a large car weigh? _____
Name three big cities in your state. _____
At what age do you register for the draft? _____
What is the quickest way to get help if your house catches on fire? _____
_____

## IV.   FORM COMPLETION

**Please try to fill out the check, stub, and deposit ticket below as follows. Do as much as you can, even if you can't do all of it. Check all of the spaces.**

1. You start with $238.56 in your bank account
2. On April 14, 1971, you deposit $53.15 cash in your account.
3. On April 23, 1971, you pay your telephone bill with a check to "New England Telephone" for $16.20.
4. Your bank charges you 10¢ per check.

| DEPOSIT TICKET | CASH | DOLLARS | CENTS | |
|---|---|---|---|---|
| Jennison C. Hall Jennifer C. Hall | CHECKS LIST SINGLY | | | 7-16 520 |
| _____19__ | | | | BE SURE EACH ITEM IS PROPERLY ENDORSED |
| | TOTAL | | | |

First national bank
Darby, New Jersey

١٦8 ٤0٧٤0

---

NO_____
DATE_____19__
TO_____
FOR_____

| | DOLLARS | CENTS |
|---|---|---|
| BAL. FWD. | | |
| DEPOSIT | | |
| TOTAL | | |
| THIS ITEM | | |
| SUB-TOTAL | | |
| OTHER DEDUCT. (IF ANY) | | |
| BAL. FWD. | | |

Jennison C. Hall
Jennifer C. Hall          _____19__  507
7-16
520

Pay to the order of _____  $ _____

_____ Dollars

First national bank
Darby, New Jersey      SPECIMEN   VOID

Memo_____

⑈⑈05 2000  98⑈⑈0 50 7⑈0   ١٦8 ٤0٧٤0   ⑈⑈00000 ٧٧5⑈⑈

**Every time you get a job, you have to complete a W4 form for the employer and the government. Please complete this form as if you were being hired right now.**

| | |
|---|---|
| Form W-4<br>(Rev. Aug. 1972)<br>Dept. of the Treas.<br>Internal Revenue Serv. | EMPLOYEE'S WITHHOLDING ALLOWANCE CERTIFICATE<br>(This certificate is for income tax<br>withholding purposes only; it will<br>remain in effect until you change it) |
| Type or print your full name | Your social security number |
| Home address (number and street or rural route)<br><br>City or town, state, and zip code | Marital status<br>☐ Single    ☐ Married<br>(If married but legally separated,<br>or wife (husband) is a nonresident<br>alien, check the single block.) |

1 Total number of allowances you are claiming........................ —————————

2 Additional amount, if any, you want deducted
   from each pay (if your employer agrees)........................ $———————

I certify that to the best of my knowledge and belief, the number of withholding allowances claimed on this certificate does not exceed the number to which I am entitled.


Signature ............................................... Date ............ 19 ......

## V. COMPLETION OF JOB APPLICATION

**PRACTICE JOB APPLICATION**
*(Please type or print legibly)*

NAME _____ PERMANENT ADDRESS _____

HOME PHONE _____ SEX _____ SOCIAL SECURITY _____

PLACE OF BIRTH _____ DATE OF BIRTH _____

HEIGHT _____ WEIGHT _____ MARITAL STATUS _____

NEXT OF KIN _____ ADDRESS _____

IMMEDIATE FAMILY

NAME              AGE         OCCUPATION         WHERE RESIDING

_____

_____

*(Please list others on back)*

PHYSICAL LIMITATIONS _____

_____

PERSONAL PHYSICIAN _____ ADDRESS _____

PREVIOUS WORKMENS COMPENSATION CLAIMS _____

EDUCATION      GRADE COMPLETED     DATES      LOCATION           SUBJECT

GRAMMAR SCHOOL _____

HIGH SCHOOL _____

COLLEGE _____

OTHER _____

MILITARY RECORD

DATES _____ SERVICE _____ TYPE DISCHARGE _____

DUTIES _____

LIST ALL CONVICTIONS FOR OTHER THAN MINOR TRAFFIC OFFENSES _____

_____

EMPLOYMENT HISTORY
(BEGIN WITH MOST RECENT JOB AND INCLUDE FOUR MOST RECENT)

EMPLOYER _____ ADDRESS _____

DUTIES OR JOB TITLE _____

STARTED _____ LEFT _____ HIGHEST PAY _____

REASON FOR LEAVING _____

EMPLOYER _____ ADDRESS _____

DUTIES OR JOB TITLE _____

STARTED _____ LEFT _____ HIGHEST PAY _____

REASON FOR LEAVING _____

EMPLOYER _____ ADDRESS _____

DUTIES OR JOB TITLE _____

STARTED _____ LEFT _____ HIGHEST PAY _____

REASON FOR LEAVING _____

EMPLOYER _____ ADDRESS _____

DUTIES OR JOB TITLE _____

STARTED _____ LEFT _____ HIGHEST PAY _____

REASON FOR LEAVING _____

MAY WE CONTACT THESE EMPLOYERS _____ YES _____ NO

JOBS FOR WHICH YOU ARE PRESENTLY QUALIFIED _____

_____

PERSONAL REFERENCES

NAME _____ ADDRESS _____

RELATIONSHIP _____ YEARS KNOWN _____

NAME _____ ADDRESS _____

RELATIONSHIP _____ YEARS KNOWN _____

NAME _____ ADDRESS _____

RELATIONSHIP _____ YEARS KNOWN _____

I CERTIFY THAT THE ABOVE INFORMATION IS CORRECT TO THE BEST OF MY KNOWLEDGE AND ACKNOWLEDGE THAT FALSIFICATION OF THIS INFORMATION WILL RESULT IN REFUSAL OR TERMINATION OF EMPLOYMENT.

DATE _____ SIGNED _____

# Appendix C:
# SELECTED WORK SAMPLE SYSTEMS

SAMPLE

| System | Developer | Description | Training | Cost |
|---|---|---|---|---|
| JEVS Work Samples | Vocational Research Institute 1624 Locust St. Philadelphia, PA 19103 (215) 893-5900 | Provides 28 work samples for special needs populations; administered over 5 to 7-day period; normative data on over 1,100 individuals; simultaneous assessment of 15 persons possible with standard hardware; supplemental hardware available | Required and included along with follow-up consultation; in cost of training; training available in Philadelphia, Atlanta, and on West Coast | $7,975 |
| VIEWS (Vocational Information and Evaluation Samples) | Same as above | Provides 16 work samples designed and normed for persons with mental retardation; incorporates individualized training to a level of competency before assessment of performance; an industrial time standard (MODAPTS) provided for each work sample to compare client productivity with average practiced professional; supplemental hardware available | Training and consultation included in cost of system (in use throughout U.S., Canada, Japan, Mexico, and Israel); training available in Philadelphia, Atlanta, and on West Coast | $7,675 |
| VITAS (Vocational Interest, Temperament and Aptitude System) | Same as above | Provides 21 work samples for disadvantaged persons, taking 2½ days to administer; assessment of 10 clients per week possible with standard hardware, up to 30 with supplementary hardware | Training included in cost; available in Philadelphia, Atlanta, and on West Coast | $8,190 |

| System | Contact | Description | Training | Cost |
|---|---|---|---|---|
| McCarron-Dial Evaluation System (MDS) | McCarron-Dial System P.O. Box 45628 Dallas, TX 75245 (214) 247-5945 | Consists of eight separate instruments that assess five neuropsychologic factors; verbal, cognitive, sensory, motor, emotional, and integration coping (adaptive behavior); provides predictive information re work potential and suggests rehabilitation strategies for disabilities related to central nervous system damage | Training of 3 days required at Dallas and selected sites | $945 (Forms packaged in quantities of 50 and may be ordered separately) |
| Hester Evaluation System (HES) | Evaluation Systems, Inc. P.O. Box 10741 Chicago, IL 60610 | Computer-based method of assessing vocational potential; consists of 20 to 27 tests measuring abilities in various fields; printout of job titles from DOT furnished; takes 5 hours to administer, 12 persons at a time | | (Cost not provided); scoring and printout packages available for: $22.50—1 copy $1000—50 at a time $1750—100 at a time |
| Talent Assessment Programs (TAP) | Talent Assessment, Inc. P.O. Box 5087 Jacksonville, FL 32207 | Provides 10 tests of perception and dexterity to measure gross and fine manual dexterity; visual and tactile discrimination, and retention of details; ages above 14 and all mental levels except "trainable;" measures attributes common to hundreds of work areas (not specific jobs); can be administered in 2½ hours, profile sheet gives Talent Quotient; Norms provided | Training required and available at the purchaser's site—1½ days | $3,300 |

SAMPLE

| System | Developer | Description | Training | Cost |
|---|---|---|---|---|
| Singer Vocational Evaluation | Singer Education Division/Career Systems 80 Commerce Dr. Rochester, NY | Series of over 20 job samples for handicapped disadvantaged, non-handicapped; each sample fitted into a carrel (work station) utilizing an audiovisual approach complete with specific equipment, tools, and supplies for completing a series of work tasks; assesses full range of person's abilities, aptitudes, interests, and tolerances for specific job areas related to DOT and OE career clusters | Recommended but not required | $1,190 and up for each work station |
| MICRO-TOWER | MICRO-TOWER Institutional Services, ICD Rehabilitation and Research Center 340 East 24th St. New York, NY 10010 | Provides 13 work samples for educable retarded through normal range, adolescents and adults, taking 3 to 5 days to complete; instructors presented on cassette tape with opportunity for questions and supplemental instructions; administered to five to ten people at a time; each work sample divided into a learning/ practice period; group discussion conducted at end of each day; profile of scores in five aptitude areas provided: Verbal, Numerical, Motor, Spatial, and Clerical Perception; Norms provided. Testing of jobs from DOT given | Not required but available at ICD (Institute for Crippled and Disabled) or at purchaser's agency at their cost | $7,223 (tests 2 people) to $17,303 (for 30 people) |

# Index

268    *Index*

Descriptive interpretation, of assessment
information, 156
Design Completion, of Non-Reading
Aptitude Test Battery, 104
Developmentally disabled
Adaptive Behavior Scale for, 117
clients as, 43–44
*Dictionary of Occupational Titles*
(DOT), 150, 152, 167–178,
169, 223
*Career Assessment Inventory* and,
146
for industrially injured client, 210,
218
Interest Check List and, 147
interpreting assessment information
with, 157, 162, 166
for job analysis, 202–203
for recommendations to client, 158
Differential Aptitude Test (DAT), 30,
105–106, 110, 111
Digit Span Subtest, of Wechsler Adult
Intelligence Scale-Revised, 88
Digit Symbol Subtest, of Wechsler
Adult Intelligence Scale-
Revised, 88
Direct job placement, for industrially
injured, 210
Direct question, in interview, 57
Disability onset, vocational functioning
model and, 6
Disability process, 212
Disability-related knowledge
in planning model, 225, 232
vocational functioning model and, 4
Discomfort Scale, of Psychological
Screening Inventory, 130
Domestic behaviors, assessment of, 114
DOT, *see Dictionary of Occupational
Titles*

Educational development, vocational
functioning model and, 3
Educational experience
interview with difficult client assessing, 242–243
in planning model, 225, 232
in vocational assessment battery, 29
Edwards Personnel Preference Schedule
(EPPS), 30, 124, 132

Emotional/behavior assessment, in Independent Living Assessment Instrument, 191, 193
Emotional characteristics of client
in planning model, 225–226,
233–234
in vocational assessment battery, 26,
30
vocational functioning model and, 4
Emotional/interpersonal values
interest assessment clarifying, 152
in planning model, 226, 234
Emotionally disabled, 127
Adaptive Behavior Scale for, 117
Employability, 8–15
occupational questions and, 10
physical questions for, 9
psychologic questions for, 9–10
socioenvironmental questions and, 10
standardized measures assessing,
12–15
Employability Evaluation Form, 12
Employability Information Sheet,
13, 31
Employability Plan, 13–14, 31
Functional Evaluation Form, 12
Job Readiness Scale, 14, 31
Job Readiness Test, 14, 31
Placement Readiness Checklist, 13,
31
Readiness Planning Checklists I
and II, 15
Service Outcome Measurement
Form, 13, 31
in vocational assessment battery, 31
Vocational Behavior Checklist for,
8–9
Employability Evaluation, 31
Employability Evaluation Form, 12
Employability Information Sheet, 13,
31
Employability Plan, 13–14, 31
Employment, *see* Job placement; Occu-
pational questions; Work experi-
ence
Environmental factors, 22
in planning model, 226, 234
in vocational assessment battery, 32
vocational functioning model and, 5
EPPS, *see* Edwards Personnel Prefer-
ence Schedule